THE UNITY OF
PHILOSOPHICAL EXPERIENCE

ÉTIENNE GILSON

THE UNITY
OF
PHILOSOPHICAL
EXPERIENCE

IGNATIUS PRESS   SAN FRANCISCO

Original English edition:
© 1937, Charles Scribner's Sons
Copyright renewed © 1964, Charles Scribner's Sons

With ecclesiastical approval

Cover design by Roxanne Mei Lum

Printed in 1999 Ignatius Press, San Francisco
ISBN 978-0-89870-748-9
Library of Congress catalogue number 99-72127
Printed in the United States of America ⊗

To my wife
E. G.

CONTENTS

FOREWORD

Harvard University celebrated the 300th anniversary of its founding in 1936; as part of the celebration Étienne Gilson (1884–1978) was invited to give the William James Lectures. He did this in the fall semester, and the lectures were published the next year as *The Unity of Philosophical Experience*.

The occasion of the James lectures was not Gilson's first visit to Harvard. Recognized as one of the great authorities on Descartes and his medieval background, Gilson, after World War I, had achieved international recognition as a medieval scholar writing studies on St. Augustine, Abelard, St. Bernard, Dante, St. Bonaventure, and, of course, St. Thomas Aquinas. While based at the Sorbonne in Paris, Gilson was first invited to Harvard in 1926, at a time when the university included among its faculty such lights as Alfred N. Whitehead, Ralph Barton Perry, and W. E. Hocking. Gilson returned again in 1927 and 1928 to teach in the fall semesters, and it was during these visits that he went to Toronto to begin the discussion with the Basilian Fathers of St. Michael's College that led to the establishment of what came to be called The Pontifical Institute of Mediæval Studies. Gilson, as director of studies, organized the curriculum to cover the range of disciplines relating to the Middle Ages: history, paleography, liturgy, theology, literature, canon law, and philosophy. Gilson regarded the founding of the Institute as one of his significant contributions to the revival of medieval studies, an interesting academic event of our time.[1]

In *The Unity of Philosophical Experience*, Gilson used the analogy of the physical scientist and the use of experiment. Just as the physical scientist sees worked out in his laboratory the consequences of certain hypotheses he has tested, so the student of the history of philosophy can see the consequences of the working out of certain premises with which a philosopher begins his philosophy.

> Thus understood, the history [of philosophy] is to the philosopher what his laboratory is to the scientist; it particularly shows how the philosophers do not think as they wish, but as they can, for the interrelation of philosophical ideas is just as independent of us as are the laws of the physical world. A man is always free to choose his principles, but when he does he must face their consequences to the bitter end.

Hence, Gilson is not writing a history of philosophy but using the resources of the history of philosophy to study different intellectual experiments philosophers have undertaken. And the lesson Gilson infers from his study is that there has been a continual temptation across the centuries for brilliant thinkers to make a similar mistake, namely, to attempt to reform the philosophy of their time according to the method and structure of another science.

To label these misadventures, Gilson coins new names: the theologism of Bonaventure, the psychologism of William of Ockham, the mathematicism of Descartes, the physicalism of Kant, and the sociologism of Comte. Gilson shows in a profound and witty way how the best intentions of these philosophers have ultimately resulted in scepticism, a loss of confidence

[1] Laurence Shook, *Étienne Gilson* (Toronto: Pontifical Institute of Mediæval Studies, 1984), pp. 176–77.

in our ability to achieve philosophical truth. But Gilson was not despairing, for he was confident that philosophers who respected the nature of philosophy and the need for it to follow its own method could succeed. His aphorism here was: "Philosophy always buries its own undertakers."

As Armand Maurer has pointed out, Gilson is using his knowledge of the history of philosophy to philosophize. In works such as *The Unity of Philosophical Experience* and *Being and Some Philosophers*, "the experience of the history of philosophy is the starting point for philosophical reflection."[2] Gilson goes on to show how a philosopher can take one principle and use it to imbalance another principle he intended to consider, throwing his system out of order. Here Gilson has a marvelous way of showing how proper it was to the philosopher to go the way he went, given his circumstances and the challenges he was facing in his time.

In his final chapter, "The Nature and Unity of Philosophical Experience", Gilson reflects on the analysis he has given of various philosophers in the Western Tradition. He grants that he has used biographical details to help understand how a philosopher came to develop his philosophy, but he says that these details belong to the history of the philosopher, not to his philosophy. Gilson treats philosophers with great respect, and even when he disagrees with their teachings he acknowledges that these teachings can be an inexhaustible source of partial truths and of acute observations.

Then, recognizing there is a basic tendency in humans to seek the truth in experience of reality, he underlines the principle that *man is a metaphysical animal*. We use our reason to go beyond particular sciences, seeking a transcendent explanation of our world.

[2] A. Maurer, "Gilson's Use of History", *Thomistic Papers*, vol. 5 (Houston, Tex.: Center for Thomistic Studies, 1990), p. 26.

In presenting what he judges to be the sound approach to reality, Gilson emphasizes that our knowledge begins with the intuition of being. This is very characteristic of Gilson's philosophizing. In the epistemological controversies of the 1930s, he had argued that we begin our intellectual life, not by reflecting on knowledge, but by the sensio-intellectual experience of things. In the somewhat autobiographical work of his later years, *The Philosopher and Theology*, he confessed, as it were, to *chosisme*, "thingness"; that is, the foundation and principle of our thinking is the recognition that there is something existing.[3] "Man is not a mind that thinks, but a being who knows other beings as true, who loves them as good, and who enjoys them as beautiful" (p. 255, below).

Gilson, therefore, was confident not only that metaphysics is possible but that he had shown the way to be followed in achieving that science.

It is now more than sixty years since Gilson presented these lectures, and generations of post–World War II students have encountered philosophy through this work. One is grateful to Ignatius Press for making this classic of our time available again.

Desmond J. FitzGerald
Professor Emeritus
University of San Francisco

---

[3] *The Philosopher and Theology* (New York: Random House, 1962), p. 18.

PREFACE

The history of philosophy is much more part of philosophy itself than the history of science is part of science, for it is not impossible to become a competent scientist without knowing much about the history of science, but no man can carry very far his own philosophical reflections unless he first studies the history of philosophy. In point of fact, the First Book of Aristotle's *Metaphysics* is also the first known History of Greek Philosophy, and it remains a perfect example of how such a history should be written. For indeed it is a philosophical history of philosophy, whereas too many modern histories of philosophy are written in an unphilosophical way. Unless it may be shown as exhibiting some intrinsic intelligibility, the endless chain of mutually destructive systems that runs from Thales to Karl Marx is less suggestive of hope than of discouragement.

It is the proper aim and scope of the present book to show that the history of philosophy makes philosophical sense and to define its meaning in regard to the nature of philosophical knowledge itself. For that reason, the various doctrines, as well as the definite parts of those doctrines, which have been taken into account in this volume, should not be considered as arbitrarily selected fragments from some abridged description of mediæval and modern philosophy but as a series of concrete philosophical experiments especially chosen for their dogmatic significance. Each of them represents a definite attempt to deal with philosophical knowledge according to a certain method, and all of them, taken together, make up a philosophical experience. The fact that all those experiments have yielded the same result will, as I hope, justify the common conclusion of the following analyses, viz., that there is a centuries-long experience of what philosophical knowledge is—and that such an experience exhibits a remarkable unity.

The fundamental convictions which lie at the basis of this book are deeply rooted in the philosophical past of its author. Yet, they might never have found public expression had not the fear of falling far too short of the standard of a famous lectureship prompted a professional historian of mediæval philosophy to trespass upon philosophical ground. I wish therefore to express my gratitude to the department of philosophy at Harvard for generously entrusting me with a lectureship whose purpose it is to honour the memory of William James. By whatever motives it may have been dictated, their choice proves at least how accurately James was describing the Harvard spirit in philosophy when he wrote to G. H. Palmer in 1901: "I think the delightful thing about us all in the philosophical department, where each has a set of *ideas*, both practical and theoretical, which are the outcrop of his irresistible idiosyncrasy, is our deep appreciation of one another, and our on the whole harmonious co-operation towards the infusion of what probably is objective truth into the minds of the students. At any rate it's genuine liberalism, and non-dogmatism." What was true of the Harvard of James, Royce, and Palmer is no less true of the Harvard of Perry, Whitehead, Hocking, Lewis, and Sheffer. When non-dogmatism shows itself generous enough to welcome even dogmatism, it has obviously reached its point of perfection.

The lectures of which the present volume is composed were given at Harvard University in the first half of the academic

year 1936–1937. I feel particularly indebted to my friends Professor Ralph Barton Perry, of Harvard University, and Rever-
end Gerald B. Phelan, president of the Institute of Mediæval
Studies (Toronto), who together have read this book in manuscript and suggested many improvements in thought as well as
in expression. My thanks are also due to Professor Daniel C.
Walsh, of Manhattanville College, New York City, and Co-
lumbia University. He has not only gone over my manuscript
and made many helpful suggestions towards clarity of expression, but he has also read the proofs.

Étienne Gilson
Institute of Mediæval Studies
Toronto, Canada
NOVEMBER 22, 1937

PART ONE

THE MEDIÆVAL EXPERIMENT

CHAPTER I

LOGICISM AND PHILOSOPHY

In the preface to his *Phenomenology of Mind*, Hegel rightly remarks that knowing a philosophical system is something more than knowing its purpose and results. Its purpose by itself is but a vague and abstract idea, or, at the utmost, the pointing out of a certain direction to be followed by a still unrealized mental activity; as to its result, it is, in Hegel's own words, "the corpse of the system which has left its guiding tendency behind it."[1] I shall therefore beg leave to lay hold at once of the matter itself and, setting aside all external considerations, begin by an analysis of the first of those philosophical experiments which, taken together, make up what I propose to call philosophical experience.

It has often been said by historians, and not without good reasons, that the whole philosophy of the Middle Ages was little more than an obstinate endeavour to solve one problem—the problem of the Universals. Universals are but another name for what we call concepts, or general ideas, and it does not require long reflection to realize that such ideas are indeed a fitting subject for philosophical speculation. Not only are concepts the very stuff of which our knowledge is made, but as soon as we attempt to define their nature, we find ourselves confronted with the central problem so well discussed by Professor C. I. Lewis under the general title *The Mind and the World Order*. What

[1] J. Loewenberg, ed., *Hegel Selections* (New York: Scribner's, 1929), p. 3.

relation is there between thought and things? More particularly, and to ask the same question in specifically mediæval terms, how is it that in a world where all that is real is a particular and individual thing, the human mind is able to distribute the manifold of reality into classes, in which particular things are contained? That such an operation is possible is an obvious fact. Man is constantly thinking in terms of genera and species. But how it is possible always was and still remains for us a very intricate problem. The great significance of Peter Abailard in the history of mediæval philosophy is due to the fact that he was the first to deal at length with that central problem: What is a class of things, or in other words, what is the essence of universality?

To such a question the easiest answer obviously was that, since things by themselves are essentially particular, the generality which belongs to our concepts cannot have any other origin but the mind. Let it be added that such an answer is undoubtedly true; its only defect is that it fails to cover the whole case. If the character of generality which belongs to our concepts is wholly and solely a product of our mind, there is nothing that answers it in the nature of things themselves; consequently our knowledge by general ideas is without an object; it is not a science, but a mere logic. True enough, it could be answered that general ideas are an artifice of the mind to handle more easily and, so to speak, at cheaper cost the enormous multiplicity of particular things; but the fact would still remain that it is a working artifice. How does it work and why? Since the human mind is able to apply a single concept to two different objects, there must be something in those objects that makes it possible for us to conceive them as one. And even if it were to be said that our so-called concepts, or general ideas, are mere words, the same problem would still remain: How is it that we can give the same name to several different things? Perhaps we do no more than name them, but they must at least be such things as can be named. In short, the generality which belongs to our concepts cannot possibly come from the mind alone; it must also, in some way or other, be found in things. What then is the nature of generality?

In order to understand the various answers given to the question by Abailard and his successors, it is very useful to know where they found it. It was an essentially philosophical question, because it was one of those fundamental problems which the human mind stumbles upon every time it tries to grasp, beyond all particular sciences, the conditions that make knowledge itself possible. The trouble is that when some scientist comes upon such a problem, he usually fails to perceive that it belongs to a non-scientific order of questions. The best that can happen is that he will dismiss it as an idle question not susceptible of a positive answer. In some cases, however, there will be a more or less successful attempt to deal with it in a scientific way, as if it were a scientific problem. After all, nothing is more natural. Arising as they do on the frontier of some particular science, problems of that kind are not easily distinguished from the science which is, as it were, their birthplace. Not fully aware that what he sees are but glimpses of problems which lie behind and beyond those which science is able to ask, the scientist naturally thinks that he is merely tracing his particular science down to its last implications.

Such an adventure, which we shall see repeated under many different forms, befell Peter Abailard in the first half of the twelfth century. Every one knows that he wrote a *History of My Calamities*, and what they were; but the novelists who have deemed it useful to rewrite that history in their own way have usually overlooked that which, according to Abailard himself, was their common origin. As he would later write to Héloïse: "Soror Heloissa, odiosum me mundo reddidit Dialectica" (Sister

Héloïse, Dialectics has made me hateful to the world). It was, at least, the origin of his philosophical misfortunes as well as of the innumerable difficulties that were to bring about the death of mediæval philosophy. Abailard's greatness lay in his acute feeling for philosophical problems; his weakness was always to deal with them as though they were logical problems. Seeking, as he did, to mould the philosophical order into conformity with purely logical principles, he was bound ultimately to fail in his undertaking and to entangle his successors in hopeless difficulties.

I wish I could make clear from the very beginning that in criticizing great men, as I shall do, I am very far from forgetting what made them truly great. No man can fall a victim to his own genius unless he has genius; but those who have none are fully justified in refusing to be victimized by the genius of others. Not having made the mathematical discoveries of Descartes and Leibniz, we cannot be tempted to submit all questions to the rules of mathematics; but our very mediocrity should at least help us to avoid such a mistake. There is more than one excuse for being a Descartes, but there is no excuse whatsoever for being a Cartesian.

Abailard's case is the first of the many cases of that kind which we shall have to discuss. The only science to be known and taught in the early Middle Ages was Logic, and the first man to realize its importance fully was Abailard. It is not easy for us to share his enthusiasm and that of his first disciples, when he discovered that human thought was submitted to necessary laws, themselves susceptible of exact definition, the knowledge of which would enable us to distinguish in all cases the true from the false. As soon as he made that wonderful discovery, Abailard decided that anything that stood in the way of the new science should be ruthlessly thrown into the scrapheap. Is not logic the science that teaches us how to think? And if it is, what mental discipline can escape its jurisdiction? Hence the reckless way in which he applied it to theology, with consequences that lie beyond the scope of the present inquiry, and to philosophy, with consequences to which, on the contrary, we shall have to devote the closest attention.

In point of fact, I am not so sure that even the logical genius of Abailard was an adequate excuse for his blunder; for the very book in which he had found the philosophical question he was going to discuss as a logician had clearly warned him that it was more than a logical question. In his famous *Introduction* to the *Categories* of Aristotle, the Greek commentator, Porphyry, had met it as an ancillary problem which arose from logic but which should be provisorily dismissed as exceeding the competency of the logician. "At present," Porphyry said, "I shall refuse to say, concerning genera and species, whether they subsist or whether they are placed in the naked understandings alone or whether subsisting they are corporeal or incorporeal, and whether they are separated from sensibles or placed in sensibles and in accord with them. Questions of this sort are most exalted business and require very great diligence of inquiry." [2] Six centuries before Abailard's times, the Latin translator and commentator of Porphyry, Boethius, had felt tempted to try a hand at those forbidden problems. "The questions", Boethius says, "concerning which Porphyry promises to be silent are extremely useful and secret, and have been tried by wise men, but have not been solved by many." [3] According to him, genera and species, that is to say our general ideas, should be considered as being incorporeal inasmuch as they are conceptions of our mind; on the other hand, Boethius added, they are joined to sensible things, and subsisting in those things inasmuch as they are

[2] As quoted from R. McKeon, ed., *Selections from Medieval Philosophers*, vol. 1 (New York: Scribner's, 1929), p. 91.

[3] Ibid., p. 91.

something independent of the mind. A clear and simple answer, indeed, but how superficial! It is very easy to say that the genus animal, or the species man, are existing both in the mind and outside the mind; the real difficulty is to know *what* they are in the mind: ideas, concepts, or names? And what they are outside the mind: subsisting ideas, forms, or mere aggregates of sensible qualities? If Boethius did not say more about the question, the reason probably is that in him the commentator was at variance with the philosopher. As an interpreter of Aristotle, he felt it his duty to speak the language of Aristotle, and therefore to say that genera and species exist only in our minds and in things. As an independent philosopher, he would rather have said that those ideas were first of all subsisting in the divine Mind. This commentator of Aristotle was basically a Platonist. As he himself says: "We have followed out the opinion of Aristotle very diligently for this reason, not in the least because we approved of it, but because this book has been written for the *Categories*, of which Aristotle is the author." [4]

When Abailard took up the problem in his turn, he found himself in an altogether different situation. He was not a Platonist: in point of fact, he knew practically nothing about Plato; but neither was he an Aristotelian, since the famous treatise of Aristotle, *On the Soul*, in which he could have found a complete answer to the question, had not yet been translated into Latin. In short, Abailard was in that blessed state of ignorance which makes it so easy for a clever man to be original. Moreover, Abailard was in a much more favourable position than was Boethius to deal with those intricate problems, for the simple reason that, being nothing but a professor of logic, there was nothing of the metaphysician in him to be ashamed of the logician. Hence the eagerness and boldness of mind with which he undertook to answer Porphyry's questions as soon as he met

[4] Ibid., p. 98.

them in the course of his own teaching. The hint of Porphyry, that this was a "most exalted business" and much above the normal grasp of the logician, was entirely lost upon him, and from the very beginning of what he called his "Logic for Beginners" he proceeded to tell his pupils how it is that our concepts and definitions can apply to real things.

I beg leave to call your attention to the precise nature of the phenomenon we are now witnessing. Here is a man unusually gifted for the study and the teaching of logic. As such, he is professionally engaged in the task of classifying our concepts according to their specific differences and of determining their various relations. What is a definition? What is a difference? What is a species? What is a genus? Those and many other similar questions were the proper stuff with which he had to deal as a logician. Yet, precisely because he was interested in classifying our concepts and determining the conditions of their various combinations, it was to be expected that he should stumble on this particular philosophical problem: What is the nature of our ideas and their relation to things? This was exactly the kind of philosophical question that would naturally arise in the mind of a logician, because it arises on the borderline that divides logic from philosophy. An almost invisible line indeed; yet as soon as you cross it, you find yourself in an entirely different country, and if you do not notice it, you get lost.

It was Abailard's misfortune to cross it, quite unaware of what he was doing. When he read Porphyry's famous sentence, "At present, I shall refuse to say concerning genera . . .", he took it for a mere precaution of the Greek author in addressing what Abailard calls "uncultivated readers", who are not yet able to inquire into such problems or to perceive their true meaning. He, therefore, quietly proceeded to discuss those philosophical questions as if he still were standing on purely logical ground. Now it was legitimate for Abailard to ask, in his own words, "how the universal definition can be applied to things";[5] but logic is not directly concerned with such problems. As a distinct science it is primarily concerned with the formal aspect of thought, not with the nature or origin of our concepts, and still less with the existence and nature of their external objects. If you ask logic to answer a philosophical question, you can expect but a logical answer, not a philosophical one, with the unavoidable consequence that your question will appear as unanswerable, and as a pseudo-question. This was precisely the kind of mistake that Abailard would make. A forward and, sometimes, a presumptuous man, he never had forewarnings while he was crossing some danger line. While yet a very young man, he had once been dared by his fellow students to teach theology without knowing it. He came back the next morning with one of the worst texts to be found in Ezekiel, and by means of syllogisms alone he explained it away. To him there never was anything like "lofty" questions or "most exalted business", because he knew logic, and there was nothing above it.

Let us now see him at work, and watch the results of his philosophical venture. What is a universal? It is, Abailard answers, that which can be predicated of several individual things taken one by one. Man, for instance, is a universal because the term can be applied to every individual man. This was a logical definition; but philosophy stepped in as soon as Abailard asked this other question: What is the nature of that which can be predicated of many? Has it even got a nature of its own? Is it a thing? Abailard's own professor of Logic at Paris, William of Champeaux, had always favoured the view that the genera and species were not mere conceptions of our mind, but real things actually existing outside the mind. In short, he was what mediæval philosophers would call a realist, not in our modern sense, but

[5] Ibid., p. 222.

in this sense, that he believed in the real existence of some element in things themselves which answers the generality of our concepts. There were some solid reasons for such an attitude. We give Socrates and Plato two different names because they are distinct as individuals; there is in each of them something that is not to be found in the other, let us say, for instance, their respective bodies. At the same time we see no difficulty in saying that both of them are men. Now on the strength of the same principle, if "Man" can be predicated with equal truth of Socrates and of Plato, there must be some element common to both. What is to be found in both of them, and accounts for the fact that both of them are men, must needs be just as real as that which makes each of them to be this particular individual. More than that, since that common element is what makes Socrates and Plato to be men, it is their very substance. Let us, therefore, say that human nature or, so to speak, "manness", is a real substance which, entirely present in every individual, is nevertheless common to all men.[6]

Though he was simply a pupil in William's class, at that time Abailard was not slow to detect a fallacy in his master's reasoning. If human nature is but partly present in Plato and in Socrates, neither Socrates nor Plato can truly be said to be a man. If, on the other hand, human nature is entirely present in one of them, it cannot be present at all in the other. Since it can be found in them neither partly, nor entirely, it cannot possibly be something, it is nothing.

Taken as a mere historical fact, such a controversy could be rightly considered as a sample of the most useless mental archeology; but it becomes highly significant as soon as we begin to see the reasons for which two men became entangled in their endless controversy. William and Abailard were equally convinced that a purely logical method would ultimately bring

[6] Ibid., p. 223.

forth an adequate answer to the question. Now logic, and quite especially mediæval logic, is ruled by the principle of contradiction, which always works when it is applied to concepts, but not always when it is applied to things. However correct my combinations of concepts may be, my conclusions cannot be more valid than my concepts. In other words, the common mistake of William of Champeaux and of Abailard consisted in not seeing that if it is necessary for a true reasoning that it be logical, it is not enough for it to be logical in order to be true. As a matter of fact, both were logically right and philosophically wrong. When I say that *Plato is a man*, and that *Socrates* also *is a man*, the word *man* can logically refer either to something that is the same in both cases, or to something that is not the same in both cases. If it is not the same, why do you give it the same name? If it is the same, how can it be found in two different things? I cannot find the slightest flaw in either one of those arguments; nor, for that matter, was Abailard or William able to find it in each other's reasoning. Hence their complete failure to convince each other in a dispute where only the more obstinate could win.

The more obstinate, of course, was Abailard. Being a rather shy and peaceful man, William of Champeaux tried to bring the controversy to an end by granting something to his cumbersome pupil. I say he tried, advisedly, because in a discussion in which logic reigned supreme, between his first position and that of Abailard there was no room left for a third. On the one side, William remained as convinced as ever that the genera and species were endowed with a reality of their own; on the other, Abailard had succeeded in convincing him that "all things are so diverse from each other, that none of them participates with another, in either the same matter essentially, or the same form essentially." William was, therefore, confronted with the hard task of preserving the real existence of the genera and species with-

out conceding their simultaneous presence in several distinct individuals. In order to get out of trouble, he simply decreed that
the genera and species should no longer be said to be present in
things *essentially*, that is to say, really, but *indifferently*. In other
words, William hoped to elude Abailard's criticism by substituting a simple lack of difference between two things for the presence of a common element in those things. The reason why
Plato and Socrates are men is this: not in the least that the same
human nature is present in both, but that "they do not differ in
the nature of humanity." [7] In short, the only reason why Socrates
and Plato are the same is that they are not different.

I quite agree that this time William of Champeaux's answer
was a most unhappy one. As Abailard immediately replied, a
mere lack of difference between two things is not enough to
account for their resemblance. For instance, Socrates and Plato
do not differ as men, which they are, but it is equally true to say
that they do not differ as stones, which they are not; and were
you to object: yes, but they are men, and they are not stones, the
ready answer would be that you are unconsciously reverting to
the first position of the question. If the reason why Socrates and
Plato are alike is a purely negative absence of difference, two
men are no more alike in what they are than in what they are
not. In point of fact, given such a case, they are not really alike,
they are merely not different. If, on the contrary, two individuals
are truly similar in this at least, that both are men, the reason for
it no longer is a mere lack of difference between them; they do
not differ, for the positive reason that both are equally sharing in
the same human nature. But then the same difficulty will occur:
If their nature is the same, how can they be different? If their
nature is the same, on what ground can we say that Socrates and
Plato are two men instead of saying that Plato is Socrates, and
that Socrates is Plato?

[7] Ibid., p. 228.

Twice defeated on his own ground by one of his pupils, William of Champeaux completely lost heart. He gave up the game and stopped teaching, the one irretrievable blunder in the career of a professor of philosophy. It was a blunder, for Abailard had clearly proved that William was wrong, but not in the least that he himself was right. After all, had he kept his patience and waited a little longer, William of Champeaux could easily have seen that both he and his pupil were asking the right question in the wrong way. Having knocked out his professor in the second round, Abailard now found himself in the always precarious position of a world champion. It was his task to say, no longer what the genera and species were not, but what they were. In other words, having clearly proved that human nature cannot be considered as a real thing, actually existing outside the mind, the problem for him was to say on what ground our mind is justified in ascribing the same nature to different individuals.

The answer given by Abailard to that question illustrates so remarkably the point that I am trying to make, that I beg to comment at some length upon it. My point is that Abailard mistook logic for philosophy; but what about logic itself? Abailard was a logician trespassing on philosophical ground because, as they knew practically nothing else, the natural approach of twelfth-century men to philosophy was logic. Yet, before study-ing logic, they had always learned something else; namely, gram-mar, with the unavoidable result that grammar was their normal approach to logic. The consequence of such a procedure was that Abailard was just as tempted to mistake grammar for logic as he was to mistake logic for philosophy. Now, what is the subject matter of grammar? It is language. Language itself is made up of words. It is the proper task of the grammarian to classify the various kinds of words of which our common speech is composed, to define their respective functions and to formulate the laws that determine their connections. As a distinct science—and it is for talking beings the most fundamental of all—grammar knows nothing but words. If you ask a grammarian a question, and if he answers it as a grammarian, your problem will inevitably be reduced by him to a mere question of words. Hence Abailard's famous sentence: "Now, however, that reasons have been given why things cannot be called universals, taken either singly or collectively, because they are not predicated of many, it remains to ascribe universality of this sort to words alone." [8] But in what sense can a word be said to be universal?

If, as Claude Bernard once wrote in his *Introduction to Experimental Medicine*, an experiment is "an observation which is either provoked, or invoked, to check up an hypothesis", Abailard's answer to the question can rightly be used as a typical case of experiment in philosophy. Before his quarrel with William of Champeaux, he had already studied logic under another professor, whose doctrine was altogether different, but equally repellent to his own mind. Roscelin, for such was the name of that first master, was of the opinion that universals were mere *flatus vocis*, that is to say, mere vocal utterances. In other words, and this is a doctrine that we shall meet again in the fourteenth century, Roscelin was turning universals into particular and concrete things; *man*, for instance, was nothing more to him than the particular noise, the physical displacement of air, which we produce when we say: *man*. With his precocious insight, Abailard very soon detected what was wrong with that theory. When we say *man*, we do much more than make a noise; we speak, and to speak is to utter sounds that have a meaning. Each one of those meaningful sounds is what we call a voice, or a word. When we ask ourselves how the word *man* can mean, at one and the same time, two radically distinct individuals, the

[8] Ibid., p. 232.

question at stake has little to do with the physical nature of the word; what is then under discussion is its meaning. How is it that a single word sometimes means several different things?

By asking such a question, Abailard was raising a very important philosophical problem, but it was a problem with which, as a logician, he had no reasons to feel concerned. As a matter of fact, since he knew that there are words whose meanings remain one and the same while they are applied to a whole class of individuals, he already knew all that he, as a logician, needed to know concerning their nature. Some words, or forms, do for a single individual, as Socrates; some do for a definite group of individuals, as man; once those elementary things had been said, it was time for the logician to begin his own work. Instead of doing so, his mind still full of his recent controversy with William, Abailard heedlessly asked himself: When we are using universal names, what are we talking about? We know that, physically speaking, all that is is individual; on the other hand, we also know that, logically speaking, our general ideas, or universals, have a meaning. Now that which they mean cannot be a thing, since it is universal. Then what is it? Ask a logician such a question, and you can be sure of the answer: that which is not a thing, is nothing. Consequently, there is nothing in reality to answer our general idea; in other words, universal names mean nothing. If William of Champeaux ever read those lines,[9] he must have been amply consoled for his own defeat by Abailard's perplexities. Having given his question that logical answer, Abailard was to fight for it to the bitter end and to maintain it in spite of all conceivable difficulties. The most obvious of his difficulties was: If universal names are without definite object, in what sense is it still true to say that they have a meaning? It was proper to remind Roscelin that words have a meaning; in a way it was equally legitimate to prove against William that what common words mean does not

[9] Ibid., p. 235.

exist; but then a third question unavoidably arises: What do you
mean by their meaning?

The true greatness of a philosopher is always proportional to
his intellectual honesty; no wonder then if it is there, in the very
centre of his difficulties, that Abailard's greatness shows itself in
full. Instead of contriving some cheap answer trying to disguise
it, he systematically destroyed each one that could have helped
him. Having proved that "man" could not point to human
nature because there is no such thing in the world, he added,
that when we hear such a name, we do not understand any one
of the many individuals which it designates, for indeed if such
were the case, there would be no difference between common
nouns and proper nouns. Thus, in Abailard's own words: "that
very community of imposition [which is typical of such a word
as *man*] is an impediment which prevents any one man being
understood in it." But since *man* does not designate any man in
particular, it can still less designate a collection of such individuals. Hence Abailard's conclusion that "in the common name
which is *man*, not Socrates himself, nor any other man, nor the
entire collection of men is reasonably understood from the
import of the word." [10] Had he been as prudent as he was
honest, our logician would have stopped asking questions about
what a signification can be where there is nothing to be signified. But prudence was so little one of Abailard's virtues, that,
having thus eliminated all possible answers, he nevertheless proceeded to answer the question.

The result was all that could be expected. According to
Abailard, the word *man* can connote both Socrates and Plato
because, distinct from each other as they may be in respect to
their essences and properties, those two individuals "are united
nevertheless in that they are men". [11] One cannot understand
even in what sense Abailard could consider it as an answer,

[10] Ibid., p. 236.   [11] Ibid., p. 237.

unless one keeps in mind the definite nature of his question. As he saw it, or rather as he himself had made it to be, the problem now for him was to find a positive cause for the existence of genera and species, but such a positive cause as would not be a thing. On the other hand, it should not be forgotten that, as a logician, his only chance was to find some dialectical escape from his difficulties. He thought he had found it in the very subtle distinction that can be drawn by the mind, between the individual reality of a man, which is a concretely existing being, and the fact that it is a man, which is positive but is not a thing. In order to understand his position, it is therefore necessary to conceive separately what Abailard would call: *to be man*. Of course, we can try, but there is slight hope of succeeding.

In point of fact, I am not quite sure that Abailard himself ever wholly succeeded in doing it. His first approach to the difficulty was through the notion of sameness. "For different things to agree", says Abailard, "is for the individuals to be the same or not to be the same, as to be man or white, or not to be man and not to be white." [12] Quite true, but what makes two men to be men, or two white things to be white? Were we to understand it in this sense, that they are both sharing in some common nature, what a triumph it would be for William of Champeaux! Abailard, of course, did not want that and he was careful to make the point as clear as possible by adding that here: "We understand nothing other than that those individuals are men, and in this they do not differ in the least, in this, I say, that they are men, *although we appeal to no essence*." [13] Quite true again, but if we appeal to no essence, what positive answer are we giving to the question? Is not this merely coming back to the second position of William of Champeaux, that there is a simple lack, or absence of difference between any two individuals belonging to the same species? Abailard himself did not

[12] Ibid.   [13] Ibid., p. 238.

think so. To his own mind, "to be man" was not nothing, and yet it was not a thing, it was a *state* or a *condition*; let us say that, rather than a being, it was a certain way of being. In his own words, "we call it the status itself of man to be man, which is not a thing, and which we also call the common cause of imposition of the word on individuals, according as they themselves agree with each other." Of course, we understand every word Abailard uses in that sentence, but if he really means to say that there is something, that is not a thing, and nevertheless is a cause, I for my own part must confess that I feel utterly unable to see his point.

There is little doubt, however, that Abailard really had nothing more to say on the philosophical side of the question. Judgments whose terms do not point to really existing substances are possible, and they can be logically correct. Yet one does not see what Abailard could gain by resorting to such logical artifices. "Often," says he, "we call those things too by the name of cause, which are not any thing, as when it is said: he was lashed because he does not wish to appear in court. He does not wish to appear in court, which is stated as a cause, is no essence." Now, I ask you, are there many reading these words who wish to appear in court? Yet I hope none of them will be lashed. The objection directed by Abailard against William at an earlier stage of the discussion is now working against his own position. If we are dealing here with a purely negative absence of wish, it cannot be considered as a cause. In point of fact, that man "does not wish to", because "he wishes not to", and he wishes it in circumstances when he ought not to wish it. The same remark applies to the question at stake; it does not help in the least to say that Socrates and Plato are in the same condition as men because they are not different in respect to that condition; what we want to know is just the reverse: if they are not different as men, it is because, as men, they are the same. To that precise objection, Abailard had no other answer than this: "We can also call the status of man those things themselves, established in the nature of man, the common likeness of which he who imposed the word conceived." [14] As it is obvious that, in this case, the real cause for the imposition of common names is not the things themselves, but their common likeness, Abailard was merely begging the question.

He could not possibly have done more by means of logic alone. I fancy that he more or less obscurely felt it, for he suddenly dropped the problem, but only to tackle a no less difficult one, and one for whose solution he was no better equipped: admitting that we have two different kinds of knowledge, that which expresses itself in common names, and that which answers common names, what is their respective value? This again was a very important and philosophically significant question, for it amounted to asking if science is knowledge of that which is universal, or of that which is particular. Unfortunately, the only help on which Abailard could rely in his endeavour to answer the second question, was his own failure to meet the first one. Unable as he was to decide whether the likeness of similar objects was something real or not, it was impossible for him rightly to estimate the value of general ideas. He tried, however, and as was usual with him, in a most intelligent way.

As he could not find in things any objective ground for the imposition of common names, Abailard looked for it in the mind. This meant nothing less than substituting psychology for both logic and philosophy. He therefore asked himself, what is the nature of those mental presentations "which the mind constructs for itself when it wishes and as it wishes", such as, for instance, the concept of man. In answering the question, Abailard could not forget his former conclusion, that the universals are

[14] Ibid.

not things. He accordingly described our concepts as being but imaginary and fictive likenesses of their real objects, "like those imaginary cities which are seen in dreams, or that form of the projected building which the artist conceives as the figure and exemplar of the thing to be found, which we call neither substance nor accident".[15] In other words, though what it represents may be something real in itself, what we call a concept has no more reality than the reflexion of some object in a looking glass. Moreover, among our concepts, some are mental presentations of a really existing thing, some are not. When I hear the word *Socrates*, for instance, I can picture to myself the particular face and figure of Socrates, with all the characteristics that make him different from Plato; my concept then has a definite object. On the contrary, when I hear the word *man*, I cannot think of any particular individual as representing human nature in its universality. What then happens is, in Abailard's own words, that "a certain figure arises in my mind, which is so related to individual men, that it is common to all, and proper to none." [16]

Such an answer was a striking anticipation of what John Locke would say much later on the same subject; but what is most remarkable is that, in a confused way at least, Abailard had some presentiment of what Berkeley's criticism of Locke would be, and that he accepted it. The strict accuracy of his philosophical language made it difficult for him not to see the difficulty that lay hidden behind his description of general ideas. In the first place, since human nature does not exist by itself, it is clear that those ideas have no object. In the second place, it is not even certain that we have such ideas at all. According to Abailard's own description of it, the general idea of "lion", for instance, should be like a picture made to show what he calls "the nature of all lions". How could this be possible in a doctrine whose fundamental assumption is that all that is is

¹⁵ Ibid., p. 239.   ¹⁶ Ibid., p. 240.

particular, and consequently that each lion has his own nature?
Again, Abailard adds that such a mental picture should be made
"representing what is proper to no one of them".[17] Now, I ask
you, can you imagine such a lion's tail as will fit the back of no
one lion in particular, and yet will generally do for all of them?
If I think of a lion with a mane, what about those lions that
have none; if I think of a lion without a mane, how could those
that have a mane be represented or even signified by it?

Abailard himself very soon reached the conclusion that he
had no general ideas. God alone has them, and that to him is the
reason why God could create, and can still keep in existence, a
multiplicity of individuals distributed among their various genera and species. As a creator, He is like an artist "about to
compose something, who preconceives in his mind the exem-
plary form of the thing to be composed". Hence, for God, the
possibility of creating an indefinite number of distinct individuals, all made in the likeness of the same idea, and thereby
belonging to one and the same species. But God is God, and
men are but men. We are unable to do what God so easily does,
that is, as Abailard says, to create those "general works" which
are the genera, or those "special states" which are the species. In
point of fact, we cannot *create* any natural and general order, but
can only *make* things that are both artificial and particular. All
that we need, and fortunately have, are particular images, plus
those composite and confused images that result in us from the
superimposition of the particular ones. Hence Abailard's ultimate conclusion, that men can have a true understanding of
what comes to the senses, whereas for all those general forms
that cannot be perceived by sense, we have much less understanding than opinion.

What is truly remarkable about Abailard's epistemology is
that, all by itself, it makes up a perfectly rounded philosophical

[17] Ibid., p. 241.

experiment. Here is one of the brightest intellects the Middle Ages has ever produced; he begins by interpreting logic in terms of grammar; then he proceeds to interpret philosophy in terms of logic, and as he fails to find a positive answer to his question, we see him ultimately reduced to a psychological solution. But was it a solution? If there is nothing in reality to answer our common concepts or, more precisely, if sameness is not something real in things, how can likeness possibly be found in our ideas of them? The difficulty was so real that Abailard himself felt it, but even his last allusion to an order of divine ideas is less an answer than a casual remark suggested to him by a short text in Priscian's *Grammar*.[18] If, as Priscian says, there are general and special forms of things intelligibly subsisting in the divine mind, the problem of their relations to the bodies in which they have been produced unavoidably arises. Had Abailard been in a position to understand the import of that problem and to realize its specific nature, he would at last have discussed a philosophical problem in a philosophical way. As he failed to do so, we cannot even guess what his answer to the question might have been. At least, there would have been one, and the history of mediæval philosophy would undoubtedly have followed another course. The ultimate result of Abailard's error was the same—that we inevitably will see following similar mistakes—scepticism. If our concepts are but words, without any other contents than more or less vague images, all universal knowledge becomes a mere set of arbitrary opinions. What we usually call science ceases to be a system of general and necessary relations and finds itself reduced to a loose string of empirically connected facts.

The upshot of Abailard's experiment is that philosophy cannot be obtained from pure logic. Such had already been the conclusion of a keen twelfth-century observer, the highly lovable English humanist, John of Salisbury. When, many years

[18] Ibid., p. 242.

after completing his studies at Paris, he returned a mature man, to revisit his old companions "whom dialectic still detained", they had not made the slightest progress. "I found them as before," says John of Salisbury, "and where they were before; they did not appear to have advanced an inch in settling the old questions, nor had they added a single proposition. The aims that since inspired them, inspired them still; they had progressed in one point only: they had unlearned moderation, they knew not modesty; and that to such an extent that one might despair of their recovery. So experience taught me a manifest conclusion, that, while logic furthers other studies, it is by itself lifeless and barren, nor can it cause the mind to yield the fruit of philosophy, except the same conceive from some other source." [19]

Let John of Salisbury's experience become our own experience. If, as I hope, we succeed in finding a number of similar cases, all of them pointing to the same conclusion, we shall perhaps be justified in turning them into a single concrete experience of what philosophy actually is, and in ascribing to it an objective unity.

[19] Joannis Saresberiensis, *Metalogicus*, lib. II, cap. 10; PL, vol. 199, col. 869. As translated by J. H. Robinson and H. W. Rolfe, *Petrarch: The First Modern Scholar and Man of Letters* (New York, 1898), p. 223.

CHAPTER II

THEOLOGISM AND PHILOSOPHY

When in the late eleventh and early twelfth centuries mediæval men rediscovered logic, they became intoxicated with the wine of formal reasoning and the abstract beauty of its laws. Hence their natural tendency to deal in a purely logical way with all possible questions. They did this in philosophy and, as was to be expected, they did it also in theology. The only difference being that there was no philosopher of note to resist the intrusion of the logicians, whereas there were a great many theologians to check their encroachments on the field of theology. In point of fact, there is hardly a single one among the great logicians of that time who has not been accused of heresy, or even condemned for it. Bérenger of Tours was condemned for his dialectical treatment of the Transubstantiation, Roscelin of Compiègne and Abailard for their dialectical interpretation of the mystery of the Trinity. Yet, Abailard himself was a moderate in those matters. At least, he considered himself as such, and it cannot be denied that one of his main intentions, when he first wrote on theological questions, was to show how such a thing could be done without harming either the necessary rules of logic or the unquestionable authority of Christian faith. It is a pity that goodwill plus logic can no more make a theologian than a philosopher. When Abailard died, a very pious and tired old monk in a Benedictine monastery, his doctrine had been and still remained, condemned by the Church. In his fight against St. Bernard of Clairvaux, not Abailard but St. Bernard was the winner.

The history of that long struggle between logicians and theologians, which went on for more than a century, would be quite irrelevant to our purpose were it not for the fact that philosophy itself rapidly became involved in it. Unaware of any dividing line between logic and philosophy, any twelfth-century professor of logic, who had never learned or taught anything but grammar and logic, would naturally call himself a philosopher. The theologians saw no reasons to worry about the mistakes made by the logicians. If there were such reasons, they utterly failed to perceive them. The only thing they were conscious of on this point was that the men who were teaching logic were also the men whom everybody called philosophers, and who were themselves convinced that philosophy is nothing but logic applied to philosophical questions. Now it was an obvious fact that if logic were allowed freely in the discussion and settling of theological questions, the unavoidable result would be the complete destruction of theology. Given their calling and the times in which they lived, these men could not be expected to see any better than the logicians themselves, what was wrong with a purely logical conception of philosophy. As theologians, their task was not to save philosophy from logicism, but, through faith and grace, to save mankind from eternal perdition. Any obstacle that stood in the way of this had to be carefully removed, be it philosophy itself. But what was the best way for theology to get rid of philosophy was a rather intricate question.

An obvious way to deal with the difficulty was to eradicate philosophy and philosophical problems from the human mind. Wherever there is a theology, or merely a faith, there are over-zealous theologians and believers to preach that pious souls have no use for philosophical knowledge, and that philosophical speculation is basically inconsistent with a sincere religious life. Among those who favour such an attitude, there are some of a rather crude type, but others are very intelligent men, whose speculative power is by no means inferior to their religious zeal. The only difference between such men and true philosophers is that instead of using their reason in behalf of philosophy, they turn their natural ability against it.

If we consider, for instance, the history of Islamic thought, Gazali will provide us with a perfect example of such an attitude. Many years before his age there had been a violent reaction in Islam against the introduction of dialectics into theology. The two spiritual groups whose ceaseless rivalry runs through the whole history of the Christian Middle Ages are already there, clearly discernible in the early history of Islamic thought. Since, according to tradition, the Prophet had said: "The first thing which God created was knowledge or Reason",[1] some Mohammedan theologians concluded that speculation was one of the duties of the believers, an argument that we shall find strictly paralleled by a similar statement in the writings of Bérenger of Tours. To other Mohammedan theologians, on the contrary, "whatever went beyond the regular ethical teaching was heresy . . . , for faith should be obedience, and not . . . knowledge";[2] an attitude that is exactly analogous to that of a large group of later Christian theologians. Gazali was the best exponent of the latter attitude, for he was brilliantly gifted for the very philosophical speculation which he thoroughly disliked. His famous *Destruction of the Philosophers*, written around 1090, is a striking confirmation of Aristotle's statement that to prove philosophy one has to philosophize, and to disprove philosophy one still has to philosophize. Against Aristotelianism, as

---

[1] As quoted by T. J. de Boer, *The History of Philosophy in Islam*, trans. E. R. Jones (London: Luzac, 1933), p. 43.

[2] Ibid.

it had been taught by Alfarabi and Avicenna, Gazali was able to turn Aristotle's own weapons in a masterly way. True, the fact that he was borrowing from a Christian commentator of Aristotle, Johannes Philoponus,[3] largely accounts for his substantial agreement with the criticism of Aristotle by later Christian theologians; but this is not our present concern. The only point in which we are interested here is the striking likeness between these two attitudes and the identity of their philosophical results. Using reason against reason in behalf of religion is by itself a legitimate, and eventually a noble, attitude; yet, if we adopt it, we must be ready to face its necessary consequences. In the first place, when religion tries to establish itself on the ruins of philosophy, there usually arises a philosopher to found philosophy on the ruins of religion. After a Gazali, there often comes an Averroës, who answers the *Destruction of the Philosophers* by a *Destruction of the Destruction*, as was the case with the famous book published by Averroës under that title; such apologies of philosophy, suggested as they are by theological oppositions, are usually destructive of religion. In the second place, philosophy has as little to gain by such conflicts as has religion itself, for the easiest way for theologians to hold their ground is to show that philosophy is unable to reach rationally valid conclusions on any question related to the nature of man and his destiny. Hence Gazali's scepticism in philosophy, which he tries to redeem, as is usually the case, by mysticism in religion. The God, whom reason cannot know, can be grasped by the soul's experience; the world, which human reason cannot understand, can be transcended and, as it were, flown over by the spirit of Prophecy. Needless to say, the philosopher, as such, has nothing against mysticism; what he does not like is a mysticism that presupposes as its necessary condition the destruction of philosophy. If, as seems to be true, mystical life is one of the

[3] Ibid., p. 159.

permanent needs of human nature, it should not only be respected, but protected against the too frequent assaults of superficial minds. Yet it remains true that philosophical knowledge is a standing need of human reason and that need too ought to be respected. It is for us the most difficult, but at the same time the most important, of all problems, to maintain all of those spiritual activities which honour human nature and dignify human life. We gain nothing by destroying one in order to save another, for they stand and fall together. True mysticism is never found without some theology, and sound theology always seeks the support of some philosophy; but a philosophy that does not at least make room for theology is a short-sighted philosophy, and what shall we call a theology wherein no provision is made for at least the possibility of mystical experience?

The obscure feeling of these necessary relations has often prompted theologians to deal in a much less radical way with philosophical speculation. Instead of attempting to kill it by discrediting the work of the philosophers, some divines have thought it better to tame and, so to speak, to domesticate philosophy by merging it in theology. I think that it would be a great mistake to seek dishonest and treacherous designs behind such a move. When theologians, whatever their particular creed may be, attempt to remodel philosophy to suit their own beliefs, they are prompted to do so by a sincere conviction that philosophy is in itself an excellent thing, so good indeed that it would be a shame to allow it to perish. On the other hand, where the revealed truth is, by hypothesis, absolute truth, the only way to save philosophy is to show that its teaching is substantially the same as that of revealed religion. The various systems whose common origin is to be found in such an attitude are almost always majestic and impressive, sometimes deep and very seldom insignificant. Owing to the seriousness of their purpose, as well as to their boldness in dealing with the highest metaphysical

problems, such doctrines have often been a source of philosophical progress. They look like philosophy, they talk like
philosophy, they sometimes are studied or taught in schools
under the name of philosophy: yet, in point of fact, they are
little more than theologies clothed in philosophical garb. Let us
call such an attitude Theologism and see how it works.

Different as they may be, owing to the various times, places
and civilizations in which they were conceived, these doctrines
resemble each other at least in this, that all of them are thoroughly intoxicated with a definite religious feeling which I beg
leave to call, for simplicity's sake, the feeling of the Glory of
God. Needless to say there is no true religion without that
feeling. The deeper it is, the better it is; but it is one thing to
experience a certain feeling deeply, and another thing to allow it
to dictate, uncontrolled by reason, a completely rounded interpretation of the world. When and where piety is permitted to
inundate the philosophical field, the usual outcome is that, the
better to extol the glory of God, pious-minded theologians
proceed joyfully to annihilate God's own creation. God is great,
and high, and almighty; what better proof could be given of
these truths than that nature and man are essentially insignificant, low and utterly powerless creatures? A very dangerous
method indeed, for in the long run it is bound to hurt both
philosophy and religion. In such a case the sequence of doctrines too often runs in the following way: with the best intentions in the world, some theologian suggests, as a philosophically
established truth, that God is and does everything, while nature
and man are and do nothing; then comes a philosopher who
grants the theologian's success in proving that nature is powerless, but emphasizes his failure to prove that there is a God.
Hence the logical conclusion that nature is wholly deprived of
reality and intelligibility. This is scepticism, and it cannot be
avoided in such cases. Now one can afford to live on philosophi-

cal scepticism, so long as it is backed by a positive religious faith; yet, even while our faith is there, one still remains a sceptic in philosophy, and were our faith ever to go, what would be left of us but an absolute sceptic?

From that point of view, no philosophical experiment is more interesting than the doctrine of the Asharites, a Mohammedan sect of the late ninth and early tenth centuries. After the first contacts had been established between Greek thought and Islamic faith, attempts were made on the part of Muslim theologians to reorganize philosophy from within in order to mould it into conformity with the fundamental articles of their own creed. The founder of the sect was Al Ashari (873–935), whom Professor T. J. de Boer describes, in his valuable *History of Philosophy in Islam* (p. 56), as a man "who understood how to render to God the things that are God's, and to man the things that are man's." I have no doubt that such was Al Ashari's honest intention; he certainly meant to do it, but whether or not he understood how to do it is an entirely different question. As a matter of fact, were Ashari to be credited with but a small part of the philosophical positions that were held later on in his school, the truth would be that his way of understanding it was to render everything to God and nothing to man. His doctrine is a remarkable instance of what happens to philosophy when it is handled by theologians, according to theological methods, for a theological end.

According to Moses Maïmonides, whose *Guide for the Perplexed*[4] is our chief source of information here, there were twelve propositions common to all Muslim theologians, some of which are directly relevant to the present inquiry. But before examining their contents it will be advantageous to ascertain the

[4] The following quotations of Maïmonides will all refer to the English translation by M. Friedländer, *The Guide for the Perplexed*, 2nd ed. (London: Routledge; New York: Dutton, 1928).

spirit in which those propositions were first formulated. "At the time when the Christian Church brought the Greeks and the Syrians into its fold," says Maïmonides, ". . . the opinions of the philosophers were current amongst those nations. . . . The learned Greek and Syrian Christians of the age, seeing that their dogmas were unquestionably exposed to severe attacks from the existing philosophical systems, laid the foundation for the science of dogmatics; they commenced by putting forth such propositions as would support their doctrines and be useful for the refutation of opinions opposed to the fundamental principles of the Christian faith." In short, as we would say today, the philosophy of these Christians was but that particular branch of theology which we call apologetics. Maïmonides then goes on to say that when the Mohammedans began to translate the writings of the Greek philosophers, from the Syrian into Arabic, they likewise translated the criticisms of those philosophers by such Christians as Johannes Philoponus, and several others. Not only did they adopt those criticisms as helping to destroy false philosophies, but "they selected from the opinions of ancient philosophers whatever seemed serviceable to their purposes", in the firm conviction that—in Maïmonides' own words—some of these doctrines "contained useful propositions for the defence of positive religion".[5] This new development gave to their theology an aspect unknown to the Greek Christian theologians; after adopting new theories, Maïmonides says, they were obliged to defend them, and consequently to build up a consistent interpretation of the world.

It was consistent enough, but was it true? Maïmonides, who with St. Thomas Aquinas is perhaps the most balanced of all mediæval theologians, has described in a masterly manner the sort of game which those men were playing. "It is not our object, Maïmonides says, "to criticize things which are peculiar

[5] Ibid., p. 109.

to either creed, or books which were written exclusively in the interest of the one community or the other. We merely maintain that the earlier theologians, both of the Greek Christians and of the Mohammedans, when they laid down their propositions, did not investigate the real properties of things; first of all they considered what *must* be the properties of the things which should yield proof for or against a certain creed; and when this was found they asserted that the thing must be endowed with those properties; then they employed the same assertion as a proof for the identical arguments which had led to the assertion, and by which they either supported or refuted a certain opinion." In short, Maïmonides concluded, these men were doing the very reverse of what Themistius rightly invites us to do, which is to adapt our opinions to things, instead of adapting things to our opinions; for this indeed cannot be done and it is a waste of time to try it.[6]

It is to be noted that Maïmonides did not stop there. Pushing his analysis further, he reached the very core of these doctrines and succeeded in isolating their germ, the primitive nucleus of all their later developments. Accusing their authors of not being interested in the real nature of things would have been a cheap criticism, though a true one. What Maïmonides has clearly perceived, with remarkable insight, is that even these men themselves were aware of the fact, and that, in a sense, their whole doctrine was but a toilsome justification of their attitude. Knowing, as they did, that their statements were open to that criticism, they assumed that it was quite useless to worry about the real nature and order of things, because things have indeed neither nature nor order. Even though its existence be convincingly established, that which actually is proves nothing at all, "because it is merely one of the various phases of things, the opposite of which is equally admissible to our minds."[7] That

[6] Ibid., pp. 109–10.   [7] Ibid., p. 110.

Maïmonides' diagnosis was accurate is best proved by a brief survey of a few at least of their propositions.

The first proposition was that all things are composed of atoms. By the word *atom*, these men understood, as did every one else, particles of matter that are small to the point of being indivisible; but they added to that classical meaning a new connotation. Not only are their atoms indivisible, but they have no magnitude; magnitude arises only when two atoms or more combine together and thus form a body. Such atoms are, therefore, very different from those of Democritus and Epicurus; having no magnitude, they have neither size nor shape of their own, and thus they cannot be used as the foundations of a mechanical interpretation of the world. Moreover they are not eternal, but created by God when it pleases Him; nor are they numerically constant, since God is always free to create new ones or to annihilate those which He has already created. In order to account for the possibility of motion, these theologians admitted that there is a vacuum, that is, an empty space wherein the atoms may combine, separate and move—that was their second proposition. Now let us join together the first two propositions: God is constantly creating anew a certain number of atoms which are separated from each other by empty space; it becomes immediately apparent from this that their existence is as discontinuous in time as it is in space. In other words, "time is composed of time atoms", each time-element being as indivisible in itself as are the atoms themselves. The consequence of that twofold position was very remarkable indeed, since it implied that just as space is made up of elements that are deprived of extension, so time is made up of elements that are deprived of duration. In such a doctrine, Maïmonides says, "time would be an object of position and order", to which remark he scornfully adds, "what can be expected of those who do not regard the nature of things?" And yet, starting from similar principles

seven centuries later, no less a man than Descartes was to reach
strikingly similar conclusions. If longer times are not made up
of shorter times, if time elements do not last, the obvious
implication is that motion itself has nothing to do with duration. Locomotion is the mere "translation of each atom of a
body from one point to the next one"; in other words, it is
much less a change in time than a transfer in space. As Descartes
himself will write in his *Principles of Philosophy* (bk. II, chap. 25),
motion is neither the force nor the action which transports, it is
the *transportation*.

I know that Descartes would object violently to such a comparison. Yet any effort on his part to stress the differences between Al Ashari's atomism and Cartesian mechanism would be
an absolute waste of time. We know these differences and we
could list them about as accurately as could Descartes himself;
but there is no need to do so, for the real question at stake is a
very different one. Descartes was a great mathematician and a
great philosopher; Al Ashari was but an intelligent theologian
poaching on philosophical ground; we are here as dispassionate
observers of the life, growth and decay of ideas in history; yet,
different in purpose and unequal in genius as we may be, all of us
are ruled by the necessity that knits together philosophical ideas.
It is true that when Descartes unconsciously came back to Al
Ashari's essential position, he was too great a man not to improve
it enormously; what he could not possibly have done, even had
he been a still greater man, was, starting from similar principles,
not to reach similar conclusions. It is not, therefore, for us to
judge Descartes, but to allow both Descartes and ourselves to be
judged by the abstract necessity of impersonal truth.

Seen from that point of view and with all due reservations as
to their differences in structure, the two doctrines under discussion were obviously bound for the same philosophical deadlock.
If they hold in common a molecular conception of matter

coupled with the assumption of a ceaselessly renewed creation of the world by God, the greatest as well as the least among men are equally bound to underwrite Descartes' conclusion, that motion is but a change in place or, as Professor Whitehead put it so well: "the simple location of instantaneous material configurations." [8] This indeed is not Al Ashari's conclusion, or Descartes' or Spinoza's conclusion, it is the conclusion of philosophy itself; and when we hear old Galenus' protest, that "time is something divine and incomprehensible", or when Maïmonides, Thomas Aquinas, Bergson and Professor Whitehead join in rejecting what they call "a distortion of nature", it is not their protests that we hear but the protest of nature itself asking justice from philosophy. For such is our common judge: reason, as judged itself by reality; and all of us are to the full extent equal and free, when we are equally swayed by it.

So true is this that, after anticipating Descartes' reduction of time and motion to space, Al Ashari had only to follow his accepted line of thought in order to anticipate the conclusions which Malebranche was later to draw from Cartesian principles. Let us assume, with Al Ashari, that bodies are mere heaps of atoms which are themselves devoid of size, shape and other qualities. In order to account for these sensible qualities by which bodies seem to differ, it will become necessary to suppose that all such qualities are as many accidents, really distinct from these atoms in which they are dwelling as in their substances. Or rather, they are not really dwelling there, for the good reason that even the atom-substances themselves do not dwell; both atoms and qualities, or substances and accidents, are constantly created anew by an all-powerful God. The consequence of this state of things is that, in a world made up of matter-atoms situated in time-atoms, what such a world is at the present

[8] A. N. Whitehead, *Science and the Modern World* (New York: Macmillan, 1925), p. 72.

moment can in no way be considered as the cause of what it will be at the next moment. What is true of the world at large is necessarily true of each one of its component parts. What I am now doing can in no way be the cause of what I shall be doing during the next instant of time; the actual position of a material body cannot account for its position in the next time-atom. In short, just as such a world is deprived of all real duration and of all real motion, so is it deprived of all efficient causality.

Why then does it look as if there were relations of causes and effects in our universe? Here I beg leave to quote in full Maïmonides' answer that you may be sure I am not forging historical analogies: "In accordance with this principle [i.e., that time is composed of time-atoms] they assert that when man is perceived to move a pen, it is not he who has really moved it; the motion produced in the pen is an accident which God has created in the pen; the apparent motion of the hand which moves the pen is likewise an accident which God has created in the moving hand; but the creative act of God is performed in such a manner that the motion of the hand and the motion of the pen follow each other closely; but the hand does not act and is not the cause of the pen's motion; for, as they say, an accident cannot pass from one thing to another. . . . There does not exist any thing to which an action could be ascribed; the real *agens* is God. . . . In short, most of the Mutakallémin [i.e., Muslim theologians] believe that it must never be said that one thing is the cause of another; some of them who assumed causality were blamed for doing so. . . . They believe that when a man has the will to do a thing and, as he believes, does it, the will has been created for him, then the power to conform to the will, and lastly the act itself. . . . Such is, according to their opinion, the right interpretation of the creed that God is efficient cause." But, adds Maïmonides, "I, together with all rational persons, apply to those theories the words 'Will you mock at Him, as you mock at man?' for their words are indeed nothing but mockery." [9]

Was it really mockery? I am not so sure that Maïmonides himself believed it. There is nothing in his masterly analysis that points to such an intention in the mind of these theologians. Malebranche certainly was a most pious priest; yet he was to teach the same doctrine. If ever there was a man who took theology seriously, it was the puritan divine Cotton Mather. Yet Cotton Mather could write: "The body, which is matter in such and such a figure, cannot affect the immaterial soul, nor can the soul, which has no figure, command the body; but the great God, having established certain laws, that upon such and such desires of the soul, the body shall be so and so commanded, *He* 'tis, who by his continual influx does execute His own laws; 'tis to his continual influx that the effects are owing." [10] Here are three theologians: a Muslim, a Catholic and a Protestant, each of whom would have sternly consigned the other two to hell, yet who could not but agree on the same philosophy, precisely because theirs was a philosophy of theologians. With a little less zeal for the glory of God, or rather, with a still greater zeal enlightened by common sense, these men would no doubt have realized that the destruction of causality ultimately meant the destruction of nature, and thereby of science as well as of philosophy. Even when it has laws, a physical world whose laws are not inscribed in the very essence of things is a world without intrinsic necessity or intelligibility, and therefore unfit for rational knowledge. Scepticism always goes hand in hand with such theologies, and it is very bad for philosophy—but is it better for religion?

[9] For this quotation, as well as the texts upon which the preceding analysis is founded, see Maïmonides, *Guide for the Perplexed*, pp. 120–26.

[10] I am indebted for my knowledge of this text (and even of its author) to the very suggestive address delivered at the Harvard Tercentenary Conference of Arts and Sciences by Professor H. M. Jones on "The Drift to Liberalism in the Colonial Eighteenth Century".

In one of his best novels, G. K. Chesterton introduces a very simple priest who finds out that a man, though clothed as a priest, is not a priest but a common thief; when the man asks him what made him sure that he was not a priest, Father Brown simply answers: "You attacked reason. It's bad theology." Father Brown was obviously a sound Thomist. No more than Maïmonides,[11] St. Thomas Aquinas was inclined to mistake religiosity for religion. He was too great a theologian to indulge in an attitude in which theology has no less to lose than has philosophy itself; but he took an interest in it, first as an artist, for there is something fascinating in a blunder so consistently executed; and secondly as a theologian, because he knew many good men infected by this same disease, some of whom would have branded him as a pagan for his stubbornness in dealing with philosophical problems in a purely philosophical way.

The propensity to see nothing in philosophy but a particular department of theology was no less common among Christian theologians than among the Muslim interpreters of the Koran. Among the innumerable representatives of that tendency whom I could quote, I should like to single out one of the most lovable figures in the whole history of mediæval thought: the great doctor of mystical contemplation, St. Bonaventura. A general minister of the Franciscan Order, St. Bonaventura was, and still remains, the most perfect exponent of Franciscan theology, that is of a theology thoroughly imbued with the religious genius of St. Francis of Assisi. Besides being one of the greatest figures in the history of speculative mysticism, St. Bonaventura was a philosopher. One can find scattered through the mass of his theological works a large number of metaphysical discussions that have become part and parcel of the history of mediæval philosophy. His idea of philosophy, however, was somewhat peculiar. We find it best expressed in the very title of one of his

[11] Maïmonides, *Guide for the Perplexed*, p. 131.

shorter mystical treatises: *On Reducing the Arts to Theology*. The Latin verb *reducere* is indeed one of his favourite expressions and for him it always means to bring—or to take—a certain thing back to God. The world has been created as an image of, and a witness to, the glory of its Creator; but the material world itself does not know it; man alone has been created with a knowing mind and a loving heart, in order that, by knowing and loving all things in God, he might refer them to their origin, which is at the same time their end. When man is thus conceived as a high priest in the lofty temple of nature, his essential function is to lend his own voice to an otherwise speechless creation, to help each thing in publicly confessing its deepest and most secret meaning, or rather its essence, for each of them *is* a word, while man alone can *say* it. What is true of things, animate or inanimate, is equally true of man and of his various activities: the ultimate meaning of our arts and techniques, of our various sciences and of philosophy itself, is to symbolize on a lower plane the perfection of the divine art and of the divine knowledge. That is what they are, but, left to themselves, they do not know it. It is the proper function of theology to bring them to a complete awareness of their proper function, which is not to know things but to know God through things. Hence the title of St. Bonaventura's treatise; the human arts should be reduced to theology, and thereby to God.

Any one with the slightest feeling for the value of the mystical life will immediately realize that St. Bonaventura was fundamentally right. That, however, is not the question. If you want a theology in order to bring all the other sciences back to God, your first requisite is of course a theology; and if you want to refer your philosophy to God, what you need first is a philosophy—a philosophy, I repeat, that is wholly and exclusively a philosophy, and which, because it is a philosophy, can be related to theology without being reduced to it. Despite his marvellous gifts as a theologian and as a philosopher, it must be said that St. Bonaventura's remarkable achievements in both sciences would have been still greater had he not failed to perceive that difficulty.

Let us consider, for instance, his discussion of the theological problem of grace and free will. This, says St. Bonaventura, is the mark of truly pious souls, that they claim nothing for themselves, but ascribe everything to God. Excellent as a rule of personal devotion, and as long as it is restricted to the sphere of religious feeling, such a principle can become dangerous when used as a criterion of theological truth. Confronted with the classical question: what is to be ascribed to grace and what to free will, St. Bonaventura was of the opinion that in such cases a theologian should always play safe. He can err in two different ways: either by giving too much credit to nature, or by giving too much credit to God. From an abstract point of view, in whichever way he may be wrong, he will be equally wrong. Not so from the point of view of religious feeling, for St. Bonaventura maintains that "however much you ascribe to the grace of God, you will not harm piety by so doing, even though, by ascribing to the grace of God as much as you can, you may eventually wrong the natural powers and the free will of man. If, on the contrary, you wrong grace by crediting nature with what belongs to grace, there is danger. . . . Consequently that position which . . . ascribes more to the grace of God and, because it establishes us in a state of more complete indigence, better harmonizes with piety and humility, is for that very reason safer than the other one." And then comes the final touch: "Even though that position were false, it would not harm piety or humility; it is therefore fitting and safe to hold it." [12]

---

[12] See É. Gilson, *La Philosophie de Saint Bonaventure* (Paris: J. Vrin, 1926), pp. 456–57.

I am not so sure that it is. The only way to ascertain what the free will can do is to define what it is. Knowing its nature, you will find in that knowledge a safe rule to define the power of the will as well as its limitations. If, on the contrary, you start on the assumption that it is safer to keep a little below the line, where are you going to stop? Why, indeed, should you stop at all? Since it is pious to lessen the efficacy of free will, it is more pious to lessen it a little more, and to make it utterly powerless should be the highest mark of piety. In fact, there will be mediæval theologians who come very close to that conclusion, and even reach it a long time before the age of Luther and Calvin. Nothing, of course, would have been more repellent to St. Bonaventura than such a doctrine; the only question here is: Was St. Bonaventura protected against it? If we allow pious feelings to decree what nature should be, we are bound to wrong nature, for how could we find in piety a principle of self-restriction? In theology, as in any other science, the main question is not to be pious, but to be right. For there is nothing pious in being wrong about God!

If piety is not theology, still less is it philosophy. Yet it cannot be denied that, as a philosopher, St. Bonaventura sometimes allowed himself to be carried away by his religious feelings. In dealing with the nature of causality, for instance, two different courses were open to him. First, he could favour the view that where there is efficient causality, something new, which we call effect, is brought into existence by the efficacy of its cause; in this case, every effect can be rightly considered as a positive addition to the already existing order of reality. Or St. Bonaventura could maintain, with St. Augustine, that God has created all things present and future at the very instant of creation. From this second point of view, any particular being, taken at any time of world history, should be considered, so to speak, as the seed of all those other beings, or events, that are to flow from it according to the laws of divine providence. It is typical of St. Bonaventura's theologism that he always clung to this second interpretation of causality. He never could bring himself to think that efficient causality is attended by the springing up of new existences. To him, such a view practically amounted to crediting creatures with a creative power that belongs only to God. An effect, says Bonaventura, is to its cause as the rose is to the rosebud. It is permissible to appreciate the poetic quality of his comparison and the religious purity of his intention, without overlooking its philosophical implications. If, in the beginning, God created, together with all that was, all that was to be, the end of the world story was in its beginning, and nothing can really happen to it; in such a system God is the only efficient cause, and this world of ours is a completely barren world, just as in the doctrine of Malebranche and of Al Ashari.

That is exactly what St. Bonaventura wanted it to be. His piety needed a world which, like an infinitely thin and translucid film, would allow the all-pervading power and glory of God to shine forth to the human eye. The same impulse that had carried him to such extreme conclusions in his interpretation of physical causality could not but prevail in his epistemology. After all, it was the same problem, because it was still a problem of causality. Here again there were two obvious ways of dealing with the question. Shall we say, as St. Thomas Aquinas was to answer, that since God has made man a rational animal, the natural light of reason must be able naturally to perform its proper function, which is to know things as they are, and thereby to know truth? Or shall we say with St. Augustine, that truth being necessary, unchangeable, and eternal, it cannot be the work of a contingent, mutable and impermanent human mind interpreting unnecessary, changeful and fleeting things? Even in our minds truth is a sharing of some of the highest attributes of God; consequently, even in our minds, truth is an immediate effect of the light of God.

In order to give his religious intuition some philosophical backing, St. Bonaventura had therefore to build up the theory of what he called divine illumination. According to his doctrine, man has been endowed by God with an intellect and with reasoning powers, that enable him to know facts as well as their various relations to each other. For instance, I know that you are men and that we are now in this very room. Such knowledge is not above the reach of the human mind, for it deals with particular facts that could be other than they are and in which there is no element of necessity. If, on the contrary, I say that man is a rational animal, I am thereby relating a certain class of beings to their eternal and necessary essence; for no irrational being could be said to be a man. In such a case, the easiest way to account for the presence of that element of necessity in a contingent reason dealing with contingent things is to suppose that Eternal Truth, or God, is permanently supplying our mind with an additional light, through which, and in which, it sees truth, as in a lightning-flash.

So far so good. Here, however, a serious difficulty arises. It does not seem that St. Bonaventura seriously worried about it, for it was but a philosophical difficulty and he probably hoped that philosophy would take care of itself. Yet it was a difficulty. Granted that we cannot know truth without some additional influx of the divine light, how are we to conceive the nature of that divine illumination? If we take it as a particular instance of the general action by which God creates and runs the world, it is but the natural light of reason, that is the human intellect itself, which can therefore know truth without any further illumination from God. If, on the contrary, we see that intellectual light as a further gift, superadded by God to the natural light of man, we make it to be supernatural. It then becomes a grace, with the result that not a single instance of our true knowledge can be considered as natural. Here again we find ourselves confronted with a scientific and philosophical scepticism that is compensated by a theological appeal to the grace of God.

In those times even the scientifically minded Albertus Magnus could see no harm in saying that all true knowledge presupposes grace of the Holy Ghost; but St. Bonaventura was not an extremist; he did not want to destroy natural knowledge if he could help it. Accordingly, he tried to steer a middle course between what he considered as two opposite dangers. But was there one? His final answer is that the divine illumination is neither general, nor special; that is to say, neither the common influence of God upon nature, nor a grace that was, so to speak, superimposed on it. Very well, but then *what* is it? One of the most brilliant among Bonaventura's disciples, the Italian Cardinal Matthew of Aquasparta, imagined that he could improve his master's answer by saying that the divine light, in which we know truth, was *more special* than the general influence of God, but still a general one. If anybody can tell me how something can be more special without being special, I shall be glad to hear it. Another Franciscan, the Englishman Roger Marston, suggested that a distinction be drawn between two aspects of that same problem: the origin of natural knowledge, and its object. His solution, then, was that scientific and philosophical knowledge can rightly be considered as natural because their objects belong in the natural order, which is not the case for theology, for instance, whose proper object is God. But Marston added that, since all true knowledge presupposes divine illumination, it is never wholly natural in its origin. More cleverly worded than those of his predecessors, Marston's answer remained substantially the same, and suffered from the same difficulty. If the truth of my judgments comes to me from God only, and not from my own reason, there is no natural foundation for true knowledge; the proper place for epistemology is not in philosophy, but in theology.

We may add that the same conclusion would apply to the desperate effort of the early Franciscan school to find a satisfactory definition of even the *object* of natural knowledge. How could anything be natural, in a doctrine where each particular being is but a mystical symbol of its Creator? In common sense, we can form the general idea of Tree, because there really are such things as trees; but in a doctrine wherein the truth of our judgments rests ultimately with the divine light, no number of particular observations could ever yield the necessary essence that we call tree. Nor will the drawing of a collection of particular circles ever provide our intellects with the necessary material for the definition of Circle. It is the divine idea of the thing that impresses on our mind the necessity of its definition. What then is the real object of natural knowledge? Is it the particular thing itself, or its idea in God? The obvious answer was in favour of the second alternative. Were it not for the presence of the divine ideas shining from on high upon human reason, no true knowledge would be possible, whereas we still would know what man is, even though there were no men, provided only the divine idea of man were shining upon our mind. As Matthew of Aquasparta made bold to say, the existence of sensible things is not necessarily required for true human knowledge; so long as the divine light is there, we can know the whole truth about things.[13]

This time we are anticipating not only Malebranche, with his famous doctrine of the "Vision in God", but Berkeley, whose radical idealism, without being affirmed or even conceived by

[13] For the preceding analysis, see É. Gilson, "Sur quelques difficultés de l'illumination Augustienne", in *Hommage à M. le Professeur M. de Wulf* (Louvain, 1934), pp. 321–31.

any member of the Franciscan school, is looming here at least as an open possibility. Perhaps it was the vague perception of that imminent danger which brought the history of the early Franciscan school to a close. This is more than a likely guess. One of its last exponents, the French Franciscan, Peter Olivi, candidly confessed that he could not find his way out of that maze. After restating the problem of divine illumination, and describing the respective positions of St. Bonaventura and St. Thomas Aquinas, Olivi concludes that, being himself a Franciscan, he feels bound in conscience to stick to the Franciscan position. Yet, he adds, I do not want to do so if that position really entails the destruction of natural knowledge. I hope that such a consequence can be avoided, but as I do not see how, I leave to greater men the task of answering the question.

Precisely such a greater man was to come in the first years of the fourteenth century. His name was Duns Scotus, and he also was a Franciscan; yet his own doctrine was, beyond all else, the death warrant of the early Franciscan epistemology. As a philosophical doctrine, it was as dead as a doornail. Theologism had killed it, and were it not for the natural forgetfulness of men, it would never have been revived. I sometimes wonder how many similar experiments will be necessary before men acquire some philosophical experience. A certain man adopts a certain attitude in philosophy, and he follows it consistently, until he finds himself face to face with unwelcome consequences. He does his best to dodge them, but his own disciples, beginning as they do just where the master stopped, have less scruples than he about letting his principles publicly confess their necessary consequences. Everybody then realizes that the only way to get rid of those consequences is to shift the philosophical position from which they spring. Then the school dies; but it is not unlikely that one or two centuries later, in some university whence history has been banished as harmful to philosophical originality, some young man, still blessed with his native ignorance, will rediscover a similar position. As he will live and write in another time, he will say very old things in a new way. Yet they will be old; his philosophy will be stillborn and neither he nor his disciples will ever be able to quicken it. The trouble is that when philosophers fail, their disheartened supporters never blame their master; they blame it on philosophy itself. *There* begins the straight road that leads to conscious and openly declared scepticism. If, by following it in history once or twice, or three times if need be, we shall have learned to avoid it in philosophy, our toilsome pilgrimage through the maze of conflicting doctrines will not have been in vain.

CHAPTER III

THE ROAD TO SCEPTICISM

While so many men were trying to base philosophy on theological foundations, a very simple and modest man was putting
everything in its place. His name was Thomas Aquinas, and he
was saying things so obviously true that, from his time down to
our own day, very few people have been sufficiently self-forget-
ful to accept them. There is an ethical problem at the root of
our philosophical difficulties; for men are most anxious to find
truth, but very reluctant to accept it. We do not like to be
cornered by rational evidence, and even when truth is there, in
its impersonal and commanding objectivity, our greatest difficulty still remains; it is for me to bow to it in spite of the fact
that it is not exclusively mine, for you to accept it though it
cannot be exclusively yours. In short, finding out truth is not so
hard; what is hard is not to run away from truth once we have
found it. When it is not a "yes but", our "yes" is often enough a
"yes, and . . ."; it applies much less to what we have just been
told than to what we are about to say. The greatest among
philosophers are those who do not flinch in the presence of
truth, but welcome it with the simple words: yes, Amen.

St. Thomas Aquinas was one of the latter, clear-sighted
enough to know truth when he saw it, humble enough to bow
to it in its presence. His holiness and his philosophy sprang from
the same source: a more than human eagerness to give way to
truth; but he was surrounded by men who did not like to do

49

that, at least not to the same degree, so that, even after him, everything went on as if truth had remained unsaid. Yet his ideas were clear and simple. Himself a theologian, St. Thomas had asked the professors of theology never to prove an article of faith by rational demonstration, for faith is not based on reason, but on the word of God, and if you try to prove it, you destroy it. He had likewise asked the professors of philosophy never to prove a philosophical truth by resorting to the words of God, for philosophy is not based on Revelation, but on reason, and if you try to base it on authority, you destroy it. In other words, theology is the science of those things which are received by faith from divine revelation, and philosophy is the knowledge of those things which flow from the principles of natural reason. Since their common source is God, the creator of both reason and revelation, these two sciences are bound ultimately to agree; but if you really want them to agree, you must first be careful not to forget their essential difference. Only distinct things can be united; if you attempt to blend them, you inevitably lose them in what is not union, but confusion.

William of Ockham's arresting personality will always provide historians of philosophy with ample material about which to quarrel. In order to add as little as possible to the prevailing confusion, I shall try to adhere as closely as possible to the simplest facts. The first of these facts, so obvious that it does not seem worth mentioning, is that Ockham was a Franciscan monk, whose most important work is a huge commentary on the *Sentences* of Peter Lombard. A second fact is that in his handling of theological problems Ockham gives great weight to the first article of the Christian creed: I believe in God Almighty. Since it is an article of faith, it is needless to say that it cannot be proved. Yet, not only did Ockham use it as a principle in theology, which was a very proper thing to do, but he also resorted to it in discussing various philosophical problems, as if any theological dogma, held by faith alone, could become the source of philosophical and purely rational conclusions. That is a third fact, and one that we should keep in mind if we wish to understand Ockham's philosophy. But what was his philosophy?

At first sight there is little or no difference between the fundamental positions of Ockham and those of his immediate predecessors. Like St. Thomas Aquinas and Averroës, he considered himself indebted to Aristotle for the principles of his philosophy. What can be more Aristotelian, for instance, than the thesis so frequently restated by Ockham, that nothing exists except that which is individual? As a matter of fact, St. Thomas himself had spent a large part of his time in trying to teach that fundamental truth to the Augustinians and Neo-platonists of his day. I would be the last one to gainsay such statements; however, they do not cover the whole case, for if Ockham was an Aristotelian, and St. Thomas Aquinas an Aristotelian, and perhaps even Aristotle an Aristotelian, this at least remains to be explained: How is it that Ockham's ultimate conclusions are so completely destructive of those of Aristotle as well as those of St. Thomas Aquinas? Were we to answer, as recently suggested, that Ockham had to criticize his predecessors, because he had to uncover and dislodge the non-Aristotelian elements which in his eyes corrupted mediæval interpretations of Aristotle,[1] such an explanation could perhaps apply to St. Thomas, but it would hardly do for Aristotle himself. Yet Aristotle's philosophy is clearly at variance with Ockham's, both in epistemology and in natural philosophy. Instead of speculating on the possible answers to that problem, we shall certainly save time and eventually reach a safer conclusion simply by watching Ockham at work, and on precisely the same problem that had puzzled

[1] E. A. Moody, *The Logic of William of Ockham* (New York: Sheed and Ward, 1935), p. 17; cf. pp. 306–7.

Abailard: What is the object of abstract knowledge; what are the so-called universals?

Shortly before Ockham's time, another Englishman had grappled with the same problem and had suggested an interesting solution. A professor of theology at Oxford, and subsequently Chancellor of the same University and Bishop of Lincoln, the much neglected Henry of Harclay was a prominent figure between 1310 and 1327. Ockham had read Harclay's *Quaestiones Disputatae* and, as we shall see, had pondered over his answer to the problem of the Universals. What he found therein was a severe criticism of the doctrine of Duns Scotus and Avicenna, which held that each concept represents an essence, that each essence has an entity and a unity of its own, and is equally shared in by all the individuals of a certain class. Roughly speaking, Duns Scotus was going back, in a much more elaborate form, to the position of William of Champeaux. Against Scotus, Harclay wanted to maintain, with Aristotle, that the general idea of animal, for instance, either is nothing or is a mere definition, by the intellect, of particular things that really exist outside the intellect.[2] As Harclay says in a striking formula: "Every positive thing outside the soul is, as such, something singular."[3] Hence the classical question: How can we draw from singular things a concept that is general?

Harclay's answer is not new to us, for he borrowed it, directly or indirectly, from Peter Abailard. Any singular thing, he says, is naturally able to affect the intellect in two different ways according as the impression that it makes is confused or distinct. I call confused an impression which does not enable us to distinguish between two individuals belonging to the same species; whereas

[2] See Thomas Aquinas, *De anima*, ed. Pirotta, n. 380, p. 133. The texts of Henry of Harclay will be found in J. Kraus, *Die Universalienlehre des Oxforder Kanzlers Heinrich von Harclay*, in *Divus Thomas* 10 (Fribourg, 1932): 36–58, 475–508; and 11 (Fribourg, 1933): 228–314.

[3] Kraus, *Die Universalienlehre*, vol. 11, p. 290.

a distinct impression entails the knowledge of an individual as distinct from every other individual. What is then the proper object of a general idea or concept? It is the really existing and singular thing itself, as confusedly known by our intellect. Man, for instance, is but the confused perception of Socrates. I am not discussing now the philosophical value of Harclay's answer, but I beg leave to suggest, from a merely historical point of view, that it might prove difficult to reconcile it with his declared purpose of going back to Aristotle. It is a well-known Aristotelian thesis that science is of the universal; if you make Aristotle say that the universal character of our general ideas is due to their confusion, you will have to face the conclusion that confusion is what makes concepts a suitable material for scientific knowledge. If there is an answer to that difficulty, it is certainly not to be found in the works of Aristotle, and how such a conclusion could be reached by merely purifying the Aristotelianism of Aristotle himself remains at least an open question.

To return to the main point, it is to be noted that Harclay's doctrine, which seems at first sight a clear case of nominalism, was nevertheless considered by Ockham as a particular variety of realism. This is a very subtle point, but well worth considering, for nothing can help us more towards a clear understanding of Ockham's own position. Harclay's doctrine represented a desperate effort to escape the conclusion that the object of our general ideas is absolutely nothing, without relapsing into realism. If such a thing could be done at all, Harclay would certainly have done it. He was not saying, like Duns Scotus, that the universals were real entities apart from their existence in individuals; nor, like St. Thomas Aquinas, that the universals are virtually present in individuals, from which they are abstracted by our intellect; but he was maintaining at least this, that the universals are the individuals as conceived in a certain way. In other words, if we suppose that our general ideas point to something that is singular, they still have things existing in reality for their objects, and consequently the universals are not nothing. Ockham saw clearly that Henry of Harclay had not really crossed the dividing line between realism and nominalism, and though the traces of realism in Harclay's position were, so to speak, infinitesimal, they did not escape the acute mind of his critic. In such a doctrine, said Ockham, the universals are still conceived as images, pictures, or representations, with which something similar corresponds in the nature of things.[4] In other words, the reason why we can form those confused pictures of things is that the nature of those things makes it possible for us to do so; general ideas still have some *fundamentum in re* and consequently the doctrine is still a realism.

Ockham's criticism of the Oxford Chancellor clearly shows us how far we must go if we would not miss Ockham's own position. As compared with him, both Abailard and Harclay were very moderate in their conclusions. What Ockham wants us to realize is that, since everything that really exists is individual, our general ideas cannot correspond to anything in reality, whence it follows necessarily that it is not their nature to be either images, or pictures, or mental presentations of any real or conceivable thing.

The special difficulty raised by Ockham was to prove of tremendous importance for the future of mediæval and even of modern philosophy. Every time philosophical speculation has succeeded in circumscribing what we might perhaps call a "pure position", its discovery has regularly been attended by a philosophical revolution. Begotten in us by things themselves, concepts are born reformers that never lose touch with reality. Pure ideas, on the other hand, are born within the mind and from the mind, not as intellectual expressions of what is, but as models,

[4] Ibid., p. 298.

or patterns, of what ought to be; hence they are born revolutionists. And this is the reason why Aristotle and Aristotelians
write books on politics, whereas Plato and Platonists always
write Utopias. Ockham himself was the very reverse of a
Platonist; in point of fact, he was the perfect Anti-Plato; yet, like
all opposites, Plato and Ockham belonged to the same species.
Neither one wanted to know up to what point the universals
could be truly said to be real; Plato wanted them to be the very
core of everything, whereas Ockham wanted them to be nothing. Ockhamism could not possibly be a reformation, it was
bound to be a revolution.

Ockham's master stroke was to perceive that the problem
could not be solved unless a new classification of the various
types of knowledge was first substituted for the old one. Hence
his division of knowledge into abstractive and intuitive, terms
that had already been used before him, but to which he was to
give a new turn and to use in a new way. In Ockham's doctrine,
an intuitive cognition is the immediate perception of a really
existing thing. It can be the perception of a material object: I
see Socrates; or of a complex of material objects given together
with their actual relations: I see that Socrates is sitting on a stone,
or that Socrates is white; but it can equally well be the mere
awareness of some psychological fact, such as a feeling of
pleasure or pain, a knowledge, an act of reasoning or a decision
of the will. It is a common character of all so-called intuitive
knowledge, to be attended by a feeling of absolute certitude. In
other words, knowledge of this kind is self-evident.

Not so with abstractive knowledge. Every knowledge that is
not an intuition is an abstraction. Such, for instance, are not
only what we usually call abstract ideas, as animal, or man,
which stand for a whole class of individuals, but even our
mental representations of mere individuals. The image or
memory of a certain fact or a certain thing, though it may

represent it with all its individual characteristics, still remains an abstract knowledge, because it abstracts from, at least, the very existence of what it represents. Were the thing there, we would not imagine it or remember it; we would see it; such knowledge would not be an abstraction, but an intuition.

Let us therefore define abstractive knowledge, in the Ockhamist sense, as a cognition, from which nothing can be concluded concerning the existence, or non-existence, of its object.[5] Should we hold that position as correct, the obvious implication would be that the only kind of knowledge which enables us to ascertain whether or not a certain thing exists is intuitive knowledge; that is to say, the immediate apprehension of some object by an internal or external perception. Intuition then is the only possible foundation of what Ockham calls experimental knowledge (*experimentalis notitia*), or scientific knowledge (*notitia scientifica*), an expression which, according to its derivation, means the sort of knowledge which causes science in us. In short, intuition alone enables us to perceive the existence or non-existence of things.[6]

The next question is: What is the nature of that special class of abstractions which we call the universals? In order to answer it, we shall have to look at the universals from two different points of view: first, that of their mode of existence, and next, that of their aptness to designate really existing things. The first part of the problem is easily solved. Since all that is real is singular, even the so-called universals have to be singular, insofar, at least, as they are really existing things. Strictly speaking, those things only are called singular that have actual existence outside the mind; but broadly speaking, the word can be applied to all that exists, either outside or within the mind. Now every time we think of man, or animal, or any other class of beings,

[5] Ockham, *In I Sent.*, prol., q. 1 (Lyons: J. Freebsel, 1495), fol. A4 recto.
[6] Ibid., fol. A4 recto, z.

something is happening in our minds; every one of our thoughts is in itself a definite modification of our mind, which is different according as we are thinking of tree, or animal, or man. In modern terminology, we would call every one of those mental happenings a psychological fact; Ockham called it a "quality of the mind". In both cases the expression is intended to signify that taken in itself, a universal is a singular and, therefore, an actually existing thing.[7]

Now let us turn to the second part of the problem: What are these universals when considered only as having meaning? The answer is that, as such, they are mere signs. Our idea of man, for instance, is something that points to any one of those individuals which we call men. Now, a sign is always something real in itself, it is a thing; but its signification is nothing real in itself, it is nothing. A signpost is endowed with actual existence, up to the very colour and shape of the letters that are painted on it, but what it means to me has no existence of its own apart from the signpost itself and my perception of it. It can likewise be said that the reality of our concepts as psychological data is an empirically observable fact, but that no intrinsic reality should be ascribed to their signification.

This was indeed a consistent answer, but not a complete one. What Ockham called a sign was really an image, or mental picture, whose function it was to signify any given individual belonging to a certain class. Now such images are rather different from what we usually call a sign. Words, for instance, are signs and, precisely because they are nothing more than that, they are largely conventional or institutional. The fact that different nations use different languages and that several different languages are sometimes in use within the same nation, clearly shows that there is no natural relation between the spoken word

[7] Ockham, *Quaestiones quodlibetales*, quodl. 5, qq. 12 and 13 (Argentine, 1491), fols. N1 and N2.

and its meaning. However, there is another fact, namely, that we learn foreign languages by relating different sets of words to a single set of concepts. Unless I have first learned it, I cannot guess that "man" is the English for "homme", but once I know it, I need not learn what you have in mind when you say "man", because I feel sure that what I have in mind when I say "homme" is practically the same. In other words, the natural signs, or concepts, used to designate concrete things are naturally comparable, even when the conventional words by which they are expressed are not. This is a fact, and it requires an appropriate explanation. Why are there natural signs or concepts which correspond to the same things in the same way in all possible human minds?

Ockham was too clear-sighted not to perceive the difficulty, but it was not easy for him to give it an answer. First he remarked that there are such natural signs. Not only men, but even beasts, naturally utter some sounds to express their feelings. Pleasure and pain, for instance, elicit from us vocal signs that may rightly be called natural signs. This, of course, is true, but does it account for that other fact, that several distinct individuals may be signified by a certain image which is almost the same in all the human minds? Ockham's answer to this question clearly shows that here he was finally at the end of his tether. Intuitive knowledge, Ockham says, is caused in us by things; now natural effects always resemble their causes, and this is the reason why we can form some idea of a cause when we perceive one of its effects. In this sense at least, one could say that even physical phenomena are the natural signs of their causes. For instance, fire can cause heat, and for that reason, heat is a natural sign of the presence of fire; so also the intuition of a certain man causes in our mind an image, which is a natural sign of its cause and, for that reason, is able to signify man.[8]

[8] Ockham, *In I Sent.*, dist. 2, q. 8, fol. 44 recto.

A less summary description of Ockham's position should take into account his acute remarks on the formation of common mental signs by the conjoint action of the particular mental signs. It cannot be denied that he achieved it by doing pioneer work in the field of psychology; but, however far he might have been able to advance along that line, the philosophical problems at stake would always have remained untouched. How is it that different individuals cause comparable impressions in our minds? Abailard's answer to that question had been that, if not in ourselves, then at least in God, there is for each class of individuals an idea, or archetype, which accounts for the characteristic features of that class. Ockham was too clever not to perceive that such a position would unavoidably bring him back to the Platonic problem of participation, and to some sort of metaphysical realism. He therefore decided to eradicate realism, even from the divine mind and to deny the existence of ideas representing the genera and the species, even in God. If the universals are nothing real, God Himself can no more conceive them than we can. A divine idea is always an idea of this and that particular individual which God wishes to create. If He freely decrees to create several individuals that resemble each other, the concrete result of such a decision is what we call a species, and that is all there is to it. We could still ask Ockham many other questions as to what makes general ideas possible, but his answers would always be the same. Things are just what they are; Nature is performing its operations in an occult way, and the will of God is the ultimate cause of both its existence and its operations.

Let us pause a moment to examine the philosophical consequences of Ockham's attitude. A pure empiricist in philosophy, he considered the will of his all-powerful God as the last argument in theology. From such a point of view, it remains both possible and desirable to describe things as they are; as we would say in our language, a positive knowledge of what is still remains possible, provided only we use appropriate methods to observe it. But *why* science, or human knowledge, is possible at all, we cannot know, because the will of God is the ultimate cause of all things, and had His free decision been different, the whole world itself would now be different.

Given, for example, a question such as this: How is it possible for things which are material to cause impressions in a soul, which is immaterial? What would Ockham's answer be? Not that this is not a question, but that it is not the first question to be asked, for what we have to know first, before discussing that problem, is whether or not the human soul is immaterial. It was commonly accepted among Ockham's predecessors, that the human soul is an immaterial, and therefore an immortal substance, which is not begotten by another similar substance, but is immediately created by God. Such a substance, these men would add, is a knowing power precisely because it is not material, and yet, through the particular body which it animates, it is able to establish relations with material things, and thereby to know them. Ockham's objection to this was that, though their position could be considered as probable, and even as more probable than the reverse, it could not be held as a certainty. The one thing we are sure of, because it is the only one we can observe, is that we do know; but that we know by means of a distinct faculty, which we call "intellect", is an entirely different question. Even granting the real existence of such a knowing power, it would still remain to be proven that its nature is not material. Were it free to follow its own inclination, our judgment would rather favour the view that what we call the human soul is a material and extended principle, like that of the other animals, and therefore no less mortal than are the animal souls themselves. Moreover, it is rather surprising to see that the philosophers who describe the human soul as immaterial are the same ones who make it the animating principle of human bodies. For what is matter, indeed, if not extension in space? And how could the soul of an extended body act as its animating principle or, as they say, be its form, if it has no extension of its own? In other words, how could the form of an extended substance be itself unextended? True, they say that the human soul *must* be immaterial, since it performs the so-called "acts of intellection" by which it draws knowledge from material things; but, Ockham rejoins, "we do not experience that intellection" which is supposed to be "the proper operation of an immaterial substance". What is the use of building up intricate theories to explain how intellection is possible, so long as we are not even sure that there is an immaterial soul and that such an operation is actually performed by it? If we want to maintain such positions, let us hold them as Christians, for it is a fact that faith expressly teaches such beliefs or invites us to accept them as true; but even though all of them should be held as articles of faith, not one of them could ever be proved.[9]

This conditional materialism, which so strangely resembles the subsequent conclusions of Locke, discloses the full meaning of the Ockhamist principle: that beings should not be multiplied without necessity. "Ockham's razor", as it is sometimes called, means first of all that one should not account for the existence of an empirically given thing by imagining, behind and beyond it, another thing whose hypothetical existence cannot be verified. Unfortunately, that very simple and, as I think, very sound methodological principle was connected in Ockham's mind with his theological conception of God as an essentially almighty God. He not only thought that the wisest philosophical attitude for us is to take things as they are, but he also

[9] Ockham, *Quaestiones quodlibetales*, quodl. 1, q. 10, fols. A5 and B1. See also quodl. 2, q. 1, and quodl. 4, q. 2, concerning the proofs of the existence of God.

believed that, whatever things are, they always might be different. Hence his firm conviction that no philosopher should waste his time in speculating on the hypothetical causes of actually existing things. If we believe that God can do anything that does not involve contradiction, all non-contradictory explanations of a given fact become equally valid, even those which are the less likely. But in that case, how can we prove conclusively that God has actually decided in favour of this rather than that possible solution?

This outlook, which gives its particular colour to Ockham's Empiricism, can help us to understand his position concerning the problem of the universals. In order to account for the possibility of abstract knowledge, Aristotle and St. Thomas had conceived an elaborate scheme, according to which things themselves were credited with virtually intelligible forms, which the human soul was supposed to abstract from things by its active intellect, and to know by its possible intellect. The self-expression of an intellect thus made pregnant with a natural form was the concept: that which is conceived by, and is born of, a human intellect, when it is impregnated with things. From Ockham's point of view, since we can perceive the existence neither of such natural forms, nor of these alleged active and possible intellects, such speculations were perfectly empty. But the worst thing about them was that they utterly disregarded the innumerable possibilities which lay open to the free will of an almighty God. We know that there are things because we feel them; we know equally well that we can use certain images as signs for certain classes of things; we also know that every one of these natural signs stands for a real or possible individual contained within that class; but beyond that we know nothing, and nothing can be known, because the reason why things are what they are rests ultimately upon the free will of God.

How far Ockham was ready to go along that line, and to

what consequences his theological attitude could lead him, may clearly be seen from his acute criticism of intuitive knowledge itself. For he was honest enough to attack even that problem and to face the consequences of his own theologism. There are abstractions, though we cannot say why. There also are intuitions; can we say why? At first sight, the question seems to be very simple. By definition, intuitive knowledge is knowledge by which we know that a certain thing is when it is, and that it is not when it is not. Therefore it seems obvious that the cause for the existence of any given intuition is the existence of its object; and this is indeed a sensible answer; nay, more, it is, in all probability, the true answer. But the question is: Is it any more than a very high probability?

That was a far-reaching question—for it seems easy enough to understand that the cause of our intuition of a thing is the existence and presence of that thing. That which is real can cause in us a mental sign of its existence; but the intuition of the non-existence of a thing raises a much more difficult problem. That a thing does not exist can well account for our having no intuition of its existence, but not for our having an intuition of its non-existence. There is a serious difference between not knowing that a thing is, and knowing that it is not. How could that which is not make us know that it is not? In order to account for negative intuitions, Ockham was compelled to push a little further his analysis of our positive intuitions. He first reminded his readers that every intuition of a really existing thing was the joint effect of two separate causes: the thing itself and our knowledge of it. In the cases in which we perceive that something does not exist, only one partial cause is left; namely, our knowledge: no wonder then if the result is different. In Ockham's own words: "When the thing is there, the intuitive knowledge of the thing, plus the thing itself, cause the judgment that the thing is there; but when the thing is not there, the intuitive knowledge minus the thing must cause an opposite judgment." [10] This was hardly an answer, for the question was, precisely, how can there still be an intuitive knowledge where there is no thing? Ockham has several times dealt with the difficulty, both in his *Commentary on the Sentences* and in his *Questions*, but his successive answers have merely driven to despair his most conscientious historians. Insofar as it is intelligible at all, his final solution seems to imply that God alone can conserve in us the intuitions of absent things, and thereby enable us to judge that they are not there. Were this the correct interpretation of his doctrine, each intuition of non-existence would entail the supernatural conservation in us, by God, of a natural intuition. Hochstetter calls it a "Verlegenheitslösung", an expedient; Abbagnano sees in it, not an answer, but rather Ockham's public admission, that a logical answer to the question was impossible. [11] I agree that it was an impossibility, at least for anybody who professes to be an Ockhamist in philosophy and forgets that Ockham himself was also a theologian. Why could not an all-powerful God conserve in us the intuition of a non-existing thing? And if this is for us the only way to account for the possibility of negative intuitions, why should we not resort to theology when we need it?

The only trouble was, that Ockham himself could not do this without endangering what was, according to his own principles, the only perfect type of evident knowledge: the intuition of that which is. If God can conserve in us the intuition of something that is not actually existing, how shall we ever be sure that what we are perceiving as real is an actually existing thing? In other words, if it is possible for God to make us perceive as

[10] Ockham, *In I Sent.*, prol., q. 1, fol. A8 recto and verso.

[11] E. Hochstetter, *Studien zur Metaphysik und Erkenntnislehre Wilhelms von Ockham* (Berlin, 1927), pp. 32–33. N. Abbagnano, *Guglielmo di Ockham* (Lanciano, 1931), pp. 6–9.

real an object that does not really exist, have we any proof that this world of ours is not a vast phantasmagoria behind which there is no reality to be found?

Ockham had touched upon the first point in the Question in which he asked: "Whether there can be intuitive knowledge of a non-existent object?" His answer was that "there can be, by the power of God, intuitive knowledge concerning a non-existent object." This, he went on to say, "I prove by an article of faith: I believe in God the Father almighty: by which I understand that everything which does not involve a manifest contradiction is to be attributed to the divine power." [12] Now, when I see a star in the sky, God is producing, at one and the same time, both that star and my sight of it; but such is God's power that He can produce separately even the things which He usually produces together. There is, therefore, no contradiction in supposing that God, who produces my sight of the star with that star, could produce it without the star. My intuition of the star is one thing, its object is another thing; why could not an almighty God produce the one without the other? True, it may be said that this would oblige God to perform a contradictory act, since intuition implies the existence of its object. To meet the difficulty, Ockham adds in another question that, in such a case, our sight of the star, or of the sky, should not really be called an intuition, but an "assent", created in us by God; not an evident assent (for this would contradict the very definition of intuition) but an assent belonging to the same species as those evident assents, which regularly attend our intuitions. [13] Whichever of these two answers represents Ockham's last position on the question, the fact remains that human knowledge would be

[12] Ockham, *Quaestiones quodlibetales*, quodl. 6, q. 6; R. McKeon, *Medieval Philosophers*, vol. 2, p. 373.

[13] *Quaestiones quodlibetales*, quodl. 5, q. 5; R. McKeon, *Medieval Philosophers*, vol. 2, pp. 368–72.

practically indistinguishable from what it is, even though all its objects were destroyed; nothing is necessarily required to make knowledge possible, but the mind and God.

The Ockhamist thesis that God can always do without intermediate causes what he usually does with such causes, had an immediate bearing on the notion of causality itself. If it is posited as a theological principle, that two really distinct things can always be created separately by God, the obvious implication is that causes can exist without their effects as well as effects without their causes.[14] A thorough application of that principle necessarily entails a complete revision of the very notion of causality. What is a cause? Most men naturally think, or imagine, that something flows out of the so-called cause and becomes an integral part of the very being of its effect. According to Ockham, there is nothing in sensible experience to confirm such a supposition. What intuitive knowledge teaches us is that every time fire, for instance, comes in contact with a piece of wood, heat begins to appear in that wood. Since there can be nothing more in concepts than there is actually in intuitions, the relation of cause to effect cannot mean more to the mind than what we actually perceive: a regular sequence between two phenomena. When the presence of a certain fact is regularly attended by the presence of another fact, we call the first one a cause and the second an effect. And beyond that we know nothing. Far from strengthening causality, those who boast that they can find something more in it are unconsciously justifying its complete denial; for such men begin by asserting that the relation of a cause to its effect cannot be reduced to a simple relation of mutual presence and of regular sequence; but when you ask them to show you something more in causality, they can find nothing. Consequently, if causality is what they say it is, the existence of what they say cannot be proven, causality is nothing.

[14] Ockham, *Quaestiones quodlibetales*, quodl. 2, q. 7, and quodl. 4, q. 6.

Here again, Ockham's criticism of a philosophical notion was powerfully backed by his theologism. He did not wish to conceive physical bodies as having an efficient causality of their own because the existence of an autonomous order of things, or order of nature, would have prescribed at least habitual limits to the arbitrary power of God. Hence the Ockhamist conception of a world in which combustion comes after fire but not necessarily because of fire, since God could have decreed once and for all that He Himself would create heat in pieces of wood, or paper, every time fire would be present in paper or wood. Who could prove to us that, even now, God does not actually do this? In point of fact, we know through faith that God does it at least in the sacraments of the Church. The sacramental words are not really the efficient causes of grace, but God decreed once and for all that every time those words are said, grace regularly follows.[15] A sacramental universe is not a self-contradictory notion; it is at least a possible universe, and we might well be living in such a world without being aware of it.

Ockham himself had no intention of advocating such a conception of the physical world. Even while he was proving that God could create the knowledge of a thing without that thing, his mind remained as far as possible from the idealism of Berkeley. At any rate, I have never been able to find in his writings the slightest intimation that he ever thought of holding it. Ockham was firmly convinced that, as a rule, our intuition of a particular object is the grasping of an actually existing thing; but, at the same time, he wanted to remind us that many cases of visions are recorded in the Bible, and that such facts should always remain for us an open possibility. It can likewise be said that Ockham's criticism of the notion of causality was much less inspired by any leaning towards Malebranche's occasionalism than by his desire to account for the possibility of miracles, or

[15] Hochstetter, *Studien*, pp. 154–55.

of such a sacrament as the Eucharist. Yet, when all is said, the fact remains that Ockham's only objection to occasionalism would be the divine ideas which it presupposes, and its excessive rationality. Finally, I fully agree that it is an overstatement to call Ockham a "mediæval Hume", for if ever there was a man whose philosophy was little concerned with the power and glory of God, that man was Hume. But, nevertheless, it would be just as great a mistake not to quote Hume in relation to William of Ockham, for there is a close affinity between their philosophical doctrines. St. Thomas Aquinas could not have accepted Hume's Empiricism without completely wrecking his own theology, whereas Hume's philosophy could have dwelt with Ockham's theology without doing it much harm. As a matter of fact, an inarticulate world such as the English agnostic's was most suitable to the arbitrary will of the English Franciscan's God; no wonder then if we find them both in the doctrine of William of Ockham.

Thus blended together Empiricism and theologism made a most explosive combination. At the top of the world, a God whose absolute power knew no limits, not even those of a stable nature endowed with a necessity and an intelligibility of its own. Between His will and the countless individuals that co-exist in space or succeed each other and glide away in time, there was strictly nothing. Having expelled from the mind of God the intelligible world of Plato, Ockham was satisfied that no intelligibility could be found in any one of God's works. How could there be order in nature, when there is no nature? And how could there be a nature when each singular being, thing, or event, can claim no other justification for its existence than that of being one among the elect of an all-powerful God? That was not the God of theology, but of theologism; for though the living God of theology be infinitely more than the "Author of Nature", He is at least that, whereas Ockham's God was not even that. Instead of being an eternal source of that concrete order of intelligibility and beauty, which we call nature, Ockham's God was expressly intended to relieve the world of the necessity of having any meaning of its own. The God of theology always vouches for nature; the jealous God of theologism usually prefers to abolish it.

Had he been only a passionate theologian, Ockham would have left us nothing more than a brilliant example of theologism, but he was at the same time a shrewd logician and a clear-headed philosopher, whose mind could not entertain a philosophy at variance with his theology. As a matter of fact, more than that, he was a great publicist whose political doctrines, deeply rooted in his theology, were dangerously shaking the lofty structure of mediæval Christendom. As a philosopher, however, it was Ockham's privilege to usher into the world what I think is the first known case of a new intellectual disease. It cannot be described as a scepticism, for it often goes hand in hand with the most unreserved devotion to the promotion of scientific knowledge. Positivism would be no better name for it, since it is chiefly made up of negations. It would be more satisfactory to call it a radical Empiricism, were it not precisely its main trouble that it is not radical enough to seek in experience that which makes experience itself possible. As this contagious disease is particularly common among the scientists of today, one might be tempted to call it "scientism", if it were not for the fact that its first result is to destroy, together with the rationality of science, its very possibility. However, since we need a label, or a sign, let us call it psychologism, and attempt to describe its meaning.

Ockham himself is a perfect case of this mental attitude and a very good model from which to sketch it. He was convinced that to give a psychological analysis of human knowledge was to give a philosophical analysis of reality. For instance, each intuition is radically distinct from every other intuition, hence, each particular thing is radically distinct from every other particular thing. Again, since no intuition of a thing can cause in us the intuition of another thing, it follows that no thing can cause another thing. It is to that settled conviction that the psychological relations between our ideas are a true picture of the real relations between things, that we are indebted for Ockham's interpretation of causality. Since the origin of causality cannot possibly be found in the thing itself, or in the intuition of the thing by the intellect, it must be explained by some other reason; and there is but one: it is what Ockham called *habitualis notitia*, and what Hume will simply call *habit*.[16] You can look at the statue of a certain man indefinitely; if you have never seen the man himself, you will never know whom the statue represents. Similarly from a merely intellectual knowledge of the abstract definition of heat, we could never deduce the fact that heat causes heat in contiguous or proximate bodies. True enough, there are such things as relations of causality, and there is an essential order of dependence between effects and their causes, for their regular succession never changes; but since there is nothing more in causality than the habitual association of ideas caused in us by repeated experience, there is nothing more than a regular sequence of events in physical causality.

That there is a striking similarity between this position and Hume's is an obvious fact, which has already been stressed by at least three different historians. Two of them, E. Hochstetter and N. Abbagnano, have even called our attention to the verbal similarity between the following lines by Ockham and a famous text of David Hume's. "Between a cause and its effect," says Ockham, "there is an eminently essential order and dependence, and yet the simple knowledge of one of them does not entail the simple knowledge of the other. And this also is

[16] Ockham, *In I Sent.*, prolog., q. 3, fol. D3, verso L.

something which everybody experiences within himself: that however perfectly he may know a certain thing, he will never be able to excogitate the simple and proper notion of another thing, which he has never before perceived either by sense or by intellect." Now let us listen to Hume: "When we reason *a priori*, and consider merely any object or cause, as it appears to the mind, independent of all observation, it never could suggest to us the notion of any distinct object, such as its effect." [17] In both doctrines, nothing was left but empirical sequences of facts outside the mind, and habitual associations within the mind, the mere external frame of a world order carefully emptied of its intelligibility.

Such a result was inevitable and will always occur whenever a philosopher mistakes the empirical description of our ways of knowing for a correct description of reality itself. That is psychologism, and however brilliantly it may conduct itself, its ultimate conclusion is that, since there is no more in reality than there is in knowledge, reality can be known, but the fact of knowledge itself cannot be understood. Now a question such as this, how do we come by our general ideas, and by our notion of causality? is no doubt tremendously important, and what psychology can tell us about it surely deserves our most careful consideration; but it cannot solve the philosophical problems which psychologism makes bold to ask, and regularly dismisses as pseudo-problems. Approached with the wrong method, a problem always becomes a pseudo-problem. In such cases, of course, we find nothing, whence we calmly conclude that there is nothing. Ockham was quite right in attempting to describe

[17] Ibid., q. 3, fol. D2, recto. F. D. Hume, *An Inquiry concerning Human Understanding*, IV, 1.27; ed. Selby-Bigge, p. 31. See also E. Hochstetter, *Studien*, p. 159; N. Abbagnano, *Ockham*, p. 172; G. M. Manser, "Drei Zweifler am Kausalprincip im XIV Jahrhundert", in *Jahrbuch für Philosophie und spekulative Theologie*, vol. 27 (1912), pp. 405–37.

the psychological process which enables us to form general ideas, or to conceive the notion of causality; but he should have stopped there and given to his psychological analysis a merely psychological conclusion. Granted that a concept is but a particular sign that stands for several individuals, it does not follow that reality is exclusively individual; otherwise, how could several individuals be signified by the same sign? Granted that our knowledge of causality is but an association of ideas, it does not follow that effects are not intrinsically related to their causes; otherwise why should there be, in their succession, that regularity which makes our associations of ideas possible? Psychologism consists in demanding that psychology answer philosophical questions. Psychology is a science, psychologism is a sophism; it substitutes the definition for the defined, the description for the described, the map for the country. Thus left without objective justification, human knowledge becomes a mere system of useful conventions, whose practical success remains a complete mystery to the minds of the very scientists who made it. Scientists themselves can afford such blunders; faith in science being what they live by, they have no need of reality. Yet, if even their intellectual life is a crippled life, what about those countless intelligences which have no science to live by, or faith left in an intrinsically intelligible world? They are all on the straight road to scepticism. Mediæval thought entered it as soon as Ockham's philosophy took deep root in the European universities of the fourteenth century. Scholastic philosophers then began to mistrust their own principles, and mediæval philosophy broke down; not for want of ideas, for they still were there; or for want of men, for there never were more brilliant intelligences than at the time of that glorious sunset; mediæval philosophy broke down when, having mistaken philosophy for reality itself, the best minds were surprised to find reason empty and began to despise it.

CHAPTER IV

THE BREAKDOWN OF
MEDIÆVAL PHILOSOPHY

Historians of mediæval philosophy have to deal with the same problems and to use the same methods as any other historians of philosophy. The only point that is distinctive about their work is that they seldom read purely philosophical books. On the contrary, an historian of mediæval theology would be unable to make much headway unless he has previously read a large number of philosophical books. A commentary on the *Sentences* of Peter Lombard, or a *Summa Theologica* of the thirteenth century, is always an organic whole in which what reason knows about God and His creation is inseparable from the teaching of the revealed text. Philosophy and theology can always be found therein in a state of more or less clear distinction, but never separated; when they did begin to resent their alliance as a suspicious promiscuity, the breakdown of mediæval culture was at hand.

If we look at the situation as a young student in theology saw it around the year 1320, it will appear to be rather confused. We have to imagine him as a thoroughly religious man, primarily concerned with the salvation of his fellow man through the word of God, for such indeed was the reason why the best among those students wanted to study theology. To be sure theological teaching was plentiful in those years at the University of Paris, but the problem was precisely to select the best theology among the many that recommended themselves to one's attention. Even the choice of a religious order was not always enough to settle the problem; a Franciscan could either stick to the old doctrine of St. Bonaventura, or he could decide in favour of Duns Scotus, unless he found it more advisable to enlist among the followers of Ockham. Were our man a Dominican he could find at the very least three theologies at his disposal. There were Albertus Magnus and Thomas Aquinas; and people were beginning to talk about a German preacher by the name of Meister Eckhart. There is never too much of a good thing, but there were too many varieties of the same thing, and the difficulty was that since Ockham was refuting Duns Scotus, the while Duns Scotus himself was correcting Bonaventura, or Thomas Aquinas straightening out Albertus Magnus, they could not all be right at the same time. But who was right?

By far the easiest way to solve the problem was to decide that every one was wrong. Many theologians began to feel that there was a serious danger for the future of religion in those scholastic wars. If theology is the science of the word of God, it is unlikely that the solving of such highly intricate problems be required in order to achieve one's own salvation. In short, the Gospel is both so simple and so safe that its teaching can only be weakened and obscured by such complications. Therefore, from that time on, the slogan of many theologians was to be: Back to the Gospel! To quote but one name, the Dutchman, Gehrard Groot, was a particularly fine example of that attitude. He considered the University of Paris as a place where a young man not only could not learn theology, but was practically bound to lose his faith, precisely because of the theologians. What he would personally advocate, instead of such dangerous studies, was the reading of the Bible, of some Fathers of the Church, such as St. Jerome and St. Augustine, and a solid training in classical Latin. There was nothing radically new in his attitude. As early as the thirteenth century the Franciscan poet, Jacopone da Todi, was complaining that Paris, whereby he meant the University of Paris, had already destroyed Assisi; that is, the purity of simple Christian life. That there were too much philosophy and too many theological discussions, was then becoming a common complaint, but Gehrard Groot did more than voice it. Himself a second-rate thinker and but an indifferent writer, he nevertheless succeeded both in expressing the inner aspirations of a large number of his contemporaries and in giving them the support of a concrete institution. As a Christian, his ideal was: *contemptus saeculi et imitatio humilis vitae Christi;*[1] his disciple, Florentius, handed it down to Thomas à Kempis, and any one who remembers the three opening chapters of the *Imitation of Christ* can consider himself fully informed about the fourteenth-century anti-scholasticism. But Gehrard Groot did more than that. At the personal request of Florentius, he organized at Deventer the first convent of the Brothers of Common Life, where his conceptions of truly Christian teaching were carried into execution. Gehrard Groot's ideal was still alive at Deventer when a young Dutchman went there in 1475 to stay until the end of his studies in 1484. His name was to become famous the whole world over as that of the greatest of all the Christian humanists: Desiderius Erasmus of Rotterdam. We read in books and dictionaries that the school of Deventer "was one of the first in Northern Europe to feel the influence of the Renaissance"; it would be more true to say that the Deventer school was one of the first influences that brought about the so-called Renaissance. After the disruption of scholasticism, a simple return to the Bible and to the study of ethical problems was one

[1] W. Mulder, *Gerardi magni epistolae* (Antwerp, 1933), pp. 26–36; on the imitation of Christ, see p. 31. See also Karl Grube, *Gehrard Grot und seine Stiftungen* (Köln, 1883), pp. 67 and 91.

of the few experiments that could still be attempted. But it could be tried in two different ways: by discrediting philosophy through criticism, or by merely decreeing that it was dead.

There was something to be said in favour of the first attitude. When theology is left without philosophy, philosophy itself has to be left without theology, and a philosophy which is allowed to go its own way is apt to brew trouble for the theologians. Averroës and his Latin followers had supported the view that philosophy, when it is given the liberty to follow its own methods, reaches necessary conclusions that are contradictory to the teachings of the theologians. Thirteenth-century scholasticism had largely been an answer to the challenge of Averroës; unfortunately, the answer was far from being unanimous. Let us consider, for instance, two problems with which philosophers were equally concerned: the eternity of the world and the immortality of the soul. Averroës had proved that the world is eternal and that there is no personal immortality. All the Christian theologians protested against his conclusions and attacked his demonstrations, but not all in the same way. St. Bonaventura attempted to prove by philosophical arguments that the world is not eternal and that the soul of each man is immortal. St. Thomas Aquinas was of the opinion that Averroës had failed to prove the eternity of the world, but that St. Bonaventura had also failed to prove that the world is not eternal; in short, philosophy cannot prove anything on that point, but it can prove the immortality of the soul. Duns Scotus' position was that neither the creation of the world in time, nor the immortality of the soul could be proved by philosophers, but that both could be proved by theologians. As to Ockham himself, he was willing to hold such conclusions as philosophical probabilities, but not as conclusively proved truths; to which he added that what cannot be proved by philosophy can still less be proved by theology, where certitude is not grounded on reason, but on faith.

The result of that state of things was a widespread feeling that theology could not afford to ignore philosophy, but should not trust it. Philosophy could not be trusted since even the most carefully balanced of all doctrines, that of St. Thomas Aquinas, was far from being unanimously received; but neither could it be ignored since Averroës and his school boasted that they could disprove religious truth. Failing an agreement as to the way in which philosophy could be made useful, there arose a general impression that it should at least be made harmless. Now the easiest way to show that philosophy could not prove anything against religion was to show that it cannot prove anything at all. Hence the current of metaphysical scepticism that runs through the late Middle Ages and whose presence can still be observed as late as the seventeenth century.

An interesting expression of that state of mind can be found in the writings of a rather obscure member of the University of Paris, Nicolas of Autrecourt. After living at the Sorbonne as a student between 1320 and 1327, he had become a lecturer in theology; but his teaching rapidly became suspect, so much so that a series of propositions extracted from one of his books was formally condemned by the Pope in 1346. Like Ockham himself and several famous Ockhamists, Nicolas had already fled for refuge to the court of King Louis of Bavaria, for there were political implications behind those abstract problems; but the only point with which we are now concerned is the philosophical attitude of our theologian and in what sense it was a scepticism.

I do not think that there ever was a single man whose mental attitude could correctly be described as pure scepticism. One is always some one else's sceptic, and the man to whom we give that name sometimes is such for lack of intellectual discipline and sometimes appears as such because his standard of truth is more exacting than our own. Nicolas of Autrecourt was certainly not a sceptic in matters of religion; and neither was he a sceptic in matters of rational knowledge: on the contrary, he had very settled ideas as to what can be known and what cannot. In fact, his attitude on that point clearly shows the new ideal of rational knowledge which was trying confusedly to express itself in the school of Ockham. It was a rather crude empiricism, examples of which could still easily be found in our own days. Nicolas of Autrecourt never admitted more than two orders of evident knowledge: what we can deduce from the principle of contradiction, and what we perceive by sense, external or internal; but he always maintained that such knowledge at least is evident. It must even be said that one of his main preoccupations was to dispel the suspicion cast by Ockham and some of his disciples on the absolute validity of intuitive knowledge. In his first letter to the Franciscan Bernard of Arezzo, Nicolas expressly states that what he is there opposing is the thesis according to which: *notitia intuitiva non requirit necessario rem existentem*;[2] whence it should logically follow that we cannot be certain of the existence of the external world, or even of our own acts.

I am quite willing to grant that Nicolas deserves to be praised for his worthy intentions of damming the rising tide of idealism and radical scepticism; but in his desire to save what little certain knowledge could be saved, he so severely restricted the field of rational certitude that practically nothing of it was left. If we suppose with him that the supreme rule of human knowledge is the principle of contradiction, there can be no degrees of evidence; we are equally sure of all that can be deduced from it, and we have no knowledge at all of that which cannot be deduced from it. Supposing then, that our sensible intuitions are unshakable facts, what can we conclude from them on the strength of the principle of contradiction?

[2] The texts are to be found in J. Lappe, *Nicolaus von Autrecourt: sein Leben, seine Philosophie, seine Schriften* (Münster, 1908), pp. 2*–6*.

In the first place, from the fact that we know a certain thing is, it is impossible to infer that another thing is, which can be shown in the following way. It is possible for one of these things to exist without the other, for the simple reason that it is not contradictory. Now from the fact that A is, nothing follows; for to say that if A is, then A is, is not an inference; but to say that if A is, then B is, is to say something that cannot be reduced to the principle of contradiction.[8] The upshot of this attitude is to leave us with two utterly independent sources of evident knowledge of such a kind that neither of them can draw anything from the other. No wonder then if, when Nicolas undertook to test the validity of Aristotle's conclusions in the light of his own principles, practically the whole body of classical metaphysics went to pieces. What is left of metaphysics if we keep only what is immediately perceived by sense, external or internal, and deduced from it by the principle of contradiction only? As Nicolas writes to his correspondent, Bernard of Arezzo: "In all his natural philosophy and metaphysics, Aristotle has hardly reached two evidently certain conclusions, perhaps not even a single one, and likewise, or much less, Brother Bernard who is not better than Aristotle." More than that, if Aristotle never reached any evident conclusions, he could not have even probable ones; for nothing can be held as probable unless it has first been evident. Now, for instance, the whole physics of Aristotle rests on the assumption that everything is either a substance or an accident; but who has ever perceived a substance? If there were substances, even peasants would see them. We don't see them, and, what is more, we cannot infer their existence from what we call their properties, or accidents, for since it has just been shown, that from the perceived existence of a certain thing, the existence of no other thing can be concluded, there is no reason whatsoever to posit unperceived substances behind their perceived accidents.[4]

[3] Ibid., pp. 9*–12*.   [4] Ibid., pp. 12*–13*.

If we go thus far, we shall have to go a little further, for a similar reasoning will clearly show that we have no evident knowledge of the fact that any thing, but God, can be the efficient cause of any other thing; we cannot even know if a natural efficient cause is merely possible; in short, after the notion of substance, we have to dismiss the notion of causality. For the same reason it is impossible to prove that a certain thing is the final cause of another thing, which eliminates purposiveness from the world. But if we dismiss both efficient causes and final causes, what will be left of the classical demonstrations of the existence of God? Obviously nothing.[5] As Nicolas says, insofar as evidence is concerned, these propositions: God exists, and God does not exist, signify absolutely the same thing.[6]

It would be a serious mistake to consider Nicolas of Autrecourt as a mere revolutionist with nothing but destructive aims in mind. On the contrary, he was most anxious to destroy scholastic philosophy in order that he could build up something else in its place. His reaction was a typical instance of what usually happens when men begin to despair of philosophy. We cannot live without ascribing some meaning to our existence, or act without ascribing some goal to our activity; when philosophy no longer provides men with satisfactory answers to those questions, the only means they still have to escape scepticism and despair are moralism, or mysticism, or some combination of both. Nicolas of Autrecourt was by no means a mystic; his was a clear case of religious moralism. His anti-metaphysicism was not prompted by any scientific ideal. In fact, I do not think that he ever suspected the tremendous possibilities which empirical methods of observation would have opened to science; on the contrary, he was much more anxious to get rid of science as quickly as possible than to usher in an era of indefinite scientific progress. He felt thoroughly disgusted at the sight of good men

[5] Ibid., pp. 32*–33*.   [6] Ibid., p. 37*.

wasting their lifetime, from youth to age, on Aristotle and
Averroës; but he felt certain that the few things which it is useful
for man to know about nature would be known in a short time
if we looked less at books and more at things. Then the best
among the members of the political community could devote
their whole care to the highest interest of morals and religion.
Were they to do so, they would keep peace and charity, the
more perfect helping the less perfect by showing them what to
do. Fully aware of how little they can know by the natural light
of reason, such men would not sin by pride, but rather would
purify both their hearts and their minds from the vices that
breed ignorance, such as envy, avarice, cupidity. At the end of a
long life thus spent in the teaching of the divine law, such pure
and wise men would be held by all as truly divine, and hailed as
the spotless mirrors of the glorious King of nature, the faithful
images of His generosity.[7]

Obviously Nicolas of Autrecourt's plan was to turn pure
formal logic against philosophy, to the greater benefit of ethics
and of practical religious life. Having borrowed from Aristotle
himself the definition of a strictly necessary demonstration, he
could easily apply it to the physics and metaphysics of Aristotle
and show that not a single thesis of the Greek philosopher had
really been demonstrated. Averroïsm, which professed to be an
expression of the genuine thought of Aristotle, was thereby
destroyed, and Christian truth was safe. This was no doubt
a plausible method, but it was a rather dangerous one, for it
implied that Christian dogmas could no more be supported by
philosophy than endangered by it. Again, it was a costly method
which obliged theologians to prove, by heaping up the most
intricate philosophical arguments, that nothing had ever been
proved by philosophers. Last, but not least, supposing that
philosophy were effectually destroyed, logic would still remain,

[7] Nicolas of Autrecourt, unprinted treatise *Exigit ordo executionis*, init.

and how could a theologian forget that, together with grammar, logic had been the first discipline to bring about theological difficulties? Why not get rid of both philosophy and logic?

Such was to be the conclusion of one of the greatest Italian poets whose name is seldom quoted in our histories of mediæval philosophy, Francesco Petrarca. Yet, if the forces that brought the career of mediæval philosophy to an end are part of that history, he ought to be there. The French historian of Petrarch, Henri de Nolhac, called him "the first modern man"; but Burckhardt also called Dante the first modern man, which shows that there have been at least two first modern men, each of whom was the very reverse of the other. For Dante was thoroughly scholastic in his culture, deeply learned in the philosophy of his time and a great admirer of Aristotle, "the master of those who know". I even think, for that matter, that he was something of an Averroïst. The second first modern man, Petrarch, was wholly different. Fifteen years after the death of Nicolas of Autrecourt, he dictated to his secretary a little book whose very title is a portent, *On My Own Ignorance and That of Many Others*. The most famous among those many others was Aristotle.

The date of the book is 1367, that is to say, two hundred and seventy years before the *Discourse on Method* of Descartes', who is supposed to have been the first to throw off the yoke of Aristotle. That yoke did not weigh much on Petrarch's mind. When some Aristotelians started a philosophical discussion in his presence, Petrarch would "either remain silent, or jest with them, or change the subject". Sometimes, Petrarch says, "I asked with a smile, how Aristotle could have known that, for it was not proven by the light of reason, nor could it be tested by experiment. At that they would fall silent, in surprise and anger, as if they regarded me as a blasphemer who asked any proof beyond the authority of Aristotle. So we bid fair to be no longer philosophers, lovers of the truth, but Aristotelians, or rather Pythagoreans, reviving the absurd custom which permits us to ask no question except whether *he* said it. . . . I believe, indeed, that Aristotle was a great man and that he knew much; yet he was but a man, and therefore something, nay, many things, may have escaped him. I will say more. . . . I am confident, beyond a doubt, that he was in error all his life, not only as regards small matters, where a mistake counts for little, but in the most weighty questions, where his supreme interests were involved. And although he has said much of happiness, both at the beginning and the end of his *Ethics*, I dare assert, let my critics exclaim as they may, that he was so completely ignorant of true happiness, that the opinions upon this matter of any pious old woman, or devout fisherman, shepherd or farmer, would, if not so fine spun, be more to the point than his." [8]

Therein lies the whole intellectual outlook of Petrarch, as clearly expressed as possible. Some of his contemporaries would accuse him of ignorance, because he declined to take interest in philosophy; but the only knowledge that really matters is that which can lead man to happiness, and no book can teach it better than the Gospel. Supposing one wishes to read something else, why not try the works of Cicero? 'Tis true that Cicero also was a pagan, and his books are full of the most dangerous errors; yet, everywhere he deals with God and the marvels of His providence, Cicero speaks much more as an apostle than as a philosopher. Besides, what is the use of teaching virtue unless we bring men to love it? Even when he is right, Aristotle is cold, and he leaves us cold, whereas it is impossible to read

[8] Petrarch, *De ma propre ignorance et de celle de beaucoup d'autres*, French trans. by L. Moulinier (Paris: F. Alcan), pp. 30–31. I am indebted for the English translation of this text to J. H. Robinson and H. W. Rolfe's *Petrarch: The First Modern Scholar and Man of Letters* (New York and London, 1898), pp. 39–40. The original Latin text has been edited by L. M. Capelli, *Pétrarque: le traité De sui ipsius et multorum ignorantia* (Paris: H. Champion, 1906).

Cicero, or for that matter Seneca, without falling in love with the beauty of virtue and feeling a bitter hatred against vice. If true philosophers are masters of virtue, Cicero and Seneca are the true philosophers.[9] Petrarch's disgust for what he calls "the noisy herd of scholastics"[10] was born of his complete mistrust of philosophy as a guide to the moral life. How indeed could we trust philosophy, if what Pythagoras had said a long time ago is true, that every philosophical proposition can be refuted as easily as it can be proved, even to this very proposition itself? Socrates modestly confessed: "There is but one thing I know, and it is that I know nothing"; and still he was bragging, for he could not even be sure of that, and Archeläus was right in adding: "for my own part I would not dare to affirm that it can be affirmed that we know nothing."[11]

Such is the moralism of the humanists, one of the classical remedies for philosophical scepticism, which, in its turn, is the outcome of all errors concerning the nature of philosophy itself. The recurrence of certain philosophical attitudes is an historical fact. It cannot be explained away merely by resorting to the influence of a philosopher on another philosopher; first, because it is sometimes impossible to prove that a philosopher was ever acquainted with the doctrine which he reproduces: it is impossible to prove that Descartes ever read St. Anselm; next, because there may be no external or material resemblance between two doctrines whose central inspiration is nevertheless the same: Malebranche never read Al Ashari and had he read him, he would have considered his doctrine ridiculous, yet Malebranche himself repeated exactly Al Ashari's undertaking; last, but not least, even when it has been proved that a man has

---

[9] Petrarch, *De ma propre ignorance*, pp. 63–65.

[10] Ibid. p. 68.

[11] Ibid. pp. 88–89. See also another text in Robinson and Rolfe, *Petrarch*, pp. 217–23.

yielded to a certain influence, the reason he did so has to be explained. Why do we rebel against certain influences while accepting some others? Not only do we accept influences, we sometimes welcome them as if, when at last they come, there had always been in us a secret hope that we might some day meet them. Reason never surrenders but to itself. Deep influences are not merely undergone, they are chosen, as in virtue of some selective affinity. Confronted with the same failure of philosophy to rise above the order of formal logic, John of Salisbury between 1150 and 1180, Nicolas of Autrecourt and Petrarch in 1360, Erasmus of Rotterdam around 1490, spontaneously conceived a similar method to save Christian faith. Logic was to them but an introductory discipline that one had to know and eventually to use against the ambitions of philosophy, but which could throw no light on the really important problems. These are the moral problems, and their answer can always be found in the Gospel, in the Fathers of the Church, and in the pagan moralists to whom the Fathers themselves were so heavily indebted. Philosophy itself, conceived as a distinct discipline, should therefore be ruled out and invited to give way to practical ethics. That was one possible solution, but there was another which consisted in resorting to mysticism; not to rule out philosophy, but to transcend it.

Here again we might feel tempted to resort to historical influences as a possible explanation for the mystical tide that swept over the fourteenth and fifteenth centuries. And it would certainly be a true explanation, for Pseudo-Dionysius, and therefore Plotinus, have played an important part in its development; but it would not be a complete explanation; for Dionysius had always been available since the translation of his writings into Latin at the beginning of the ninth century, many theologians had written commentaries on his works, and yet no one had ever found therein what the men of the fourteenth and fifteenth centuries were to read in his books. No one, except perhaps Scotus Erigena; but the periodical revivals of Erigena themselves are not without causes: his presence becomes perceptible every time, and as soon as some one needs him, whereas for those who have no use for him, he will stand for naught. I am not quite sure that Eckhart needed Erigena, but he certainly was predetermined to receive the message of Dionysius the Areopagite, and he received it gladly.

That God is infinitely above anything we can think and say about Him, was a universally accepted doctrine in mediæval theology. St. Thomas Aquinas had made it the very foundation of his doctrine. We do not know what God is, but only what He is not, so that we know Him the better as we more clearly see that He is infinitely different from everything else. This principle, however, can be used in two different ways. We can, with St. Thomas Aquinas, posit it at the beginning and at the end of our theology; it will then act both as a general qualification applying to all theological statements, and as an invitation to transcend theology, once we are through with it, by entering the depth of mystical life. Yet, between his initial statement that God is, strictly speaking, unknowable, and his ultimate endeavour to experience by love that which surpasses human understanding, St. Thomas Aquinas never forgets, that if we do not know God, the reason is not that God is obscure, but rather that He is a blinding light. The whole theology of St. Thomas points to the supreme intelligibility of what lies hidden in the mystery of God. Now, if God is intelligible in Himself, what little we know about Him may be almost nothing, but it is not nothing, and it is infinitely more important than all the rest. In short, even when St. Thomas Aquinas uses reason as a means to a mystical end, he does not use it in a mystical way. Reason is made to throw light everywhere it shines; where darkness becomes invincible, reason gives way to love, and there is the

beginning of mystical life. Not so with Eckhart. Fully convinced that if God is unknowable for us He must be unknowable in Himself, the German theologian was bound to use
reason as a mystical means to a mystical end. Eckhart's writings
are full of dialectical arguments, and much of the material he
uses is borrowed from St. Thomas Aquinas, but the spirit of
Thomism is gone, for instead of being used as a light on the
field of theology, philosophy has nothing else to do in Eckhart's
doctrine but to throw darkness upon God and so surround
Him with the cloud of unknowingness. The God of Meister
Eckhart is not posited as simply beyond the reach of human
knowledge, but, in a true neoplatonic manner, as escaping all
knowledge, including His very own. Taken in Himself, God is
die wüsste Gottheit, the wilderness of Godhead; and though it be
true that God is eternally expressing Himself in an act of self-
knowledge, the fact remains that God's infinite essence is un-
fathomable, even to God, for He could not know Himself
without turning His infinite essence into a definite object of
knowledge. Now, considered as known, the wilderness of
Godhead is not only subjected to limitation, but to number;
God as knowing and God as known are two, so that God no
longer is the simple and absolute Divinity. The only way to
reach God, insofar at least as it is possible for us to do so, is
therefore to transcend all mutual limitations and all distinctions;
it is to go, not only beyond the multiplicity of finite things, but
even past the Trinity of the divine persons. It is only when
man reaches that silent wilderness where there is neither Father,
nor Son, nor Holy Ghost, that His mystical flight comes to an
end, for there lies the source of all that is: beyond God, in the
fullness of the Divinity.

Such an achievement would necessarily remain beyond the
grasp of even the greatest mystics, were it not that God has
created man in His own image and likeness. There is, in each

one of us, a spark of the divine essence, that shines upon the very apex of what we call intellect, and makes us partakers of the divine light. Uncreated and uncreatable as the Divinity itself, that spark is more one in us with its divine source than it is with the very intellect in which it dwells. In short, were man nothing but that light, he would be God. Such a mystical conception of human understanding was exactly what Eckhart needed in order to overcome all the distinctions that stand in the way of man's absolute surrender to God. The divine spark is in us both as the source of our longing for God, and as the force that brings us back to God. Since it is God in us, it is the wilderness of God urging us from within, to seek Him beyond shape, place, time and even existence. Every particular thing, for as much as it is, is the negation of what it is not; how then could we raise God above all determinations and negations, unless we posit Him even above all affirmations? God is so supremely existing, that He is nothing. Such is the deepest meaning of Meister Eckhart's theology, whence it follows, that just as piety consists in ridding ourselves of all things for the love of God, theology consists in ridding God Himself of shape and shapeliness, things and thingness, existence and existences, until we reach the absolute nakedness of His divinity.

We read in his *Sayings*, that "Meister Eckhart met a lovely naked boy. He asked him whence he came. He said, 'I come from God.' ... 'Who art Thou?'—'A King.'—'Where is thy kingdom?'—'In my heart.'—'Mind no one shares it with Thee.'—'So I do.'—He took me to his cell and said: 'Take any coat Thou wilt.'—'Then I should be no King' (said he), and vanished. It was God Himself that he had had with him a little spell." [12] The religious beauty of such lines is not only above criticism, it is

<hr/>

[12] Meister Eckhart, *Sermons*, ed. F. Pfeiffer (Leipzig, 1857); trans. C. de B. Evans (London: J. M. Watkins, 1924–1931), sermon 94, p. 235; tract 19, p. 412; sayings, p. 438.

even above praise. Yet, how could we forget that other naked
boy, whom his friends had seen, not in a vision but in the flesh,
giving back to his father what money he had left, to even the
clothes he had on? The young Francis of Assisi also was a naked
king, but his God was not a naked God; and that is why, having
given up everything but God, he had both God and everything
else: Brother Sun and Sister Moon, and the air, and the cloud
and the wind. As the God of St. Francis had not been stripped
by man of his own intelligibility, creation itself remained intelligible, and desirable and lovable for the sake of its creator; but
since the God of Eckhart was a wilderness, Eckhart's nakedness
was that of destitution, and like God Himself he could be but
the king of a waste land.

This is exactly what nature had to become when, in the
fifteenth century, Nicolaus Cusanus applied Eckhart's theological principles to philosophy. His main ambition was to bring to
an early end the philosophical and theological dissensions which
were then growing so dangerous for the unity of the Church. In
point of fact, it was not difficult in those times to see that
Christendom was threatened with ruin; but Nicolaus Cusanus
was still hoping that the disaster could be avoided, if only men
could bring themselves to look upon their quarrels as insignificant philosophical and theological differences. After all, what
was it all about? Some of his contemporaries felt convinced that
they knew the whole truth concerning God; others, on the
contrary, were busy proving that the first ones did not know
anything about Him. Hence their endless disputes, followed by
doctrinal condemnations, heresies and schisms. Nicolaus was
clever enough to perceive that the trouble with those men was
that they were all equally dogmatic, no less in their negations
than in their assertions.

When a man of critical mind undertakes to refute the conclusions of metaphysicians, he obviously labours under the

delusion that there is in the mind an order of absolute truth, wholly different from metaphysical conjectures. His critical attitude toward philosophy might change, however, were he a bit more critically minded, for then his first question would be: Is there any case in which exact and precise truth can really be arrived at? An exact truth would be an adequate mental presentation of its object; but the known object and its knowledge in the mind are two distant realities, and who has ever found in nature two things that were really two, that is to say, distinct, and yet identically alike? Likeness is always a matter of comparison, and therefore of degree and approximation. No thing so closely resembles another that a third one could not still more closely resemble it. In our comparisons there is always something that is *like that*, but *that* it is not and cannot be. Now if truth requires a perfect adequation of the knowing mind to the known thing, it is an indivisible. There can be no question of more and less about it; either knowledge is absolutely identical with its object, and then it is true; or it is not wholly identical with it, and then it is not at all true. But we were just observing that no two things could possibly be both distinct and identical at one and the same time. Consequently, truth is impossible.

This, of course, does not mean that any statement that can be made about a thing is no better than any other one. As soon as we rid ourselves of that truth obsession, we begin to deal with approximations that are comparable both to each other and to reality. Strictly speaking, they have no truth value, but granting that all of them are excluded from that indivisible point, some of them are closer to it than others. In this sense, the notions of more and less regain their whole significance and do apply to our judgments. Each of them stands to truth in the same relation as a polygon of n sides to the circle; whatever the number of its sides, no polygon is a circle: it is not at all a circle;

yet as you go on increasing the number of its sides, it grows less and less different from a circle, the which nevertheless it will never be. Such also is human knowledge, and to become more and more clearly aware of its nature is the proper task of the philosopher. Basically, philosophy is but a *docta ignorantia*: a learned ignorance, and the more we learn about our own ignorance, the more we learn also about philosophy.[18]

The same conclusion holds true if we turn from definitions to judgments, but for another reason. To judge is to affirm, or to deny, a certain relation between two things, or two different aspects of reality. Of course one has to do it, but how far it takes us is another question. Whatever their different systems may be, almost all philosophers agree that the first cause of the world is God. Moreover, they describe God as the Absolute. If God is the Absolute, the cause of the world at least is secure from our judgments, for the Absolute is outside and above all relations. It is therefore useless for us to resort to the principles of identity and of contradiction in order to ascribe something to God, or to deny something of His nature. There is nothing which the Absolute is not, but there is also nothing which the Absolute is without being at the same time everything else. It is correct to say, for instance, that God is a being than which no greater can be conceived, but if He is the Absolute, He must needs be at the same time, and for the same reason, a being than which no smaller can be conceived. God is the coincidence of opposites, and therefore He is above both the principle of identity and the principle of contradiction. In short, God is unthinkable: "I have learnt that the place wherein Thou art found unveiled is girt around with the coincidence of contradictories, and this is the wall of Paradise wherein Thou dost abide. The door whereof is guarded by the most proud

[13] Nicolaus Cusanus, *De docta ignorantia*, bk. 1, chap. 4. Cf. bk. 2, chap. 1; ed. E. Hoffmann and R. Klibansky (Leipzig, 1932).

spirit of Reason, and, unless he be vanquished, the way will not lie open."[14]

The upshot of the situation is that our judgments are almost as powerless to express relations between things as they are to describe God. Taken all together, things make up what we call the Universe. Now the Universe is an effect whose cause is God. This is the very reason why it is a Universe, that is to say, not a mere plurality of unrelated things, but a universality of many-related things. The trouble is that, in point of fact, things are not only many-related, but universally related. Taken as a whole, the Universe must bear to God the same likeness that all effects bear to their causes, and just as all the divine ideas are co-related, so also all the corresponding things must needs be co-related. More than that, since every one of the divine ideas is but a particular expression of God as a whole, so also must every particular thing be considered as a restricted but global expression of the Universe. The sun is the Universe in a restricted way, and the same thing can be said of the moon, and of the earth; in a word, the Universe is identical with itself in each particular aspect of its diversity.[15] From such a point of view, even the old problem of the universals at last becomes intelligible, and that in virtue of its very unintelligibility. What was the difficulty? It was, we remember, to understand how a certain species can be wholly present in every one of its individuals. But the whole world is so made, that each singular being is there the concrete expression of a totality! The old principle of Anaxagoras still holds true: everything is in everything. The only difference is that we know much more clearly than Anaxagoras himself why his principle was true. God is in the

[14] Nicolaus Cusanus, *The Vision of God*, chap. 9; trans. E. G. Salter (London and New York, 1928), pp. 43–44.
[15] Nicolaus Cusanus, *De docta ignorantia*, bk. 2, chap. 4; ed. Hoffmann-Klibansky,, pp. 72–75.

Universe as the cause is in its effect, and the Universe is in God as effects are in their causes; moreover, and for the same reason, the Universe is in every one of its parts, for every one of its parts is the Universe, with the consequence that, as a restricted Universe, each particular thing is every other particular thing.[16]

Such as Nicolaus Cusanus conceived it, the world was in great danger of becoming almost as unthinkable as God Himself. However much we may regret it, human understanding is so made, that when it tries to conceive a thing as being both itself and its opposite, it ceases to understand. This, of course, was exactly the point which Nicolaus wished to make; not in the least that the world is intelligible to us, and how, but rather that the world is not intelligible, and why. It is not intelligible, and such is necessarily the case, at least if it is to fulfill its proper function, which is to manifest a God who surpasses all understanding. The universal mystery of things is but a concrete expression of the supreme mystery of God.

Such was the last word of mediæval philosophy, and I am far from being blind to its magnificence, or deaf to the secret truth of its message; I am merely pointing to the fact that it was a complete abdication of philosophy as a rational discipline. I do not say that the fourteenth and the fifteenth centuries were periods of sterility in the history of the human mind; on the contrary, these late scholastics were obviously headed for entirely new and highly important discoveries. It is not by mere chance that the first attempts to prove that the earth is moving, or to give anything like a scientific description of motion itself, were the work of Ockhamists; and no one can read Nicolaus Cusanus without feeling that with him, Pascal, Leibniz and the infinitesimal calculus had already become open possibilities. But was it impossible to pave the way to science without destroying philosophy?

[16] Ibid., bk. 2, chap. 5, p. 76; and chap. 8, pp. 88–89.

This at least is a fact, that as soon as the scholastics gave up all hope of answering philosophical problems in the light of pure reason, the long and brilliant career of mediæval philosophy came to a close. Despite its great achievements in other fields, the sixteenth century counts for very little in the history of philosophy itself. And no wonder. Rational metaphysics was dead; positive science had not yet been born; nothing was left to which the men of those times could still resort, but imagination. This is the reason why, whereas St. Thomas Aquinas and Duns Scotus have still so much to tell us, Giordano Bruno, Telesio and Campanella have become hardly readable to anybody who is not professionally obliged to read them. Besides, the most sincere expression of the philosophical attitude of the Renaissance is not to be found in such books. We find it rather in the endless list of treatises wherein an open philosophical scepticism was coupled with a more or less complete abdication of philosophy as a rational discipline. The generalized scepticism of the Renaissance was bound to follow from such doctrines as their necessary conclusion. After Petrarch's *Confession of His Own Ignorance* and Nicolaus Cusanus' treatise on *Learned Ignorance*, Adriano di Corneto will prove in his *De vera philosophia* (1509) that Holy Writ alone contains true science and that philosophy cannot teach it. In 1535, an obscure man, who went by the name of Bunel, was maintaining that nothing is less safe than philosophy, whether it deals with natural or moral problems; now that same Bunel once presented an old man with a copy of the *Natural Theology* of Ramon Sebond, and that old man in turn asked his son to translate it from the Latin into French; which was done. The name of the young translator was Michel de Montaigne: Montaigne, *the* sceptic in Emerson's gallery of representative men. The first edition of the famous *Essays* was published in 1580, soon followed, in 1581, by the *Nothing Known* of Sanchez, and in 1601 by the first edition of

Charron's book, *On Wisdom*, which was but a better ordered exposition of Montaigne. Even leaving aside the publication of Sextus Empiricus' *Hypotyposes*, and so many other treatises which it would be easy to cite, the most superficial glance at the literature of that period attests the complete triumph of a universal scepticism.

Analyzing the philosophical situation as it was around 1340, an ideal observer could safely have predicted the complete breakdown of scholastic philosophy. Nothing is easier for us than to show in a few sentences how those events came to pass, and why similar results may safely be expected every time philosophers make the same mistakes. It does not even require a demonstration to make it clear; it is a flat truism that all attempts to deal with philosophical problems from the point of view, or with the method, of any other discipline will inevitably result in the destruction of philosophy itself. Yet such abstract statements usually fail to convince those who hear them, and sometimes even those by whom they are made. One of the greatest uses of history of philosophy is precisely that it brings us their experimental demonstration. By observing the human mind at work, in its failures as well as in its successes, we can experience the intrinsic necessity of the same connections of ideas which pure philosophy can justify by abstract reasoning. Thus understood, the history of philosophy is to the philosopher what his laboratory is to the scientist; it particularly shows how philosophers do not think as they wish, but as they can, for the interrelation of philosophical ideas is just as independent of us as are the laws of the physical world. A man is always free to choose his principles, but when he does he must face their consequences to the bitter end. During the Middle Ages, the exact place of philosophical speculation had been clearly defined by St. Thomas Aquinas; nothing, however, could have obliged his successors to stay there; they left it of their own accord, and they were quite free to do so, but once this had been done, they were no longer free to keep philosophy from entering upon the road to scepticism. The Renaissance at last arrived there. But man is not naturally a doubting animal; when his own folly condemns him to live in uncertainty concerning the highest and most vital of all problems, he can put up with it for a certain time; but he will soon remember that the problems are still there clamouring for solutions. Usually a young hero then arises who decides that the whole business has to be done all over again, like Descartes; he may eventually start his experiment by the same blunder that had brought on both scepticism and his own struggle to get out of it, like Descartes; so that the same old cycle will have to revolve in the same old way until philosophers are willing to learn from experience what is the true nature of philosophy.

PART TWO

THE CARTESIAN EXPERIMENT

CHAPTER V

CARTESIAN MATHEMATICISM

In spite of their various interpretations of Cartesianism, histories of philosophy usually agree that "more than any other
figure in the seventeenth century, Descartes marks the transition
from the Middle Ages to the modern world."[1] Commonplace as
it may be, the statement contains a solid nucleus of historical
truth; for, although mediæval thought had already been slum-
bering for two centuries when Descartes began to write, he was
the first to build up a new system of ideas and to open formally
a new philosophical era. His predecessors had done little more
than to distrust scholastic philosophy, and, as they knew no
other one, to extend their distrust to philosophy itself. Descartes
brought to the world the unexpected revelation that, even after
the breakdown of mediæval philosophy, constructive philosophical thinking was still possible. Ever since the fourteenth
century there had been men to criticize Aristotle, but Descartes'
ambition was quite different: it was to replace him.

That statement needs, however, to be qualified. In the first
place, Descartes marks the transition from the Renaissance,
rather than from the Middle Ages, to the modern world. In the
second place, he does not even mark the transition from the
whole Renaissance to the modern world, but, quite exactly,
from the scepticism of Montaigne to the modern period of
constructive thinking in philosophy. The line that goes from

[1] R. M. Eaton, ed., *Descartes Selections* (New York: Scribner's, 1927), p. v.

Nicolaus Cusanus and Bruno to Leibniz does not run through Descartes, but Cartesianism was a direct answer to the challenge of Montaigne's scepticism. The long list of passages of the *Discourse on Method* that are but an echo of the *Essays*, clearly shows how conversant Descartes was with the work of Montaigne. What can be more modern, for instance, than the opening sentence of the *Discourse*? "Good sense is of all things in the world the most equally distributed, for everybody thinks himself so abundantly provided with it, that even those most difficult to please in all other matters do not commonly desire more of it than they already possess." Was not this the first article of the charter of independent thought? If, as Descartes immediately added, good sense, or reason "is, by nature, equal in all men"[2] why should it ever submit to authority? True, but the fact remains that the first lines of the *Discourse* are borrowed from Montaigne's essay "On Presumption" (*Essays*, bk. II, chap. 17): "of all the gifts made to man by Nature, the most justly distributed is judgment (or sense), for no man is ever displeased with what amount of it he may have received." I quite agree that Descartes read his own thought into the text of Montaigne, but rather than an objection to my thesis, it is the very point I hope to make: the philosophy of Descartes was a desperate struggle to emerge from Montaigne's scepticism and the very form of the *Discourse on Method* is enough to suggest it. Written in the untechnical French of a seventeenth-century gentleman, Descartes' first intention had been to call it, *A History of My Mind*. A perfect title indeed, not only for the *Discourse*, but for the *Essays* as well. In fact, the *Discourse* was one more essay written by Descartes as an answer to Montaigne's *Essays*.

What was the last conclusion of Montaigne? That there was a wisdom, but very different in kind from that of the schools. Deeply perturbed by the religious and political dissensions of

[2] Ibid., p. 2.

his time, and above all by the disruption of moral unity result-
ing from the Reformation, Montaigne had traced back the
common source of those evils to dogmatism. Men are so cock-
sure of what they say that they do not hesitate to eliminate
each other, as if killing an opponent were killing his objections.
Montaigne has been, and still is, the master of many minds, but
the only thing we can learn from him is the art of unlearning.
It is very important, and nowhere is it better learned than in
the *Essays*; the trouble with the *Essays* is that they never teach
anything else. As Montaigne sees it, wisdom is a laborious
training of the mind, whose only result is an acquired habit not
to judge. "I can maintain a position", says Montaigne, "I cannot
choose one." Hence his practical conservatism. If a religion is
there, why should we change it? It cannot be proved; but the
next one will not be more proved, and that one at least is there.
There is nothing more dangerous than to touch a political
order once it has been established. For who knows whether the
next will be better? The world is living by custom and tradition; we should not disturb it on the strength of private opinions which express little more than our own moods and
humours, or, at the utmost, the local prejudices of our own
country. A well-made mind is never fully convinced of its own
opinions, and therefore doubting is the highest mark of wisdom. Not "I know", or even "I don't know", but "What do I
know?" This is doubting.

Such it is as Descartes describes it in the *Discourse*, the program which he followed at the College of La Flèche was well
adapted to convince him that Montaigne was right. As soon as
he had achieved the entire course of these studies, he realized
clearly that he had learned nothing that was clear, certain, or of
any use in life. Then, says Descartes, "I found myself embar-
rassed with so many doubts and errors that it seemed to me
that the effort to instruct myself had no effect other than the

increasing discovery of my own ignorance." [8] As has been seen, many others before him had already made the same discovery, but what had been their ultimate conclusion was only a starting point for Descartes. True enough, at the end of his studies, he found that he was a sceptic. He had to be one, for it was the fashion; but he was a sceptic waiting for something better than scepticism. The purely negative wisdom of Montaigne could not possibly be complete wisdom, but it was the first step to a complete one. True wisdom should be positive, not made up of what we do not know, but grounded on the fullness of what we do know. The problem therefore was to find a knowledge such as would stand the acid test of Montaigne's universal scepticism, for that at least would be an unshakable certainty. But was it possible to find it?

If Descartes had not felt confident that it was, he would not even have thought of asking the question. When he left La Flèche, his ideas were probably much less definite than would appear from the *Discourse*. Memoirs are always a reconstruction of the past in the light of the present. Yet the germ of what now is the present must have already been there in the past, and a man who writes his memoirs, knowing himself from within as he does, has a right to stress that continuity. We shall, therefore, not be far from the mark if we simply say that Descartes left La Flèche with a general feeling of disappointment, but not of despair. In point of fact, even before he could clearly formulate his philosophical problem, Descartes had already found, if not the answer, at least what was later to give him the answer. The course of study established by the Jesuits made provision for forty-five minutes of mathematics a day during the second of the three years of philosophy. It was not much, but that little proved more than enough for such a boy as the young Descartes, not only because he had genius, but also because the teaching

[3] Ibid., p. 4.

of mathematics at La Flèche seems to have been rather intelligent.

In all the colleges of the Jesuits the great authority in mathematics was Father Clavius. We do not know if even so brilliant a student as Descartes would be invited by his teacher to
use the ponderous treatises of the so-called "Modern Euclid",
but there is solid evidence that he read them a little later, and
very likely before 1519. Descartes found there not only a complete exposition of the more modern theories in algebra and
geometry, but also a good deal of the results that had already
been achieved by the Greeks by means of the analytical method.
As G. Milhaud says: "If Descartes was dissatisfied with the
teaching of the School, was not his very dissatisfaction, and his
craving for another kind of learning, partly due to what he had
learned?"[4]

Milhaud's statement is undoubtedly right; I wish to add only
this, that besides his first stock of mathematical knowledge,
Descartes inherited from Clavius something much more valuable—the spirit of mathematical learning. Let us only read the
introduction of Clavius to the 1611 edition of his complete
Mathematical Works: "The mathematical disciplines demonstrate
and justify by the most solid reasons everything they may call for
discussion, so that they truly beget science in, and completely
drive out all doubts from, the mind of the student. This can
hardly be said of other sciences, where most of the time the
intellect remains hesitating and dubious about the truth value of
the conclusions, so manifold are the opinions and so conflicting
the judgments. Leaving aside other philosophers, the many sects
of the Peripatetics are enough to prove it. All born of Aristotle,
as the various branches of a common trunk, they disagree so
completely with each other, and sometimes with Aristotle himself, who is their source, that it is quite impossible to know what

[4] G. Milhaud, *Descartes savant* (Paris, 1921), p. 235.

Aristotle was really after, or whether his philosophy was primarily concerned with words or with things. Such is the reason why, among his interpreters, some will follow the Greeks, some others will favour the Latins, or the Arabs, or the Nominalists, or the so-called Realists, and yet all boast that they are Peripatetics. I suppose that every one sees how far all that is from mathematical demonstrations. The theorems of Euclid, as well as those of the other mathematicians, are just as purely true today, as safe in their results, as firm and solid in their demonstrations, as they already were in schools many centuries ago. . . . Since, therefore, mathematical disciplines are so exclusively dedicated to the love and cultivation of truth, that nothing is received there of what is false, nor even of that which is merely probable . . . there is no doubt that the first place among sciences should be conceded to Mathematics."[5]

This was not yet Cartesian philosophy. Clavius had certainly nothing more in mind than what he wrote in his introduction. Yet it was a provoking statement, even though he himself did not know it. There are innumerable sects in philosophy, there are no sects in mathematics; philosophers are always dealing with mere probabilities, mathematicians alone can reach demonstrated conclusions; such statements do not imply the slightest suspicion of what Descartes' own move was going to be. It was an unpredictable move, yet so natural after what Clavius had said, that it assumed at once an outward appearance of necessity. Instead of concluding with Clavius that mathematics was the first of all sciences, Descartes' own inference was that mathematical knowledge was the only knowledge worthy of the name. Hence his conclusion, "not, indeed, that arithmetic and geometry are the sole sciences to be studied, but only that in our search for the direct road towards truth, we should busy

[5] See É. Gilson, *Descartes: Discours de la méthode, texte et commentaire* (Paris: J. Vrin, 1930), p. 128.

ourselves with no object about which we cannot attain a certitude equal to that of the demonstrations of arithmetic and geometry." [6]

The whole philosophy of Descartes was virtually contained in that initial decision, for the *I think, hence I am* is the first principle of Descartes' philosophy, but it is his pledge to mathematical evidence that led Descartes to the *I think*. This, I am afraid, was one of those initial decisions, which beget systems of philosophy where everything is conclusively justified, except their very principle. If we need a philosophy whose certitude is equal to that of mathematics, our first principle will have to be the *I think*; but do we need such a philosophy? And supposing we do, can we have it? In other words, are we sure that everything that *is* is susceptible of a mathematically evident interpretation? The answer, of course, is arbitrary. You have a full right to bet on the affirmative, but it is gambling, and if by any chance you happen to be wrong, you will be playing a losing game from beginning to end. Everything will be mathematically proved in your philosophy, save only this, that everything can, and must be, mathematically proved.

There, at any rate, lies the deepest root of the Cartesian philosophy. If anything can be truly said to express its innermost spirit, it is what I venture to call "Mathematicism", for Descartes' philosophy was nothing else than a recklessly conducted experiment to see what becomes of human knowledge when moulded into conformity with the pattern of mathematical evidence. We would waste our time in asking Descartes for a rational justification of his attitude, for there was none, except that he was weary with scepticism; but it is interesting to watch him on his way towards his decision, for it helps in understanding how he reached it. Descartes did not jump from the mathematics of Clavius directly to his own mathematicism; something very

[6] Eaton, *Descartes Selections*, pp. 43–44.

important happened to him in the interim which accounts for the apparent rashness of his conclusion.

The professor who taught Descartes mathematics at La Flèche was a certain Father François, S.J., who was interested particularly in applied mathematics. Practical applications and, wherever possible, concrete demonstrations were according to him the best way to make that science understood by young students. He wanted them, as he wrote in his *Treatise on Quantity*, "to eye-witness his demonstrations." Judging from the books he has written, his pupil must have heard a lot about land surveying, topography, hydrography, and hydrology. This is precisely what Descartes suggests in two passages of his *Discourse*, where he says that mathematics had been taught him chiefly as a means of furthering all the arts and of diminishing man's labour. I would not be surprised to learn that these Jesuits had read Francis Bacon. It is typical of Descartes, however, that he should immediately react against that attitude. His personal interest in mathematics was entirely due to what he calls there "the certainty of its demonstrations and the evidence of its reasoning"; and of course mathematics should have its applications, but of a loftier order than drawing maps, digging canals or building bridges.[7] That such was really his feeling, even at that early date, is wholly confirmed by the fact that, as soon as he left La Flèche and went to Holland, he became interested, not in mathematics applied to engineering, but in mathematics applied to physics.

Descartes was by no means the first to enter that field of research; nor was he the only one to follow that line of thought around the year 1618. Yet these who then called themselves "physico-mathematicians" were very few in number, and when one stumbled upon another, both experienced the pleasant feeling of meeting one of the initiated. Such was, for instance, Isaac Beeckman, a young Dutchman whom Descartes happened

[7] Ibid., pp. 5 and 7.

to meet three or four years after he himself had graduated from La Flèche. Fortunately for us, Beeckman used to keep a diary, where we can read that in November, 1618, he had just hit upon a young Frenchman by the name of René, who had been delighted to meet for the first time in his life another man equally interested in solving physical problems by means of purely mathematical demonstrations. Physico-mathematicians are scarce, Beeckman sadly remarks (*physico-mathematici paucissimi*), and, he adds, "neither had I myself ever had any conversation on that topic with anybody but him."

His acquaintance with Beeckman became an important factor in Descartes' evolution, in this sense at least, that the questions which his new friend asked him to answer directed his mind towards purely theoretical problems. As a matter of fact, on March 26, 1619, Descartes could already write to Beeckman that he had just discovered four demonstrations, all of them important and entirely new, in the field of geometry. He immediately began to make the first of his truly Cartesian moves. Having found the solution of four geometrical problems, Descartes felt immediately that it should be possible to find a more general method applicable to all geometrical problems whatsoever. Such was the first mental shock he received from his personal studies in mathematics, and the first one of those always wider concentric circles that were to spread around each one of his discoveries. From that very moment he himself could feel that he was up against a task of tremendous difficulty, but he felt confident that it could be done: "My project", he then wrote to Beeckman, "is unbelievably ambitious, but I cannot help feeling that I am sighting I know not what light in the chaos of present-day geometry, and I trust that it will help me in dispelling that most opaque darkness." [8]

[8] Descartes, *Oeuvres complètes*, ed. Charles Adam and Paul Tannery (Paris: Cerf, 1897–1910), vol. 10, pp. 157–58.

Yet full light was not to shine in Descartes' mind until the end of the year 1619. He had by then left Holland, and was going to Germany, where it was his intention to serve as a free officer in the army of Maximilian. There he found many soldiers, but very few battles. In these happy times Turenne had not yet taught the world that a winter campaign was a possibility. His army having nothing to do, Descartes himself had to spend the better part of that winter in a quarter where, as he says in the *Discourse*, since he found no society to divert him and had no cares or passions to trouble him, he remained the whole day shut up alone in a stove-heated room where he had complete leisure to occupy himself with his own thoughts.[9] His natural inclination brought him back to mathematics, and, more precisely, to the huge problem of a universal method in geometry which, so far, had not yet received its solution.

He was really pursuing what we call today analytical geometry. How far advanced Descartes was in its discovery on the night of November 10, 1619, no one knows. What, on the contrary, is certain, is that during that very night he felt clearly not only that what he had dreamed of could be done, but that he was actually doing it. Right or wrong, Descartes could not help feeling that he had found such a method by which geometry, taken as a whole, would rapidly be brought to completion. As he himself had written to Beeckman eight months before, there would be almost nothing left to be discovered in geometry (*adeo ut pene nihil in Geometria supersit inveniendum*); such had been his "incredibly ambitious" project, and there it was now, before his eyes, a concrete reality. "I was filled up with enthusiasm", says Descartes in one of his personal notes. And no wonder. He was twenty-three years old and, alone with his own thoughts in the solitude of an unknown German village, that young man had just made an epoch-making mathematical discovery.

[9] Eaton, *Descartes Selections*, p. 10.

The strong wine of intellectual enthusiasm went to his head. Fully convinced that he had virtually completed geometry by combining it with algebra, Descartes proceeded on the spot to another and still bolder generalization. After all, his only merit had been to realize that two sciences hitherto considered as distinct were but one; why not go at once to the limit and say that all sciences are one? Such was Descartes' final illumination. He suddenly realized that he had found out, together with a universal method of solving all problems whatsoever, what was to be the work of his lifetime. All sciences were one; all problems had to be solved by the same method, provided only they be mathematical, or could be dealt with in a mathematical way; last, but not least, such a universal restoration of human knowledge was bound, out of its own nature, to be the work of a single man. He himself was that man, for he was the only one to know the true method, the only one therefore who owned the key to a rational explanation of reality. During the same night Descartes had dreams where he ventured to find a confirmation of his extraordinary and almost supernatural mission. Was that, as has been suggested by a modern historian, the Pentecost of reason? It merely was the Pentecost of mathematical reasoning, and less a Pentecost than a deluge. In the joy of a splendid discovery, mathematics began to degenerate into mathematicism and to spread as a colourless flood over the manifold of reality. Descartes was a great genius, but I sometimes wonder if his dream were not a nightmare. At any rate, it will be seen later that the men of the eighteenth century had their doubts about it.

The memory of that eventful night was still vivid when, seventeen years later, Descartes was writing in the *Discourse* the history of his mind; but the long train of thoughts by which he then justified his philosophical endeavour had lost the fire and glow of his first enthusiasm. A mature man, he was now taking less interest in the dramatic side of his discoveries than in their contents. Yet even in that public confession of a philosopher, where decency restricted him to mere allusiveness, the salient points of the drama still remain clearly discernible. One of the first considerations that occurred to him, Descartes says, was that there is often less perfection in works "carried out by the hands of various masters, than in those on which one individual alone has worked."[10] Clearly enough, he had not lost his inner conviction that God had entrusted him with the task of achieving human knowledge and that the only way for him to succeed was to go at it single-handed. Such was the first act of that philosophical play. During the second one, we are called to witness the birth of the famous method. A man can be convinced that he is about to complete the whole body of knowledge, and that he will do it the better by doing it alone, but there would be no end to such a task unless it be carried in a simple and consistent way. It clearly results from the *Discourse* that his discovery of analytical geometry gave Descartes the clue which was to guide him always. He had successfully combined the analysis of the ancients with the algebra of the moderns; the next move had to be obviously the further combination of both with logic. The Cartesian method was the upshot of that experiment; a method, says Descartes, which, "comprising the advantages of the three, is yet exempt from their faults".[11] And that was the end of the second act.

In 1619 the third act was only beginning, and it was to extend itself over a long period of years. Descartes was dedicated to the proposition that all sciences are one, which means that he had no choice between knowing them all and ignoring them all. He could see now why Montaigne had found himself condemned to a complete scepticism. In a way, Montaigne had been right, in this at least, that since he had not found the key to universal knowledge, he rightly felt that he knew nothing at all. Now,

[10] Ibid.   [11] Ibid., p. 16.

however, a positive wisdom was more than a bare possibility. It was there, virtually implied within the method, which itself was but a normal use of the natural light of reason. Wisdom, that is to say, neither chronic doubting nor the mere heaping up of an indefinite number of facts, but reason itself, which "suffers no more differentiation proceeding from" its various subjects "than the light of the sun experiences from the variety of the things which it illumines".[12]

Nor was that all. If all sciences are one owing to the unity of their common method, Descartes was not only condemned to knowing all, but to knowing all with an absolute certainty. Born in mathematics, the method had to yield results that were mathematically true. This time, Descartes was answering the challenge of Father Clavius. The Jesuit, simple and modest old scholastic that he was, had argued: necessary knowledge is better than mere probability; mathematical knowledge alone is necessary; mathematical knowledge is better than all other knowledge. That was not original, but it was true. The young Descartes was following a much more risky way: true knowledge is necessary; mathematical knowledge alone is necessary; hence all knowledge has to be mathematical. Whatever such a reasoning may be worth, the fact remains that Descartes was thereby eliminating from knowledge all that was mere probability. The second of his *Rules for the Direction of the Mind* is an explicit statement of that important item of his program: "Thus, in accordance with the above maxim, we reject all such merely probable knowledge and make it a rule to trust only what is completely known and incapable of being doubted." The standard sciences would henceforward be arithmetic and geometry, in the new form they had just been given by the young mathematician.[13]

From now on Descartes had his whole life carefully planned ahead of him. First he would try his method for a number of

[12] Ibid., p. 38.   [13] Ibid., p. 50.

years on a large number of different subjects; next, he would see about building the complete body of sciences and, before his death, the whole business should have been brought to completion. The first trouble was that, in order to extend mathematical certitude to all sciences, Descartes had to tamper with mathematics itself. In point of fact, the gigantic stretching out of mathematical method had for its first result to put an early end to Descartes' own career as a mathematician. While he had allegedly found the means to solve all problems, Fermat was laying down the foundation of such an insignificant detail as the differential calculus, which both Leibniz and Newton were soon to bring to completion. His friends, who sincerely admired him, were trying vainly to make him see that there were still a few problems which his own method could not solve; Descartes would not listen to them, or rather he could not. He got *the* method, and that was an end to it.

Thus directly inspired by mathematics, the new method could not be universalized without undergoing a deep transformation. It had been a great idea to substitute algebraic signs for geometrical lines and figures, but algebraic signs would never do in metaphysics, not always in physics, still less in biology, in medicine and in ethics. Descartes was therefore confronted with the necessity of extracting from his mathematical method that which would be applicable to all possible problems. The very nature of his own discovery invited him to think that it could be done without altering the nature of mathematical reasoning. Having succeeded in eliminating figures from geometry, he felt inclined to believe that quantity itself could be eliminated from mathematics. It was necessary for him to do that, at least if he wished to extend the mathematical method even to such problems as metaphysics and ethics, where no quantity is involved. Now, if quantity had to go, the algebraic signs by which it was expressed were bound to fall out of the picture, with the result that nothing was to be left of mathematical reasoning but order and measurement where matter is concerned, and order alone where the mind is not dealing with material objects. "Method", says Descartes, "consists entirely in the order and disposition of the objects towards which our mental vision must be directed if we would find out any truth." [14]

Let us, with Descartes himself, call that method "Universal Mathematics";[15] it certainly was universal, but could it still be called mathematics? Descartes felt sure it could, because he was aiming at a complete liberation of knowledge from its objects. According to Aristotle and the Scholastics, each science was both defined as a distinct branch of knowledge and determined in its method by the definite nature of its own object. Biology, for instance, was distinct from mathematics as a science because its proper object was life, and not quantity; for the same reason it was supposed to use a different method from that of mathematics, because what is more than simple quantity cannot be studied as if it were nothing else. Of course you can do it up to a point. You can do it exactly insofar as biological facts can be expressed in terms of quantitative values, but no further. Descartes' own position was to be just the reverse. Since according to him all sciences were one, being but varied expressions of the same human reason, nothing could warn him that he was taking a chance in totally disregarding the rights of the object. Mathematics has something to say everywhere, because quantity is everywhere; and not only in physics, or in biology, but, indirectly at least, even in sociology and in ethics. Statistics, for instance, have a definite part to play in social and moral sciences. But if you go one step further, and deprive mathematics itself of its proper object, it becomes a science of the relationships of order between all possible objects. Is that still mathematics, or is it logic?

[14] Ibid., p. 56.   [15] Ibid., pp. 54–55.

At first sight, this is but a question of names. Shall we restrict the name of mathematics to the logical relations of order that apply to real or possible quantity, or extend the name of mathematics to all relations of order? Yet names have a dreadful power of suggestion. They are invitations to deal in the same way with what we call by the same name. By calling "universal mathematics" a method, which had been extracted from geometry, algebra and logic, Descartes was pledging himself to the task of making all problems "almost similar to those of mathematics",[16] as if the extreme simplicity of the object of mathematics was not partly responsible for the evidence of their conclusions. The evidence of mathematics depends upon both their complete abstract generality and the specific nature of their object. Because of its complete generality, the mathematical method can be indefinitely generalized, but, if we want it to yield evidence, it cannot be indiscriminately extended to all possible objects. These logical laws of abstract order which, applied to quantity, yield the exact science called mathematics lead to nothing but arbitrary generalizations when they apply to objects more complex than quantity. This, at least, is what happened to Descartes, and the result of his bold experiment was scientifically as well as philosophically disastrous.

The principle that lies at the root of Cartesian mathematicism is that, since the most evident of all sciences is also the most abstract, it would be enough to make all the other sciences as abstract as mathematics in order to make them just as evident. This, I am afraid, was a sophism because it disregarded the most important aspect of abstraction. To abstract is not primarily to leave something out, but to take something in, and this is the reason why abstractions are knowledge. Before stretching mathematical methods to nonquantitative objects, one should therefore remember that our abstract notions validly apply to what

[16] Ibid., p. 27.

they keep of reality, not to what they leave out; next, one should make sure that the content of these nonquantitative concepts constitutes an object as completely analyzed, or analyzable, as numbers, figures or positions in space; last, but not the least, one should keep in mind that all conclusions drawn from incompletely analyzed or incompletely analyzable objects, logically correct as they may be, shall lack the specific evidence of mathematical conclusions. Everybody is free to call mathematics any logical ordering of more or less confused notions, but he will have made mathematics arbitrary in its results instead of making the results of other knowledge mathematically evident.

This is exactly what Descartes himself did. In order to make the objects of philosophical knowledge as similar as possible to those of mathematics, he reduced their number to three: thought, extension, and God. Moreover, in order to make them as simple as our notions of number and space, Descartes decreed that the whole content of each of them was such as can be exhausted by a simple intuition. This, of course, was a bold decision. Even number and space are far from being perfectly simple; but the notion of thought is a hopelessly confused one, and that of God is little more for us than the sign of that which surpasses human understanding. Yet, if Descartes wanted to achieve anything like a mathematical metaphysics, these concepts had to be held by him as so many clear and distinct ideas, which every mind can see within itself and see in the same way, provided only it pays attention to them. This is precisely what drove Descartes to the famous doctrine that our clear and distinct concepts are, in his own words, as many "simple natures", each of them endowed with a definite essence of its own, and wholly independent from the minds in which they dwell. From that time on, philosophy was to be the mathematical knowledge of the necessary order there is between the so-called *simple natures*, or fundamental ideas of the human mind.

How Descartes managed to do it, and how far he was successful in his undertaking, are points we will set aside for later consideration. What I now wish to suggest is that, by so doing, Descartes put his money on the actual existence of a set of intellectual intuitions, or pure ideas, quite independent of any empirical reality. Moreover, supposing, as he did, that these mental essences are the very stuff human knowledge is made of, the slightest error about them had to affect science as a whole, from physics to medicine and to ethics. Last, but not least, the nonexistence of these ideas, or of their internal necessity, remained an open possibility, in which case the whole structure of mathematical philosophy would be left in the air without any foundations.

Descartes himself never entertained any doubts as to the absolute validity of his position. True enough, he met much opposition in his own life time and he often provoked it, but he was so sure of his answers that, on the whole, he must have lived in a state of intense intellectual satisfaction. Take, for instance, his metaphysics; Descartes saw no difficulty in writing that "it is *at least* as certain that God . . . is, or exists, as any demonstration of geometry can possibly be." [17] In fact, he had already written to his friend Mersenne on November 25, 1630: "As for me, I dare well to boast of having found a proof of God's existence which I find entirely satisfactory, and by which I know that God exists, more certainly than I know the truth of any geometrical proposition." As to his physics, it had been deduced a priori from evident philosophical principles; no flaw could possibly be found in it; nor for that matter in his biology, and Descartes felt so sure of himself on those points that he had announced his method as an infallible way to find a mathematically demonstrated medicine. As early as 1630, he wrote to Mersenne that he was now headed for "a Medicine grounded on infallible demonstrations". There, however, he found himself in a pecu-

[17] Ibid., p. 33.

liar position: unless he lived long enough he would not have time to complete his mathematical medicine, but so long as he had not done it, he could not be sure to live long enough to do it. That was a vicious circle. Rather, it was a race against time, and Descartes was bound to lose.

He finally did, but he had put up a good fight. In a letter of January 25, 1638, to his friend Huygens, Descartes seems seriously concerned with the problem of how to last until the time of his medical discovery. What was worrying him then was that, while he had hitherto considered that death could not take from him more than thirty or forty years of life at the utmost, he now felt sure that an early death would shorten his life by more than a century. And then he did an awful thing. He broke the sacred rules of the Method and set about writing an "Abridged Medicine" before his physics had been completed. He just wanted a short delay that would take him to the time of his really demonstrated medicine. After that, lasting for a century would be the easiest thing in the world. This, I think, is the only point where Descartes had time enough to realize that all was not well with his philosophy. In 1646 he wrote to Chanut that though he had spent much more time on medicine than on ethics, he was making more headway in ethics than in medicine. Thus, Descartes modestly concludes: "instead of finding the means to preserve my life, I have found another one, far more easy and more safe, which is not to be afraid of death." A very useful discovery indeed, but a rather old one, and one which does not require the brains of a physico~mathematician. When he died, on February 11, 1650, Descartes was but fifty-four years old. Death had won the race by a long margin; yet it was perhaps better for him that he should die at a time when his doctrine had not yet been openly disproved by facts. Merciful death took the great dreamer away still full of his dreams. For they were dreams, and it did not take much time for the fact to be known.

In 1650 both Spinoza and Locke were eighteen years old: Spinoza, who was to use a still more geometrical method than Descartes himself, and nevertheless to reach thereby completely different conclusions; Locke, who was to undermine the very foundations of Cartesianism and to provide the French eighteenth century with a new philosophical orthodoxy. For a mathematically proved system of metaphysics, this was hardly a success. But the worst of it is, that even the scientific part of Cartesianism was also doomed to an early destruction. When Descartes died, Leibniz, who had already been born, was destined to prove that the Cartesian laws of motion were mathematically wrong, from which it followed that, grounded as it was on erroneous mechanics, Cartesian physics had no scientific value whatsoever. Yet, what has perhaps been the most striking of Descartes' scientific failures took place already during his own lifetime. W. Harvey had just discovered the circulation of the blood, and the modest little book wherein he submitted his conclusions to the learned world (1628) will always remain as a perfect example of scientific demonstration. Harvey was no less admirable in not explaining what he did not understand than in clearing up all the rest. Descartes read the book, and immediately took sides with Harvey, against those who were opposing his conclusions. He certainly could see the truth when he forgot his universal mathematics. The trouble was that Harvey's description of the motion of the heart, still today perfectly correct, could not very well fit in with the mechanical biology of Descartes. The learned world was then called upon to witness that surprising spectacle: Descartes, who had not discovered the circulation of the blood, explaining it to Harvey, who had made the discovery, and adding to it as many mistakes as he was adding explanations. Yet, Descartes was so sure of himself that he made public his wrong theory in the fifth part of his *Discourse*, where it is expounded at length as a perfect instance of mathematical demonstration in biology. A more blindly trusted method never took anybody to more consistently wrong conclusions.

There would be no excuse for reviewing the failures of such a great man as Descartes, were it not done for other purposes than to debase him. But nobody can either debase him or raise him above his real level. Descartes alone has a right to judge Descartes, and he alone can do it. Any one who is at all acquainted with him will probably agree that Descartes' absolute devotion to truth would feel hurt by any attempt to palliate his defeat; but what he would certainly resent more deeply than anything else is the cheap generosity of his liberally minded historians. Descartes was not a liberal mind. He was most generous, he was charitable, he was unreservedly tolerant; yet he always took ideas seriously, which means that while granting any one full freedom to hold as true what he himself knew to be false, he could not bring himself to think, or to say, that what he knew to be false might after all be true. In dealing with such a man, straight honesty is the only mark of respect he would appreciate. Were we to tell him: "There is not much left of your physics and still less of your biology, but the spirit of Cartesianism will live forever in mathematical physics; as for your metaphysics, it is neither better nor worse than many other ones, but it remains full of the most stimulating suggestions", Descartes would probably answer: "Thank you. But I fail to see how the spirit of Cartesianism can be all right if Cartesianism itself is all wrong. From the very beginning I pledged myself to give mathematically true demonstrations of everything; to which I added that I had no use for mere probabilities; and last, I made it a point that Wisdom was one, so that where one science is right, all sciences are bound to be right, while where one is wrong, all the others must be wrong. That, and nothing else, was my message to the world, and it is the standard by which I have a right to be judged. You can praise Montaigne by saying that he was partly right, not me. I was in the world to rid the world of Montaigne; don't you grant me the benefit of his indulgent scepticism; there is nothing that I hate more. I promised an infallible method; if I failed to fulfill completely my promise, I failed completely; say it." But it will be less unpleasant to let facts speak for themselves and, rather than judge Descartes, merely register their own verdict.

CHAPTER VI

CARTESIAN SPIRITUALISM

When Descartes at the age of twenty-three first conceived his project of a universal mathematics, he was fully aware of its unusual importance. He even considered it as "the most important in all the world", so much so that he decided to spend several years in preparing himself for the work. For nine years, he did nothing but study particular questions, especially in mathematics and in physics, without paying the slightest attention to what was then considered as philosophy and philosophical problems. Nor was it until 1628 that he began, in his own words, "to seek the foundation of a philosophy more certain than the vulgar".[1] But then he worked so fast that within three or four months his whole system of metaphysics was completed.

That it took him so little time to succeed in his undertaking was of course an effect of his philosophical genius; but it was no less an effect of the very nature of philosophical knowledge itself, such as Descartes conceived it. Philosophy had to become a department of universal mathematics; now mathematicians deal with nothing but ideas, and ideas can be dealt with much more rapidly than concrete facts. The first important point was precisely to realize that the new philosophy, unlike the old one, but like mathematics, would always go, not from things to ideas, but from ideas to things. What is a circle, to the mind of a

[1] Eaton, *Descartes Selections*, p. 27.

mathematician? Is it this and that circle, such as I can imperfectly draw on a piece of paper or on a blackboard? Obviously not— the real circle is the definition of a circle, and nothing else. It may be that no material figure ever answered that definition in reality; what the mathematician is interested in is something different: the essence, or true nature of the circle, as is to be found in its definition, and only there. Let us therefore state this first principle, whose consequences will run not only through the whole body of Cartesian philosophy, but through the whole body of modern idealism as well: all that can be clearly and distinctly known as belonging to the idea of a thing can be said of the thing itself. As a matter of fact, it *is* the thing.

But what is it, to know something *distinctly*? When a mathematician knows a circle, he knows not only what it is, but, at the same time, what it is not. Because a circle is a circle, it has all the properties of the circle, and none of those that make a triangle a triangle, or a square a square. Philosophers should therefore proceed on the same assumption: as mathematicians, they will always proceed not only from thought to existence, but from distinct thoughts to distinct existences. In other words, since it is the nature of ideas to be mutually exclusive in mathematics, each containing everything that comes under its definition, and nothing more, so it follows that it must be in the nature of real substances, in philosophy, to be mutually exclusive, each containing everything that comes under its definition and nothing more.

Thus, when Descartes made up his mind to get down to brass tacks and reconstruct the world, the only material at his disposal was: ideas, clear ideas, and distinct ideas. That was the main reason why he could do it so quickly; for to him, as to the mathematician, the only problem was henceforward to be: With what idea should he begin, and in what order should he put the succeeding ideas? Now, even there, mathematics could help. If we consider the very essence of mathematical reasoning apart from the fact that it applies to numbers, figures and symbolic signs, it can be reduced to very simple rules, which are the rules of reason and of plain common sense itself.

The first is to divide up each of the problems we examine into as many parts as possible. In other words, we should never try to solve a complete problem as such, without first having tried to solve the different problems it implies. The second rule is, having thus divided our problems, to conduct our reflections in due order, that is to say: to begin with those objects that are most simple and easy to understand, in order to rise little by little to the knowledge of the most complex. The whole problem, then, becomes a problem of *order*; finding out the natural order of ideas, and, where none can be found, devising one of our own as a substitute. A fictitious order, known as such, is better than none, since it can help us to connect long stretches of the natural order, even though we had no knowledge of their real connection.

Now, what was the first of all particular problems, for a man who needed nothing but ideas to rebuild the world? It was to decide whether or not something can be evidently known; and not, this time, in the order of abstract speculations, such as mathematics, but in the real order of actually existing things. And what was the only way to solve that problem? By finding some judgment of existence that would withstand even the most extravagant objections of the sceptics. When he reached that point Descartes—or was it only a young boy of sixteen who had heard of it at La Flèche?—remembered that long ago, another man had found himself in a similar difficulty, and had discovered a way out. St. Augustine too had known such a time in his life, when a man with a passionate love for certitude has to surrender to the evidence that he is sure of nothing. Like Descartes then, and before him, St. Augustine had become a sceptic in spite of himself, but he had also succeeded in his effort to discover a decisive answer to scepticism. It is to be found in his *Soliloquies*, book II, chapter I. Reason is leading the discussion with Augustine: "You, who wish to know yourself, do you know at least that you are?—I know it.—How do you know it?—I don't know.—Are you a thing that is simple, or that is composed?—I don't know.--Do you know whether you are moving or not?—I don't know.—But do you know that you think?—Yes, I know that.—Consequently, that you think at least is true.—It is true.—You know therefore that you are, that you live and that you think."

Such also was the first evidence which Descartes laid down as the unshakable cornerstone of his philosophy: I think, hence I am. For let us suppose with Montaigne that everything else is false, or at least doubtful; let us even suppose that the creator of this world be a very powerful and very cunning deceiver, who ever employs his ingenuity in deceiving me: "Then without doubt I exist, also if he deceives me, and let him deceive me as much as he will, he can never cause me to be nothing so long as I think that I am something." [2] Even in this, Descartes was repeating what Augustine had said in another text, *On Free Will*, book II, chapter 3: "First, I ask you, in order to begin with what is the most evident, whether you are, or not? And in this you cannot fear to be deceived in your answer, because in case you did not exist, you could not possibly be deceived." And again, in his *City of God*, book XI, chapter 26: "If I am wrong, I am, for he who does not exist, cannot be deceived; thus, from the very fact that I am deceived, it follows that I am. How then could I possibly be deceived in believing that I am, since it is an obvious thing that I am so long as I am deceived?"

In 1641, when Descartes restated his first principle in his *Meditations in First Philosophy*, one of those whom he had per-

[2] Ibid., p. 97.

sonally invited to send him their objections, namely, Arnauld—
the great Arnauld—was not slow in pointing out the fact that
St. Augustine had already said the same thing many centuries
ago. Descartes did not seem to relish the remark: "I shall not
take up time here", he said in his reply, "by thanking my
distinguished critic, for bringing to my aid the authority of St.
Augustine, and for expounding my arguments in a way which
betokened a fear that others might not deem them strong
enough." [3] Arnauld could have surmised as much: quoting an
authority against Descartes' clear and distinct ideas would have
been a foolish thing to do, but quoting an authority in their
favour was worse: it was an insult.

Not only did Descartes himself resent it, but even Blaise
Pascal was to raise a vigorous protest against it in his famous
treatise *On the Geometrical Spirit*: "Indeed, I am far from saying
that Descartes is not the true author of that principle, even if it
were true that he came by it only through his reading of that
great saint. For I know all the difference there is between
writing a word at random, without devoting to it fuller and
broader reflection, and perceiving within that word an admirable series of consequences, that prove the distinction between
material nature and spiritual nature, so as to make it the firm
and sustained principle of a whole Physics, as Descartes claimed
he was doing. . . . That word is as different in his own writings
from what it is in the writings of those who said it casually, as a
man full of life and strength is from a dead man." [4]

When he wrote those glowing lines, Pascal himself had
already made his own discoveries concerning conical sections;

[3] This text has not been included by Prof. Eaton in his *Descartes Selections*; it
is found in the *Philosophical Works of Descartes*, ed. E. S. Haldane and G. R. T.
Ross (Cambridge University Press, 1912), vol. 2, p. 96.
[4] Blaise Pascal, *Pensées et opuscules*, ed. L. Brunschvicg, 4th ed. (Paris:
Hachette, 1907), p. 193.

he was a young mathematician and physicist of genius, who could not foresee that an older and more mature Pascal, having made other discoveries in a higher field than that of science, would some day write this short sentence: "Descartes useless and uncertain."[5] He understood Descartes perfectly, he admired him, he loved him, and he was right; but we can safely conclude from what he says, that when he wrote his treatise *On the Geometrical Spirit*, he knew little, if anything, of the work of St. Augustine. For it is hardly fair to consider as written at random, a statement four times repeated by St. Augustine, in four different books, at the end as well as at the beginning of his long career. Nor is it possible to maintain that Augustine failed to see in his own principle a series of important consequences, since he used it to defeat scepticism, as did Descartes; to prove the existence of a spiritual soul, as did Descartes, and, like Descartes again, to prove the existence of God. As to the other consequences, if St. Augustine was not able to perceive them in his principle, it is perhaps simply that they were not there. He had no need of Pascal to feel that the rest would be useless and uncertain.

Descartes, on the contrary, had nothing to warn him that he was in danger. His principle was a true principle, not in the ancient sense of an abstract and universally valid statement, but in the new Cartesian sense of a "beginning", or "starting point" for the attainment of real knowledge. Besides, it undoubtedly was the first principle, since it could be known without our knowing anything else, while nothing else could be known without our first knowing it: whatever else I may happen to know, I think; hence I am. Furthermore, it was the perfect type of a clear and evident knowledge, since such a principle could not even be doubted without being at the same time proved: if I

[5] Blaise Pascal, *Pensées*, trans. W. F. Trotter (London: J. M. Dent, 1931), p. 28, no. 78.

doubt that I am, I think; hence I am. Last, but not least, it provided Descartes with his first opportunity to show what it means for an idea to be "distinct". But this point requires further explanation.

First let us come back to our mathematical definition of knowledge: "When we say that something is contained in the nature or concept of anything, that is precisely the same as saying that it is true of the thing or can be affirmed of it." [6] In the present case, I know that I am; but I know it only because I know that I am thinking. If I now ask myself that new question: But *what* am I? the only legitimate answer will be: I am a thinking thing. Whether that thing be called a thought, or a mind, is immaterial to the problem at stake. What matters, is the fact that I can rightly ascribe to my own nature all that is evidently contained in the nature of a thinking thing. And what is a thing that thinks? "It is a thing which doubts, understands, conceives, affirms, denies, wills, refuses, which also imagines and feels." [7] To know that I am such a thing is to have a clear idea of myself as a thing which thinks, but to have *a distinct* idea of it is something else, and no less important: I have a clear idea of what I am as soon as I realize what it is to be a thinking thing, but in order to have a distinct idea of it, it is just as necessary to realize what a thinking thing is not. In short, clearness comes to ideas from the fact that we ascribe to them all that belongs to their nature, distinction comes to them from the fact that we deny to them all that does not belong to their nature.

For instance, such philosophers as Aristotle and his followers assure us that our soul is an animating force, which exercises various operations in and through our body: nutrition, motion,

[6] *Reply to II object.*, in Haldane and Ross, eds., *Philosophical Works*, vol. 2, p. 53. The "quid" of the Latin text has been substituted, in our own translation, for the "attribut" of the French text.

[7] Eaton, *Descartes Selections*, p. 100.

sensation. Now we cannot ascribe such functions to the soul without associating its idea with that of a body.[8] But do we even know that we have a body? The idea of body is in no way contained within the clear idea of thought; it should therefore be excluded from it, if we want it to be a distinct idea. And since we pledged ourselves always to affirm or to deny of things themselves, all that can be affirmed or denied of their clear and distinct ideas, to say that the idea of the soul implies nothing that pertains to the body is precisely the same as to say that the soul is really distinct from the body. Substances are as radically exclusive of each other as are our ideas of those substances. When the philosopher deals with metaphysics, he has no need of knowing whether he has a body, since, in case he had one, his thought would not have anything to do with it. When he deals with physics, he would do better to forget that he has a soul, because, in case there were bodies, his soul would not have anything to do with them. As the soul is nothing but thought, so also the body is nothing but extension in space according to the three dimensions. Metaphysics then is pure spiritualism, and physics pure mechanism. In this sense it is true to say, with Pascal, whose insight here into the meaning of Descartes' method was truly deep, that Descartes made his "I think" the firm and sustained principle of a whole physics.

Let us add that paving the way to a purely mechanical physics, biology and medicine was the thing in which he was most interested, and this may perhaps account for his readiness in asking metaphysics to pay the price for it. First of all, since a thinking substance has nothing in common with bodies, it would be better to avoid even the word soul. "Soul" always suggests some connection with a body; even "Spirit" is not so good, for it is equivocal and is frequently applied to what is corporeal. It would therefore be better to call "Mind" that

[8] Ibid., p. 98.

substance in which thought immediately resides, or rather which *is* thought.[9] Mentalism, if the word were received, would therefore be a better denomination than spiritualism for Descartes' metaphysics.

Again, once it is accepted that the Mind is purely thought, it becomes obvious that it cannot cease to think unless it cease to be. A thing whose nature it is to think, either thinks, and is, or does not, and is not. Hence this new consequence, which Descartes always upheld, against all objections, as standing and falling together with his whole system: the mind is always thinking. If we do not feel that way, we certainly are wrong, since it follows from the clear idea of the mind and from its very definition.

But it is impossible to go that far with Descartes without going a little further. If the thinking thing is conceived as radically distinct from the body, that substance, or mind, would be exactly what it is, and think as it does, even if there were no bodies in the world, either its own, or any other one. Where then does that mind find its ideas? The necessary answer is: in itself, and nowhere else. There is in the mind a natural aptness to grasp by a direct intuition such ideas as represent true, eternal and unchangeable essences: the mind itself, for instance, or God, or the Body conceived as pure extension, the Triangle, and so on.[10] In the description of that first class of notions we can easily recognize the attributes of the divine ideas in St. Augustine. But whereas, according to St. Augustine, ideas were shining above the mind, they are now conceived by Descartes as being in the mind. Other ideas, we make up at pleasure, and they are mere products of our imagination: centaurs, chimeras for instance: they are "fictitious" ideas. There remains a third group, made up of our so-called sensations. These seem to come to us

[9] In Haldane and Ross, eds., *Philosophical Works*, p. 53.
[10] É. Gilson, *Descartes: Discours de la méthode*, p. 328b.

from without, but we are sure that, in a way at least, they do not, because that would be self-contradictory and impossible. How indeed could a distinct substance receive anything from another distinct substance? What, then, is a sensation? At the utmost, an innate idea awakened within the mind on the occasion of some change that takes place in a body. If there are bodies, a thing which we do not yet know, they cannot be the *causes* of our ideas; they are but occasions for the mind to conceive them; therefore, as Descartes himself says, even sensation "must have been there beforehand." [11]

Descartes' conception of man as an angel, or disembodied thinking substance, swept Europe, and was soon received as immediate evidence by the greatest thinkers of his time. Stripping themselves both of their bodies and of their souls, they became magnificent minds who, theoretically at least, did not feel indebted to their bodies for any one of their ideas. Leibniz in Germany; Malebranche in France; Spinoza in Holland, were such minds, and all of them had nothing but innate ideas. For all of them, like Descartes himself, were living under the spell of Cartesian mathematicism. Even apart from his philosophical deductions, had not Descartes himself proved that he was right by inventing analytical geometry? For if Descartes had made that remarkable discovery, it simply was because he had used reason, instead of imagination, to study matter itself and its properties. By so doing, he had done more than deduce from some principles the conclusion that man is a mind, he had given an experimental demonstration of it. Descartes' mentalism reigned supreme in French philosophy until about the first third of the eighteenth century, when a sudden change brought its domination to a close.

A few years ago, when a severe storm had cut off all traffic

[11] Ibid., p. 327a. Cf. Descartes, *Oeuvres complètes*, ed. Adam and Tannery, vol. 7, part 2, p. 359.

between Great Britain and the rest of Europe, the London *Times* summed up the tragedy in this simple headline: *Continent Isolated*. In a way, the Continent always is. This, I suppose, accounts for the fact that from time to time some Frenchman has to rediscover England. It always comes to him as a shock. Such an adventure befell Voltaire, when he crossed the Channel and went to London in 1728. As he would later write in the Fourth of his *Philosophical Letters*, "When a Frenchman arrives in London, he finds things very much changed in philosophy, as in everything else." [12] Thus, says Voltaire, very few people in London read Descartes, whose writings have indeed become obsolete; and if you ask them for an opinion on that great mathematician, they will answer you that he was a "dreamer".[18] Surprising destiny, indeed, for the philosopher of good sense, of clear and distinct ideas, and of mathematical evidence, to be finally condemned on such a charge! But between Descartes and Voltaire had come another philosopher, to whose doctrine Voltaire himself was very soon to become a convert.

He was an Englishman, and his name was John Locke. When I say that he was an Englishman, I mean much more than the bare facts that he was born in England near Bristol, in 1632, and lived and died there in Oates (Essex) in the year 1704. Locke was as thoroughly English as Descartes was thoroughly French, and they proved themselves to be English and French even in their respective ways of approaching philosophical problems. We may feel surprised to hear a mathematician of genius branded as a dreamer; but what was good about Locke, Voltaire tells us, was precisely that he was *not* a mathematician: "There was never a more sober and more methodical intelligence, nor a more exact logician than Mr. Locke; yet he was no great

[12] Voltaire, *Lettres philosophiques*, ed. G. Lanson (Paris: Hachette, 1917), vol. 2, p. 1.
[13] Ibid., p. 5.

mathematician." [14] And, as late as 1749, Condillac would repeat the same thing in still more forceful terms, in his *Treatise on Systems*: "We have four famous metaphysicians: Descartes, Malebranche, Leibniz and Locke. The last is the only one who was not a geometer, and how far superior to the others he was!" Not being a geometer, he would not yield to the temptation of deducing human nature from some abstract principle, which all his predecessors had done. "All those praters having written the Romance of the Soul," Voltaire concludes, "a wise man has come who modestly wrote its history." [15]

To write a mere history of the soul, such, indeed, had always been Locke's design. By profession a physician, he naturally advocated what he himself once called: "a historical, plain method"; [16] that is to say, a method of observation and of description, chiefly dealing, in his own words, with "particular matters of fact", since such facts "are the undoubted foundations on which our civil and natural knowledge is built". His ambition was therefore to follow a moderate Empiricism; for even in his Empiricism Locke was a moderate. As he saw it, the problem came back to the steering of a middle course between two opposite errors. Some men lose the improvement they should make of matters of fact, by merely crowding them in their memories instead of lodging them in their understandings; others, on the contrary, having no patience with facts, "are apt to draw general conclusions and raise axioms from every particular they meet with". [17] One of Locke's editors, J. A. St. John, commenting upon this text, observes that: "of the two methods here described, the former is that of the Germans, the latter that

[14] Ibid., letter 13, vol. 1, p. 166.

[15] Ibid., p. 168.

[16] J. Locke, *Essay concerning Human Understanding*, bk. 1, chap. 1, introd., no. 2, ed. J. A. St. John, 2 vols. (London, 1877), vol. 1, p. 129.

[17] J. Locke, *On the Conduct of the Understanding*, 13; cf. 25; in ibid., vol. 1, pp. 55 and 76–77.

of the French; and perhaps nearer home we might find examples of both." [18] The fact remains, however, that Locke's own
ideal was to shun both, and that he did it to the best of his
ability.

His celebrated *Essay Concerning Human Understanding*, published in the year 1690, remains a remarkable example of what
can be done by a man who takes hints from carefully gathered
material, and carries them to his intellect to be judged. As
Locke himself was later to write to Stillingfleet: "All that I can
say of my book is, that it is a copy of my own mind, in its
several ways of operation." Descartes had written his *Rules for
the Direction of the Mind* without even suspecting that he might
be wrong in eliminating from the mind all that is not clear and
distinct, and yet, does not what is confused and obscure equally
belong to the mind? As a consequence, before setting down his
own rules for the *Conduct of the Understanding*, Locke felt himself
obliged to inquire into the original of those ideas "which a man
observes, and is conscious to himself he has in his mind; and the
ways whereby the understanding comes to be furnished with
them"; for he saw that such an inquiry would enable him to
ascertain "what knowledge the understanding has by those ideas,
and the certainty, evidence and extent of it". Even opinion,
even faith, all the reasons and degrees of assent; in short, each
particular mode of intellectual life has to be taken into account.
It was to be the work of a true physician; a complete anatomy,
physiology and pathology of human understanding.

When John Locke submitted the conclusions of Descartes to
the rules of his own method, he did not find much in them that
he could keep as truly proved. Descartes had taught that, from
the very nature of the mind, it necessarily follows that all our
ideas are innate. What ideas? The general principles of human
knowledge, such as: what is, is; and it is impossible for the same

[18] J. Locke, *Essay*, in ibid., vol. 1, p. 55, note.

thing to be and not to be? But children, idiots, and even many a normal man, die without ever coming to the knowledge of such principles. Yet they have souls, they have minds; how could those notions be imprinted on their minds, and yet remain unknown to them? As Locke says, it "is to make this impression nothing".[19] In fact, there are no principles, no ideas which are innate, not even the idea of God; all of them come to us from both sensation and reflection. External material things are the objects of sensation, and the operations of our minds within are the objects of reflection. And such "are to me", Locke concludes, "the only originals from whence all our ideas take their beginnings".[20]

As soon as we reach that point, and Locke reached it in the very first chapter of his *Essay*, the fate of Cartesian philosophy is a settled thing. Descartes maintains that it is necessary for the soul always to think; if it is necessary, it ought to be so; unfortunately, it is a fact that the soul is no more always thinking than the body is always moving. The question is about a matter of fact, and it is "begging it to bring, as a proof for it, an hypothesis, which is the very thing in dispute".[21] How about men who sleep without dreaming? Are we going to say that they think, but do not remember that they think? If they do not remember it, how could it be proved that they think? After all, it is not even evident that the soul is nothing but a thinking substance, radically distinct as such from a merely extended body. It thinks, but it also wills; it has a power of putting body into motion by thought, that is to say, motivity. And not only motivity, but mobility as well, since every one "finds in himself that his soul can think, will and operate on his body in the place where that is, but cannot operate on a body, or in a place a hundred miles

[19] *Essay*, I, 2, 5; in ibid., vol. 1, pp. 136–37.
[20] *Essay*, II, 1, 4; in ibid., vol. 1, p. 207.
[21] *Essay*, II, 1, 10; in ibid., vol. 1, pp. 211–12.

distant from it".[22] The coach that carries your body from Oxford to London carries at the same time your soul, so that it
constantly changes place during the whole journey between
those points. What indeed does Descartes mean, when he says
that the mind has nothing to do with the body? He does not
even know whether his body itself is able to think or not. Since
mobility belongs to souls, why should not thought belong to
bodies? There is no contradiction in supposing that God could,
if he pleased, "give to certain systems of created senseless
matter, put together as he thinks fit, some degree of sense,
perception, and thought".[28] In other words, let us say we have
no positive reasons to believe that matter is a thing that thinks,
but when Descartes says that a thinking matter would be a
contradiction, he goes far beyond the limits of what we know,
and of what can be proved by the power of human understanding.

We have got so used to those sudden changes of perspective
in the history of philosophy, that we look at them as if they
were inseparable from philosophy itself. More than that, we feel
tempted to view philosophical revolutions as the normal signs
of its inexhaustible vitality. One should not forget, however,
that the radical destruction of what has been held as absolute
truth by many minds is bound to have a destructive effect on
these minds themselves. Descartes had succeeded in convincing
the greatest thinkers of his time, that scholastic philosophy had
completely failed to prove the existence of God and the spirituality of the soul; then he had proved both in his own way. I
would not say that every one had been convinced by his demonstrations; there still were sceptics, and obscure scholastic teachers
in colleges, to oppose his views; but the strange fact was, that
Descartes had precisely succeeded in convincing many thinkers

[22] *Essay,* II, 23, 20; in ibid., vol. 1, pp. 436–37.
[23] *Essay*, IV, 3, 6; in ibid., vol. 2, p. 144.

who were not of the *hoi polloi*. He had convinced Malebranche, who was a great philosopher and a priest; Arnauld, who was a remarkable theologian and a Jansenist; Bossuet, who was a great orator, a bishop and the fierce adversary of the Jansenists; and Fénelon, who was also a bishop, and a great writer, but who could agree neither with the Jansenists, nor with Bossuet. Around the end of the seventeenth century, Cartesianism had become the scholasticism of all those who prided themselves on being up to date in philosophy. When, on the contrary, Locke's criticism began to undermine the influence of Descartes, these people remained convinced that an intelligent man could not be a scholastic, but it also became apparent that he could not easily keep on being a Cartesian. What then was to become of the existence of God and of the immateriality of the soul? If neither Descartes nor the scholastics had been able to prove them, it was to be feared that they could not be proved at all.

Edward Stillingfleet, Bishop of Worcester, provides us with a vivid illustration of what was then a not uncommon state of mind. He had been persuaded by Descartes that innate ideas were the only means to prove the existence of God; Locke was now trying to prove that there are no such ideas; but then, asked Stillingfleet in his *Discourse in Vindication of the Doctrine of the Trinity* (1696), how are we to refute the atheists, if there is no innate idea of God? To which Locke replied, that if there really were in man an innate idea of God, there would be no atheists: "I would crave leave to ask your Lordship, were there ever in the world any atheists, or not?" That was enough to settle the whole question.

Anybody can see at once the fallacy in Stillingfleet's position on the question. A philosopher has no right to say: the existence of God must be proved; it cannot be proved unless we have innate ideas; hence we have innate ideas. It works the other way around: What ideas have we? Then, and only then, can the existence of God be proved? But I have not quoted Stillingfleet as a great philosopher; I merely called him in as a witness to the mental distress in which men found themselves, when Locke began to threaten Cartesianism with the same ruin it had brought upon scholasticism. When Stillingfleet wrote to Locke: "If this be true, then for all that we know by our ideas of matter and thinking, matter may have a power of thinking, and . . . then it is impossible to prove that the spiritual substance in us is immaterial", what could Locke say to remove the Bishop's fears? Not very much indeed. In true Ockhamist spirit, he answered that it is highly probable that immaterial thinking is not the attribute of some solid, corporeal substance, though the contrary cannot be proved to be an impossibility: "But your Lordship thinks not probability enough . . . your Lordship seems to conclude it demonstrable from the principles of philosophy. That demonstration, I should with joy receive from your Lordship, or any one." [24]

Of all the discoveries made by Voltaire on the other side of the Channel, there was none in which he felt more interested than in Locke's hypothetical materialism. That was just the sort of stuff he wanted. One cannot fully account for his impassionate backing of the "wise Locke" against old Descartes, unless one takes into account the very definite service which Voltaire was expecting from Locke. Of course, Descartes had rid the world of scholasticism, and that was good. Voltaire was always grateful to some one for destroying something. But Locke had destroyed Descartes, and that was better, for it meant the destruction of even the scholastic conclusions which Descartes had attempted to vindicate in his own way. Such as we still can see him in Voltaire's *Philosophical Letters*, Locke had become there a sly, cunning materialist, who had concealed his game in an artful

[24] The texts are to be found in *The Works of John Locke*, ed. J. A. St. John, vol. 2, appendix, pp. 339–411.

way. Let him say that materialism is a possibility, Voltaire thought to himself, everybody will soon realize that it is an obvious reality.

In point of fact, the main responsibility for the spreading of materialism throughout the whole eighteenth century does not rest with Voltaire, and still less with Locke, but with Descartes. He had assumed the heavy task of giving a mathematical demonstration of the spirituality of the soul. The better to do it, he had begun by turning the old scholastic soul as the form of the body into a disembodied mind. Now that the Cartesian mind was dead, the body was left without either a mind or a soul. It was a mere machine; and Descartes himself had always said it was; but Descartes had not foreseen that his human machine would some day lose its mind, and would therefore be asked to produce even thought.

The mathematicism of Descartes then began to bring forth unexpected, yet necessary, consequences. If you set about dissecting concrete reality into as many separate things as there are distinct ideas, the substantial unity of man disintegrates into two really distinct substances: his mind, and his body. Let us now suppose that you fail in your mathematical demonstration to prove that there is such a separate mind, it will then be impossible for you to prove it in any other way. You have no right to appeal to what is going on in your body in order to prove that there is a mind: the existence of a *soul* could be proved in that way, not that of a *mind*. Since its existence can be established neither mathematically nor empirically, the obvious implication is that there is no mind.

Thus, by seemingly paradoxical yet necessary consecution of ideas, the materialism of La Mettrie was ushered into the world by the mathematical spiritualism of Descartes. In his famous book *Man a Machine* (1768), La Mettrie will openly claim Descartes for his direct ancestor: "This celebrated philosopher, it is true, was much deceived; no one denies that. But at any rate he understood animal nature; he was the first to prove completely that animals are true machines. And after a discovery of this importance, demanding so much sagacity, how can we without ingratitude fail to pardon all his errors?" [25] Thus, according to this unforeseen disciple, the upshot of Cartesianism is, that man is a machine that thinks: "What an enlightened machine!" La Mettrie exclaims! [26] It certainly was, and Descartes would have been surprised to meet it. Yet he would perhaps have been still more surprised to read in the papers of Du Marsais this "Cartesian" description of a philosopher: all men are machines; the only difference there is between a philosopher and other men is, that a philosopher is a machine which, "owing to its mechanism, reflects on its own movements". In short, Du Marsais concludes, every man is a watch, but a philosopher is a self-winding watch. [27]

Fathers are sometimes surprised at their own children; yet La Mettrie and Du Marsais were legitimate sons of a father whose body had already lost its soul. But it was in the nature of Cartesian mathematicism that it could disintegrate into two opposite ways, and it actually did. While the body was losing its Mind in France, the Mind was losing its body in Great Britain. To find the abstract connections between the ideas that turned such an improbable consequence into a philosophical necessity is the problem to which we have now to turn our attention.

[25] O. de La Mettrie, *Man a Machine*, French and English text, ed. G. C. Bussey (Chicago: Open Court, 1912), p. 143; English text only, repr. 1927. Cf. the earlier English translation, 3d ed. (London: G. Smith, 1750).

[26] *Man a Machine*, p. 56.

[27] See also W. H. Wickwar, *Baron d'Holbach: A Prelude to the French Revolution* (London: G. Allen, 1935), p. 70.

CHAPTER VII

CARTESIAN IDEALISM

Descartes had proved his existence to be that of a thing that thinks. Being a geometer, the only opportunity he had now to make any headway was to discover, within the nature of his mind, other natures which he could submit to his analysis. What is it, to be a thing that thinks? It was, to be knowing a few things, ignoring many others, willing, desiring, imagining and perceiving. For a psychologist, such as Locke for instance, what a wonderful field for exploration! But Descartes was working towards something else, and the incredible variety of psychological facts was of little interest to him, because he knew that all of them were nothing but particular varieties of thought, that is to say, that they were fundamentally one and the same thing.

After wandering to and fro among his ideas, unable to decide which one he should single out as coming next in the order of deduction, Descartes made up his mind to go back to his starting point. After all, the only thing he was sure of was that he was a doubting thing, that is, a thinking substance, a mind. But there might be more knowledge involved in the act of doubting than the bare certitude of mind and of its existence. He who doubts knows that he does not know as perfectly as he would like to know. He must therefore have in mind at least some confused feeling of what perfect knowledge should be, that is to say, the idea of perfection. Now, by carefully observing that new notion, he rapidly becomes aware that there is, present to his mind, a very remarkable idea: that of a perfect being, in other words, of a being in which all conceivable perfections are to be found. Such is God, whom we conceive as a supreme being, eternal, infinite, immutable, all-knowing, all-powerful, and creator of all things which are outside himself.[1] What is there, in us, which is the origin of such an idea?

It cannot be our mind, for a doubting, and consequently imperfect, mind cannot be the model from which it draws its own idea of perfection. It cannot be any of the material things existing outside our mind. True, philosophers commonly believe that the best proofs, not to say the only proofs, of the existence of God, are those that prove Him to be the necessary cause of the physical order. But, first, even could such demonstrations be made, we, at least, could not attempt to make them; all we know, so far, is the existence of our own mind, and since we are not yet sure that there is an external world, how could we use it to prove the existence of God? Furthermore, supposing that it could be done, such a proof would still not be a demonstration of the existence of a perfect thing, for the world of matter is not perfect, or eternal, or actually infinite in perfection. Why then should its first cause, if there be one, be infinite and perfect?

And yet, as everything has a cause, there should be a cause of our idea of God. It should be such a cause as contains within itself at least as much perfection as there is to be found in its effect; in other words, the model from which our idea of perfection is copied should be at least as perfect as the copy itself. It must therefore be a perfect being, endowed with all the perfections that are found in our idea of its nature: supreme, eternal, infinite, all-knowing, all-powerful, creator of all things which are outside of Himself; in short, such a being must necessarily be that which we call God.

[1] Eaton, *Descartes Selections*, p. 113.

The very idea of perfection, which is identical with our idea of God, is therefore in our minds as an objective reality, for whose existence no other conceivable cause can possibly be found but that of an actually existing God. That it is a reality, and not a fiction of the mind, is obvious from the fact that it appears to us as a true "nature", endowed with a necessity of its own, just as our ideas of a circle, or of a square. Some people say they do not know whether or not there is a God, but even these people would agree that, if there is a God, He must of necessity be a perfect and infinite substance, and that, together with the principle of causality, is the only thing required for our demonstration of His existence.

Let us therefore conclude that God, in creating us, placed the idea of perfection within us "to be as the mark of the workman imprinted on his work". Nothing, after all, is more natural, for, as Descartes says in his second *Meditation on First Philosophy*, "from the sole fact that God created me, it is most probable that in some way He placed his image and likeness upon me, and that I perceive this likeness (in which the idea of God is contained) by means of the same faculty by which I perceive myself." [2] In other words, as is always the case when we are dealing with truly geometrical deductions, we are not so much deducing as perceiving intuitions within other intuitions; for since the very act of doubting implies the notion of perfection, which is one with the notion of God, we have just as much right to say: *I doubt, hence God is*, as to say: *I doubt, hence I am*.

Even at this distance from Descartes, it seems to me that we still can understand his philosophy as he himself understood it: an initial intuition, then more intuitions flowing from the first by means of a deductive process; and finally, a powerful effort of the mind to eliminate deduction itself by reintegrating its successive stages in that first single intuition. The whole body of

[2] Ibid., p. 125.

human knowledge was present to his mind, and he could see it at a glance, grounded as it was on the truth of its first principle, and sharing in its evidence. What else, and what more is there to be found in mathematical certitude? Nothing at all. Here, for instance, is the idea of God; it is possible to prove, as we have done, that an actually existing God is its only conceivable cause; but a mere analysis of the content of that idea would be enough in itself to prove the existence of God. For if our notion of God is identical with the notion of perfection, how could we not see that existence is involved in that idea, as one of the perfections which it signifies or connotes? I am no more free to think of God as non-existent, than I am to think of a triangle whose three angles would not be equal to two right angles. Existence pertains to God, whether or not I wish it, as necessarily as geometrical properties pertain to geometrical figures. I cannot think then of God otherwise than as existent,[3] and since all that is true of the idea of a thing is true of the thing itself, existence belongs not only to the idea of God, but also to God.

We are now in a better position to understand in what sense Descartes could say that "it is at least as certain that God, who is a being so perfect, is, or exists, as any demonstration of geometry can possibly be."[4] It is even more certain than any mathematical truth, for as long as I did not know God as a perfect being, I could not be sure that my Creator was not systematically deceiving me in mathematics as in everything else. At any rate, it is an obvious fact that the existence of God is better known to me than even the existence of the external world, since I know that there is a God, but I do not yet know whether or not there is an external world.

This was precisely the point at which Descartes found himself confronted with an entirely new and very difficult task. Up

[3] Ibid., Fifth Meditation, pp. 138–39.
[4] Ibid., p. 33.

to his time, no philosopher had denied flatly the existence of material things; Descartes himself, of course, had never entertained any real doubt as to their actual existence; but he was forbidden by his own principles to take it as an established fact. Like the rest, it was in need of being proved, and it could not have been proved at an earlier stage of the deduction. The mind first, God next, then, and only then, the external world. Such was the order. Why should Descartes have worried about it? He himself believed in the existence of matter, and he knew that every one else would keep on believing in it anyway. Besides, was he not about to prove it? The only difference would be that men, henceforward, would know it instead of believing it, and for a philosopher at least, that was the proper thing to do.

Having thus made up his mind, Descartes looked about for a proper starting point towards that new goal. Of course, as he still was but a mind, he could begin only with an idea, and the idea to be tried first was obviously that of matter. What is matter? Taken in itself, that is, as a clear and distinct idea, it is pure extension in space according to the three dimensions. Now, however carefully I examine that idea, I cannot find in it anything from which I can deduce the existence of its object. Unlike the idea of God, it does not represent anything so perfect that I could not be the cause of my idea of it. Why should not a mind be able to form the notion of matter, even though there were no actually existing matter? We shall therefore have to try something else.

Besides his idea of matter, Descartes could find in his mind another representation of the same object, for which he was indebted, not to his reason, but to his imagination. Apart from our abstract notion of extended bodies, we can picture them to ourselves, as we do circles, triangles, and so on, when we begin to study geometry. Now here, the problem is different; for there is nothing in the mind, taken as a mind, to account for its having an imagination. According to its nature, it should not have images, but ideas only. In order to account for the obvious difference between pure intellection and imagination, we might be tempted therefore to suppose, that there is a body, to which mind is conjoined and united. Pure intellection then would be a turning of the mind inward upon itself, while imagining would be a turning outward towards the body and beholding there something that is foreign to its own nature. To tell the whole truth, there is no other convenient explanation for the presence of an imagination within a mind. It is therefore highly probable that body exists; but we do not yet have a demonstration of its existence; even that idea of corporeal natures which I find in my imagination is a distinct idea, since geometers had nothing else whereon to build their science until analytical geometry was discovered. If it is a distinct idea of something which, unlike God, is only equal and even rather inferior in perfection to the mind, how could we deduce from its presence in the mind the actual existence of its object?

Our last hope then rests with sensation, and, this time, we are bound to succeed in our undertaking. It is true that sensations like our ideas and images are to be found within the mind, and that is why we can use them as a new starting point, but they are very different from all our other thoughts, both in their content and in their origin. First of all, they are but confused representations of some qualities, to which no distinct idea can be attached. Let us take, for instance, the feeling of pain. Where is pain, and what is it? If I am hurt by a piece of wood, or steel, it is obvious that the pain itself is not in the wood, or the steel. It cannot be anywhere else but in my mind; but how are we to account for the fact that a mind experiences such a feeling? A mind is a thing that thinks, not a thing that feels; as such, it can form clear and distinct ideas, as for instance the idea of extension, but it cannot form sensations like pain and pleasure, or smell, or taste, which cannot be measured and numbered, or become the fitting objects of any true science. Besides, it is a fact that the mind does not form sensations at will, as it does ideas, and even images; sensations come to the mind in the most various and unexpected ways, as though they were caused in it by something that is outside of it. In this case, then, we can safely say, that the mind not only surmises but actually experiences its union with something foreign to its own nature, i.e., a body, through which it becomes related to all other bodies. We might still fear of being deceived in our conclusion, did we not know that God's existence, proved in the way in which we have proved it, entails the existence of a supremely perfect being, who cannot allow us to be deceived. Now he would deceive us if, while we have both a natural inclination to believe that there is a world and a rational justification for that belief, that world did not exist.

Descartes' demonstration was as good as it possibly could be; its only defect was that it was a demonstration. As soon as Descartes published it, it became apparent that, like Caesar's wife, the existence of the world should be above suspicion. As long as it never occurred to any one to prove it, every one was sure of it, but the first attempt to prove it turned out to be the first step towards the denial of its existence. Descartes had endeavoured to prove something that could not be proved, not because it is not true, but on the contrary, because it is evident. Let us add that it is evident to a soul, not to a mind; and since Descartes was but a mind, he could no longer accept as evidence that which is such only to a soul, to a spiritual principle substantially united to a body; nor could he hope to find in mind, that is in a thinking substance distinct from, and exclusive of, the body, ground for the demonstration of its existence.

If sensations belong to the mind itself, nothing but the mind should be needed to account for their existence, but then there would be no reason to suppose that there is a material world. If, on the contrary, sensations are in us as coming not from the mind, but entering it from without, the so-called mind is not a true mind, but a soul, which immediately perceives the existence of bodies, as a certainty that neither can be proved, nor needs proof. Descartes had tried to find some possible position between the two horns of the dilemma; but there was none. He wanted a mind, at once so radically distinct from matter that the existence of matter would have to be proved, and so intimately conjoined with matter, through feeling, that the existence of matter could be proved. Even metaphysicians know that you cannot eat your cake, and have it; so, as soon as Descartes' successors realized his failure, they devoted themselves to the task of finding a new answer to the questions.

These successors were three in number, and all three were great metaphysicians: Leibniz, who was at the same time a great mathematician, for he discovered the differential calculus; Spinoza and Malebranche. All three were fully alive to the fact that Descartes had failed to account for the existence of sensations; as Leibniz said: "At that point, Monsieur Descartes withdrew from the game." And yet, not one of them was able to perceive that Descartes' failure was due to the fact that he had dealt with concrete substances as geometers deal with abstract definitions. They took up the game at exactly the same point where Descartes had dropped it, they kept the same hand with the same three cards, the mind, matter and God, and as Descartes himself had already played the first two, and failed, they had but one card left; which accounts for the fact that all three of them played the same card. They had to explain everything by God. The problem, as they saw it after Descartes, could be reduced to very simple terms. Mind and matter are in reality two completely distinct substances; that, at least, Descartes had fully demonstrated. On the other hand, it seemed to be a fact that there was some sort of connection between mind and matter; but the possibility of such a connection could never be found in those two substances themselves, since they were by definition mutually exclusive. Now outside of those two substances, there was still another one, and only one, namely God; through God, therefore, should proceed the unknown force that linked mind to matter and matter to mind.

That is the reason why Leibniz, Spinoza and Malebranche, despite the fact that they spent a good deal of their time in refuting each other, can be considered as having formed a distinct school, the Cartesian school. Leibniz said that God, in His perfect wisdom, had ordered all things from the very beginning, in such a way that every modification in a certain body would be accompanied by a certain modification in a corresponding soul. He called his system pre-established harmony.[5] Spinoza went still further: he decided that thought and extension were two attributes of one and the same infinite substance, flowing from that substance with the same necessity, and according to the same law, so that every mode of extension had to find its equivalent in a corresponding mode of thought. God, being the only true substance, was therefore the common source of those parallel attributes.[6] For this reason his system was often called metaphysical parallelism. As to Malebranche, he rejected Leibniz' solution on the ground that if God has pre-established a universal harmony, there was no room left for free will; and he rejected the system of Spinoza (whom he once called: "le misérable Spinoza", the wretched Spinoza) because to conceive mind and body as two finite modes of two attributes of the divine substance was to identify them with God. It was pantheism. But where could he find another solution?

[5] Leibniz, *The Monadology*, art. 80.

[6] Spinoza, *Ethics*, part 2, prop. 1–3; in B. Rand, ed., *Modern Classical Philosophers* (Boston: Houghton Mifflin, 1924), pp. 168–69.

Malebranche was greatly helped in finding one, by an expression that had already been used, but only in a casual way, by Descartes, and even by St. Augustine. Why not say that God has established such laws, that on the *occasion* of some change taking place in our bodies, some other change should necessarily take place in our souls? According to such a doctrine, which is commonly called *occasionalism*, matter and its modifications are but occasions for God to give us corresponding sensations and corresponding ideas. In a way, it can be said that Malebranche had answered the question, but his answer was fraught with fearful consequences, some of which he had not been able to foresee.

Let us begin with those which he himself perceived, and accepted. The first consequence is, that since we know everything through God, or, as Malebranche would say, in God, our knowledge is not directly related to actually existing things, but only to their ideas in God. Of course, we know *that* things are, and *what* they are; but since material substances, by their own natures, are entirely foreign to thinking substances, it might perhaps be better to say that, owing to God, we know everything about them, but do not know them.

This is so true that even were the external world annihilated by an act of the divine will, the character of physics as an exact science would not be changed. For indeed, physics is not a knowledge of the external world in its actual existence and its own reality, but rather a science of that intelligible idea of matter which is in God, and through which alone we know the properties of matter as well as its laws. Science is what it is, and always will remain such, whether there be an external world or not.

The second consequence of occasionalism is, that I do not know my own body any more than I know other bodies. To me, my own body is just as much part of the external world, that is to say, just as foreign to my mind, as every other body. I do not see my body, except through the ideas and sensations I have of it impressed upon my mind by God. Another way of expressing the same fact would be to say that the body which our soul *sees* is not the same as the body which our soul *animates*; for the body it animates is a concrete and material thing which, as such, can be neither felt nor known by the mind, whereas the body the mind knows is but the intelligible nature of the same body, in God.

From those two consequences there follows a third, the importance of which for the ulterior development of meta-physics was immediately perceived by some of Malebranche's contemporaries. It is that Descartes was wrong in saying that God would be a deceiver, if He made us falsely believe that external bodies make themselves known to us through sensa-tions. What had happened was simply this: Descartes admitted that sensations were actually caused in us by external bodies. That he admitted it, is strange; for, just as he had been the first to prove the real distinction of mind and body, he also should have been the first to realize that no action of a body upon a mind is conceivable; but he did admit it, and as he felt sure that he was right, he decreed that if he, Descartes, could be wrong when he was sure he was right, *then* God would be a deceiver. Unfortunately there was a third possibility, which Malebranche was not slow to see. On Descartes' principles, we know, as an evident truth, that the external world is not the cause of our knowledge of it; on the other hand we know, with equal certainty, once more from Descartes' own demonstrations, that God is not a deceiver. Whence it follows, as a third evident truth, that Descartes was wrong. He was wrong in considering as an evident truth our natural inclination to believe that bodies can act upon our minds. True, there is in us such an inclination, and it was put in us by God, and it is a deceiving inclination, yet the presence in our mind of such an inclination is no proof that God is a deceiver. To ask why it was put there by God is irrelevant to the question; the only thing that matters is the fact that God has not given us that inclination, as a rational evidence to be accepted by reason. On the contrary, God has given us, together with that natural inclination, the natural light of reason, by which we can question the truth-value of that inclination, and prove that it has none. Descartes should have reached that conclusion from his own principles; if he did not reach it, it is because he was deceiving himself, not because he was being deceived by God.[7]

Now let us recall what has already been said about Descartes' demonstration of the existence of an external world. It is well worth remarking that Descartes himself had considered Malebranche's vision in God as a possibility, but had rejected it on the ground that "since God is not a deceiver, it is very manifest that He does not communicate to me these ideas immediately and by Himself.[8] On the contrary, Descartes had said, God not only did not give me a faculty with which to recognize that this is the case, but he gave me rather a very great inclination to believe that these ideas were sent to me by corporeal objects. Hence his conclusion: as I have that natural inclination, and, on the other hand, as I have no evident knowledge that it is a deceitful one, "I do not see how He [God] could be defended against the accusation of deceit, if these ideas were produced by causes other than corporeal objects. Hence we must allow that corporeal things exist." [9] It is clear that, with the

[7] Malebranche's argument is the stronger, for Descartes himself, by his rejection of secondary qualities, had been obliged to admit that: "notwithstanding the supreme goodness of God, the nature of man, as it is composed of mind and body, cannot be otherwise than sometimes a source of deception." Eaton, *Descartes Selections*, p. 163.

[8] Ibid., p. 154.

[9] Ibid.

failure of this last argument, the whole Cartesian demonstration of the existence of an external world goes to pieces. How then are we going to prove it?

To that question, Malebranche's answer was simply: we are not going to prove it, because it cannot be proven. It was a very bold step, but at the same time it was obviously an inevitable one for any one who wanted to be truer to Descartes' principles than Descartes himself had been. As a matter of fact, the founder of the school lived long enough to see one of his first disciples arrive at the same conclusion. Regius, a Dutch professor of philosophy, and a great admirer of Descartes, said, and even printed, that according to the new philosophy: "it was naturally doubtful, whether or not corporeal things were actually perceived by us." But, he added, "that doubt is removed by the divine Revelation in Holy Scriptures, since it cannot be doubted that God has created heaven and earth.[10] When he read that statement, Descartes was furious; reminding Regius that he had given conclusive proof of the existence of the world in his writings, he added that his proofs could be understood at least by such people as "are not like the horse and the mule which have no understandings".[11] That, at least, could be proved by the Bible.

Unfortunately, there soon appeared another Cartesian horse, or mule, in the person of Géraud de Cordemoy, who in his interesting essay: *On the Distinction of Mind and Body, Sixth Discourse*, expressed surprise to hear that some people are not quite sure of having a soul; the real problem, says Cordemoy, is rather to prove that we have a body; without faith in divine revelation, how could we be sure of it? Thus, when Malebranche came third in the series, there was very little left for him to do, except confirm, by deeper and more convincing proofs, an opinion generally received in the French Cartesian school.

[10] Descartes, *Oeuvres*, ed. Adam and Tannery, vol. 8, part 2, p. 344, no. ix.
[11] Ibid., pp. 356–57. Cf. Ps 21:9, in the revised Douay edition.

In his *Conversations on Metaphysics and on Religion* (1688), Malebranche devoted the Sixth Conversation to a proof of the existence of bodies by means of divine revelation. The obvious objection was, that by doing so he was substituting religion for philosophy; but Malebranche knew several answers to that reproach. Since he had already proved that we receive our sensations directly from God, he was bound to consider sensations themselves, as some sort of natural revelations.[12] This was even the reason why Malebranche, far from being ashamed because he could not find a demonstration of the existence of matter, took great pride in proving at least that it is impossible to prove it.[13] Bodies cannot be directly perceived by our minds; on the other hand (and this is where Spinoza was wrong), their existence cannot be concluded from the nature of God, since God has created them, not by any necessity of nature, but rather by a free decision of His will. How then could we prove an existence that can be neither perceived nor deduced? It is a radical impossibility. But we know there is a God, and we believe that He is the Christian God; consequently, we should also believe that what He says in the Holy Scriptures is true. We are, then, bound in conscience to believe that "in the beginning, God created heaven and earth", together with the millions and millions of creatures contained therein. We should therefore hold, as an article of faith, that the external world is, or exists.

Just as Descartes had been labelled a "Dreamer", so Malebranche was commonly to be called a "Visionary". Yet he immediately found an audience, even in England, where J. Norris supported Malebranche's views, in his *Conduct of Human Life* (1690), with the unexpected result that the Quakers immediately recognized their own doctrine in Malebranche's

[12] N. Malebranche, *Dialogues on Metaphysics and on Religion*, VI, 8; trans. M. Ginsberg (London: G. Allen and Unwin, 1923), p. 165.
[13] Ibid., VI, 4; p. 166.

doctrine of the Vision in God.[14] Norris himself, who was a good scientist, was then accused of being a Quaker, which he denied, not however without adding, that were the Friends able to elaborate their doctrine into a clear system, it would not be so different from his own opinions.[15] This is why, in his Second *Philosophical Letter*, Voltaire introduces the famous Quaker, who justifies his own doctrine of inspiration by saying, that God gives us all our ideas. "Eh!" Voltaire says, "here is Father Malebranche true to life."—"I know thy Malebranche," the Quaker rejoins, "he was a bit of a Quaker, but not enough."[16] Such was Malebranche's reward for having pledged himself always to follow the pure evidence of reason. As Faydit said of him in a then oft-quoted verse:

> He who sees all in God, there, sees not he is mad.

That was not the worst. According to an old tradition, when Malebranche was in the last year of his life (1715), and already very weak, a young Irish philosopher waited upon him. His name was George Berkeley. Having published his own *Essay towards a New Theory of Vision* (1709), it was only natural that he should carry on a serious philosophical discussion with Malebranche. We are not sure what the topic of the discussion was, but we should not be very far from the mark in supposing that it ran something like this: "Father, I quite agree with you that God gives us all our ideas, including sensations, and that, consequently, the existence of a material world cannot be proved. But then, why are you so keen on upholding its existence? The existence of *what*? You have proved conclusively to us that the

---

[14] See also J. Locke, *Remarks upon Some of Mr. Norris's Books Wherein He Asserts P. Malebranche's Opinion of Our Seeing All Things in God*; ed. J. A. St. John, vol. 2, pp. 459–71.

[15] Voltaire, *Lettres philosophiques*, ed. G. Lanson, vol. 1, p. 31, note 14.

[16] Ibid., p. 25.

so-called matter 'neither acts, nor perceives, nor is perceived.' Then, *what* is it? You say it is an occasion. But since matter has nothing in common with mind, God could not possibly find there even an occasion to do something in our minds." [17] "Then you add that we should at least believe what Revelation tells us about it; but Revelation tells us nothing at all about it; all it says is, that God created heaven and earth, not that he created an unknown and unknowable substance, called matter, that lies hidden behind our own ideas and our own feelings. Nothing will be changed in the usual interpretation of Holy Writ whether there be, or be not, external things." [18] Ideas, then, and spirits, make up the whole of reality, and outside of them, there is nothing; nay, not even an outside. [19]

If young Berkeley did use such an argument, which I have borrowed from his later criticism of Malebranche, the account given by Stock of their interview is not entirely lacking in probability: "In the heat of the disputation," says Stock, "he [Malebranche] raised his voice so high, and gave way so freely to the natural impetuosity of a man of parts, and a Frenchman, that he brought on himself a violent increase of his disorder, which carried him off a few days after." [20] If the story is true, it is a good one; if it is not true, it is better than true, for it should

[17] See G. Berkeley, *Of the Principles of Human Knowledge*, part 1, nos. 67–79; ed. A. C. Fraser (Oxford: Clarendon Press,1901), vol. 1, p. 43.

[18] Ibid., nos. 82–85; vol. 1, pp. 302–4.

[19] The idealistic implications of Malebranche's vision in God had already been seen by Locke: "What he [Malebranche] here means by the sun is hard to conceive; and according to his hypothesis of seeing all things in God, how can he know that there is any such real being in the world as the sun? Did he ever see the sun? No; how then does he know that there is a sun which he never saw?" J. Locke, *An Examination of P. Malebranche's Opinion of Seeing All Things in God*, no. 20; ed. J. A. St. John, vol. 2, p. 425.

[20] A. C. Fraser, ed., *The Works of Berkeley* (Oxford: Clarendon Press, 1871), vol. 4, p. 73. See also a shorter account of the same story in the 1901 edition, vol. 1, p. 43.

have happened. No wonder then, that De Quincey inserted it in his famous Essay on *Murder as One of the Fine Arts*.[21] What a murder case, indeed: "Murder by Metaphysics!"

Whether the sudden revelation that he had always been an unconscious idealist actually killed Malebranche or not, the fact remains, that while Locke was bringing Descartes' reign to an end on the continent, the geometrical distinction of mind and body was reaching on Irish soil the last stage of its natural evolution. Like all philosophers, Berkeley felt rather interested in those points of his own system on which he was at variance with Malebranche and Descartes, but his radical idealism was none the less a natural and necessary offspring of the "I think, hence I am." In spite of Berkeley's own protests, his contemporaries, and particularly his friend Doctor Clayton, had no difficulty in finding him a place among the members of the Cartesian family. In the *Essay on Spirit*, printed in 1750, and attributed to Clayton, we read that the opinion of Spinoza was, that "there is no other substance in nature but God; that modes cannot subsist, or be conceived, without a substance; that there is nothing in nature but modes and substances; and that therefore everything must be conceived as subsisting in God. Which opinion, with some few alterations, has been embraced and cultivated by Father Malebranche and Bishop Berkeley."[22] Clayton was right, save only in this, that if Malebranche, Berkeley, and let us add Leibniz, had made God the only knowing, acting, and subsisting reality, Spinoza had played no part in their decision. The responsibility for so much metaphysical trouble behind all those systems rests with Descartes and his geometrical metaphysics. Every one is free to decide whether he shall begin to philosophize as a pure mind; if he should elect to do so the difficulty

[21] *De Quincey's Works* (Boston: Riverside Editions, 1877), vol. 2, p. 551.

[22] Fraser, *Works of Berkeley*, vol. 4, p. 324, no. 55. Compare J. Locke, *Remarks upon Some of Mr. Norris's Books*, no. 16; ed. J. A. St. John, vol. 2, pp. 468–69.

will be not how to get into the mind, but how to get out of it. Four great men had tried it, and failed. Berkeley's own achievement was to realize at last, that it was a useless and foolish thing even to try it. In this sense at least, it is true to say that Berkeley brought Descartes' "noble experiment" to a close, and for that reason his work should always remain as a landmark in the history of philosophy. But Descartes was not only a metaphysician, he was also a physicist; and we shall now see how, after destroying our natural belief in the existence of the world, Descartes' mathematicism was to destroy our natural belief in physical causality.

CHAPTER VIII

THE BREAKDOWN OF CARTESIANISM

No one who knows the ulterior destiny of Descartes' doctrine can read without surprise the heedless sentence with which his Sixth *Meditation* begins: "Nothing further now remains, but to inquire whether material things exist."[1] So far was he from fearing any difficulty on the point that, when some readers told him he was headed for trouble, Descartes refused to believe it. Yet, he had been duly warned. "What must the union of the corporeal with the incorporeal be thought to be?" Gassendi had asked him: "How will that which is corporeal seize upon that which is incorporeal, so to hold it conjoined with itself, or how will the incorporeal grasp the corporeal, so as reciprocally to keep it bound to itself . . . ?" True, you say that you actually experience such a union when you *feel* pain, but then "I ask you how you think, that you, if you are incorporeal and unextended, are capable of experiencing the sensation of pain?" In short, to conclude in Gassendi's own words, "the general difficulty always remains, *viz.*, how the corporeal can have anything in common with the incorporeal, or what relationship may be established between the one and the other."[2]

To Gassendi's most pertinent objections, Descartes had simply answered: "At no place do you bring an objection to my

---

[1] Eaton, *Descartes Selections*, p. 145.
[2] Gassendi, *Fifth Objections*, in Eaton, *Descartes Selections*, pp. 245–46.

arguments."[3] Such blindness in such a genius would remain a mystery, did we not know that Descartes' real purpose, in proving the existence of an external world, was less to prove the existence of something outside of the mind, than it was to make clear that nothing exists outside of the mind but geometrical extension. As he himself understood it, his distinction of mind and body had to cut both ways; first, it had to prove that nothing of what belongs to the nature of corporeal substance can be ascribed to the mind; and secondly, which was what Descartes wanted above all, it had to prove that the converse is true: that nothing of what belongs to the nature of the mind should be ascribed to corporeal matter. In other words, if Descartes never worried very much about his demonstration of the existence of matter, the reason is that in his mind, the real problem had never been: Does matter exist? but, rather: Of what do we prove the existence in proving that matter exists? And the answer was: extension in space according to three dimensions; whence it follows that matter is that, and nothing else.

Thus, Descartes was resorting once more to his fundamental principle: what is true of the concept of a thing is also true of that thing.[4] The only existence I can conceive outside of my mind is that of extension; consequently, what is outside of my mind is nothing but extension. Hence the title of his Sixth and last *Meditation*: "Of the existence of material things, and of the real distinction between the soul and body of Man."[5] And the precise point, which he wished to make in his demonstration, may clearly be seen from its carefully worded conclusion: "Hence we must allow, that corporeal things exist. However, they are

[3] Eaton, *Descartes Selections*, p. 262.

[4] Descartes, *Reply to Objections II*, ed. Haldane and Ross, vol. 2, p. 57, prop. 1; and p. 53, defin. 9.

[5] Eaton, *Descartes Selections*, p. 145.

perhaps not exactly what we perceive by the senses, . . . but we must at least admit, that all things which I conceive in them clearly and distinctly, that is to say, all things which, speaking generally, are comprehended in the object of pure mathematics, are truly to be recognized as external objects." [6] We shall then have to remove from the idea of matter all the so-called "qualities", such as weight, hardness, colour and so on, for they do not arise from the body alone, and, therefore, they do not actually belong to it. [7] In the same way, and for the same reason, shall we have to eliminate from matter the so-called "natures", or "forms", which were supposed by Aristotle and his mediæval followers to be in animate and inanimate bodies, as the internal causes of their motions, growth, nutrition, generation and sensations. What are such "natures", or "forms", but disguised souls, ascribed by men to matter, as if all natural bodies were made up of a body and a soul? True, it is in man a natural illusion to conceive all things after the pattern of man; nevertheless, it is but an illusion. Man alone has both a body and a mind; as to physical bodies, they are nothing but bodies, that is to say, variously shaped particles of extension, arranged according to various orders, and occupying certain places in space. Even living bodies, animals, for example, are mere machines, and our human body itself, when considered apart from the mind to which it is united, is nothing but a machine.

The ultimate conclusion of Descartes' metaphysics provided him, therefore, with the first principle of a purely geometrical and mechanical conception of the physical world, which was the very thing he wanted. Let us then suppose with him a matter created by an all-powerful God. There is no reason to conceive an extension beyond which no further extension could

[6] Ibid., p. 154.

[7] Descartes, *The Principles of Philosophy*, II, 2–4; in Eaton, *Descartes Selections*, pp. 290–91.

be found, and even no possibility of doing so, whence it follows that we can say, as we do in the case of the idea of matter we have in the mind, that matter itself is indefinitely extended and the material world has no limits. On the other hand, since matter is identical with extension, there can be no empty space in the world; for, where there is space, there is extension, and consequently there is matter; not only therefore is the world of matter indefinitely extended in space, but it is full. Last, but not least, as we cannot conceive a particle of extension so small that it could not be conceived as capable of being divided into still smaller parts, we are bound to think of material bodies as indefinitely divisible. In short, there are no atoms, which makes motion possible in a perfectly full world. A material movement is always a complete circle of infinitely small particles of matter moving together so that, as similar to the case of a perfectly full streetcar, where no man can get in without another man getting out, each particle of matter successively occupies every one of the places left vacant by the previous one. All natural motions in material bodies are therefore whirling motions; each of them is a "vortex".

Beyond these intrinsic properties of matter, the only metaphysical hypothesis we need to assume is that, when God created matter, He caused a certain amount of movement in it. Given that fundamental assumption, all the laws of physics will be deduced with mathematical evidence; observations and experiments having no part to play, other than to clear up every successive point of the deduction, or to provide us with more facts to be deduced from the same principles. Having created the world with a certain amount of motion, God, who is immutable because He is perfect, still preserves in the world just as much motion as there was on the day of creation. Every moving thing, then, as far as lies in it to do so, continues to move as it was once moved, keeping its whole motion when it comes in contact with a stronger body, and communicates to weaker bodies just as much motion as it loses by their impact. Such motion is not the external manifestation of some energy hidden within the matter; such a fancy is inconsistent with straight mechanism and would bring us back to the scholastic illusion of "forms", or "natures". Ultimately it would mean that some "souls" are animating matter from within, setting it in motion and stopping it at will. A purely geometrical idea of motion reduces itself to a change of place; a body then will be said to be moving, when it passes from the vicinity of those bodies that are in immediate contact with it, into the vicinity of others.[8] Motion, as Descartes says, is nothing but "the *transportation*, and not either the *force* or the *action* which transports." And the reason why he says so is obvious: "motion is always in the mobile thing, not in that which moves."[9] Bodies in motion keep what motion they have received until they communicate it to other bodies according to very simple laws; it would be even more correct to say that motion passes through bodies, from some to others, for mobile bodies are in motion, they are moving things, not movers; so much so that the sole mover of the whole world is not himself in motion: He is the immutable preserver and mover of moving matter, *viz.*, God.

The better to explicate the full meaning of such a philosophical revolution, allow me to take you back, for a few moments, to the mediæval world which Descartes was attempting to replace. According to St. Thomas Aquinas, the physical order was essentially made up of "natures", that is to say, of active principles, which were the cause of the motions and various operations of their respective matters. In other words, each nature, or form, was essentially an energy, an act. Now it is an obvious fact that such a world was no fit subject for a purely

    [8] Ibid., II, 25; Eaton, *Descartes Selections*, p. 301.
    [9] Ibid.

mechanical interpretation of physical change; dimensions, positions and distances are by themselves clear things; they can be measured and numbered; but those secret energies that had been ascribed to bodies by Aristotle and St. Thomas, could not be submitted to any kind of calculation. Should they be allowed to stay there, and this indeed was to Descartes the main point, there would remain in nature something confused and obscure, and in science itself a standing element of unintelligibility. As a geometer, who wanted physics to become a department of his universal mathematics, Descartes could not possibly tolerate such a nuisance. Forms, natures and energies had to be eliminated then from the physical world, so that there should be nothing left but extension and an always equal amount of motion caused by God.

How thoughtful and accommodating a God indeed was Descartes' God! All-powerful, He had created just the kind of world which Cartesian philosophy could explain; immutable, He was preserving things with so conscientious a regularity that Descartes could unfold the whole explanation of his world without bothering any more about Him. Pascal had clearly perceived that deep intention, when he wrote that in all his philosophy, Descartes "would have been quite willing to dispense with God. But he had to make Him give a fillip to set the world in motion; beyond this, he has no further need of God." [10] However true this may be, it should not be forgotten that if, in a sense, the Cartesian God does not do much in the world, since science can freely develop itself as though there were no God, in another sense it is just as true to say that God does everything in it. Like Descartes' God, the God of St. Thomas was a continuous creator of all things; but the things He had created, and which He was still keeping in existence, were "natures", that is to say, active causes, true causes. Indebted to Him for

[10] Pascal, *Pensées*, trans. W. F. Trotter, p. 23, no. 77.

their actual existence, their operative powers and even the very efficacy of their operations, they nevertheless were efficient causes, and such operations could truly be said to be their own. Thus, what God has to keep in existence, in a Thomistic world, is a set of enduring, active natures, each of which is an original power with a sufficient capacity to do its own work. Not so in the world of Descartes. Once all individual sources of energy had been expelled from it, nothing was left therein but extension and its laws; not natures, but Nature, that is to say, those changes that happen in the various parts of matter. As to the "laws of nature", they were nothing more than the divinely and freely created rules, in accordance with which these changes occur; the Divine activity, which does not itself change, remained, in fact, the only active cause still to be found in such a world.[11]

Of those two Descartes, the Descartes who would have been quite willing to dispense with God, and the Descartes who wanted to ascribe all causality to God, which one was the true Descartes? Both; for Descartes was quite willing to give everything to God in metaphysics, if that were necessary in order to have nothing but extension left in physics. As he himself had no use for physical energy of any kind in his purely mechanical physics, what Descartes needed in metaphysics was a monstrous and despotic God, whose proper function it would be to draw from matter all that was not bare and naked extension in space. The actual condition of such a world, in any given moment, would then require no other explanation than the creative and preserving power of a God who would make it to be so; what such a world is now does not follow from what it was in the instant immediately preceding, nor is it a cause of what it will be in the next one. In short, the existence of such a world is not a continuous duration of permanent substances, but a succes-

[11] Descartes, *The World*, VIII; in Eaton, *Descartes Selections*, p. 322.

sion of disconnected and instantaneous existences, each of which has no other cause than the creative power of God.[12]

I wish I could honestly tell you that Descartes' sacrifices in the field of metaphysics were repaid a hundredfold by his discoveries in the field of physics. But it was not to be so. Truth is one, and bad metaphysics seldom pays, even in the interests of science. Immediately after Descartes, Leibniz proved that even the Cartesian laws of impact were scientifically wrong, and precisely because Descartes had failed to grasp the importance of such notions as form, force and energy.[13] As soon as Newton published his *Mathematical Principles of Natural Philosophy*, in 1687, it immediately became apparent that Descartes' physics was a thing of the past. Aristotle's physics had lasted twenty centuries, Descartes' lasted about thirty years in England, and not much more than sixty years on the Continent. True, there were still some belated Cartesians both in England and France during the first third of the eighteenth century, but the real scientists regarded them as curious specimens of an actually extinct race. When the worthy Fontenelle was so heedless as to compare Descartes with Newton, English public opinion felt very indignant and blamed it on French national prejudice. "This", said a letter to *The London Journal* in 1723, "is just as if a comparison had to be made betwixt a Romance and a real History, between a scheme of mere suppositions and a set of real truths; between conjectures, imaginations, mere reveries, and plain facts, visible laws and known experience."[14] From that

[12] This is the reason why, as Spinoza was to see very clearly, bodies should not be considered as "substances" in a Cartesian world: Spinoza, *Ethics*, part 2, prop. 13, lemma 1.

[13] On the Leibnizian meaning of those notions, see the important text quoted in H. W. Carr, *Leibniz* (Boston: Little, Brown and Co., 1929), pp. 77–79.

[14] The text is quoted, together with several others to the same effect, by G. Lanson, in his edition of Voltaire's *Lettres philosophiques*, vol. 2, pp 9–10.

decision there was to be no appeal, even in France. Around the year 1732, Voltaire became a convert to Newton's physics, French public opinion followed him, and hardly a single one of the physical laws laid down by Descartes in his *Principles of Philosophy* has been held as valid by any scientist since that time. As a matter of fact, Descartes' physics was an almost complete failure; yet his metaphysics of nature was to give a new turn to natural philosophy.

As we should expect, it is to France that we must turn in order to witness the beginnings of those new developments. In 1664, one of Descartes' disciples, Louis de la Forge, published a posthumous work of the master: *Man by René Descartes*, to the text of which he added an interesting commentary of his own. In 1666, the same de la Forge published his own *Treatise on the Spirit of Man, Its Faculties, Its Functions and Its Union with the Body according to the Principles of René Descartes.* In chapter 10 of his book, de la Forge proved that, on Descartes' own principles, the physiological modifications of our body could not be more than "occasional causes" of our feelings, but in chapter 16 he raised another question, which proved to be a very important one. Philosophers are always wondering how a mind can act upon a body, and a body upon a mind; but a body itself is just as distinct a substance from another body, as it is from a mind; how then are we to account for the fact that one body seems to act upon another body? True, we see, or at least we believe we see, that some material things, which are in motion, communicate some of their own motion to other bodies; but have we any clear and distinct idea of *how* that can be done? We have absolutely none; instead we perceive clearly and distinctly, that it is a contradiction to posit such direct communication between two distinct substances. What actually happens is not that body A is acting upon body B, but that God, who was preserving both A and B in contiguous places, is now conserving them apart, that is, in separate places, on the occasion of their former contiguity.

Thus initiated by Descartes and de la Forge, the breakdown of physical causality soon became an accomplished fact with Géraud de Cordemoy. No one did more than that obscure man to bring into the open those essential implications that had always been involved in Descartes' principles. As soon as he began to deal with the question, in his treatise *On the Discerning of Mind and Body*, he was able to settle the whole case at once, and he made a thorough job of it. Two axioms, and it was done. First axiom: a thing cannot have by itself that which it can lose without ceasing to be what it is. Second axiom: a body can gradually lose its motion until no motion at all be left, without ceasing to be a body. Conclusion: no body has by itself any motion. Cordemoy's conclusion indeed reached the very root of the problem, and helps us to realize the deep meaning behind Pascal's irony. Descartes had no need of God, save only "to give a fillip to set the world in motion". But, for that at least, he was in very great need of God.

Descartes, we remember, had planned to give geometrical explanations of all phenomena, even life; but he met with difficulty from the very beginning of his undertaking. How indeed could he extend pure geometry even to mechanics, since pure geometry deals with extension only, while mechanics deals with extension plus motion? Motions do not belong in the geometrical order; they come from without, as something new that cannot possibly be deduced from the bare essence of extension. True, extended things are actually moving, but they are not moving as extended, that is to say, in virtue of their own essence as extended things. Descartes himself knew that so well that he did his very best to palliate the difficulty; if we saw him reducing motion itself to a transportation from place to place, passively undergone, it was because he wanted to leave nothing in bodies but relations of place and distance, that is to say, geometrical relations. Yet, transportation itself still remained a fact to be accounted for. Transportation by what? No "what" could be found in extension itself, since motion does not belong to extension as such. Then, transportation by whom? The only possible answer obviously had to be: by God.

This was Cordemoy's final answer. Since no body can move another body, and as the only other kind of substance we know of is mind, the cause of all motions in space must needs be a mind. Not our mind, which cannot move even its own body; then it must be God. The conclusion flowed so necessarily from Descartes' method, that in the last third of the seventeenth century all Cartesians received it as a truth conclusively proved. We find it quoted as "the principle of the Cartesians" in the anonymous pamphlet: *Letter of a Philosopher to a Cartesian*, which was printed in 1672. According to the 32nd article of the *Letter*, all Cartesians agree that God alone is able to cause motion. We fancy that cannon balls bring walls down; they do not. No gun in the world, no gun powder, no cannon ball, no engine, no man, even no angel, is able to move anything, be it a straw. God alone can do it.

When Malebranche took up the problem in his turn, he could do little more than provide his contemporaries with new demonstrations of the same conclusion. As a matter of fact, other great minds of the time were intent upon working out some answer to the Cartesian problem of the "communication between substances". Spinoza, for instance, identifies Nature with God (*Deus sive natura*); individual things therefore are nothing but "modes by which the attributes of God are expressed in a certain determined manner, that is, they are things which express in a certain determined manner the power of God whereby God exists, and acts." [15] Bodies, therefore, do not

[15] Spinoza, *Ethics*, part 3, prop. 6.

act, they merely exhibit particular modes of God's action. Leibniz's famous monads "have no windows, through which anything could come in or go out"; there is then "no way of explaining how a monad can be altered in quality or internally changed by any other created things".[16] Hence Leibniz's conclusion, that "the influence of one monad upon another is only ideal, as it can have its effect only through the mediation of God," [17] or in still fewer words: "There is only one God, and this God is sufficient." [18]

If Malebranche's answer to the question was to exercise a particularly deep influence on eighteenth-century philosophy, it is because he, at least, still believed in the existence of a concrete and actually subsisting world of matter. To him, matter was not simply a confused perception, as it was to Leibniz; nor would he reduce bodies to what they were for Spinoza, *viz.*, finite modes of a purely intelligible extension, which itself is one of the attributes of God. Even knowing, as he did, that it could not be proved, Malebranche clung through faith to the conviction that God had created, after the pattern of its intelligible idea, an actually existing substance, that was something in itself, apart from its idea in God and from our knowledge of it. Malebranche was thereby compelled, by his own position, to deal with the nature of causality in the material world, and, of course, to deny it.

According to Malebranche, the first step to the conclusion that bodies cannot act upon bodies is the realization that we have no idea whatsoever of what such an action could be. As a true Cartesian he insists that we consult the idea which we have of bodies, and always remember that "one must judge of things by the ideas which represent them."[19] Now the idea of an

[16] Leibniz, *Monadology*, 7; ed. R. Latta (Oxford, 1898), p. 219.

[17] Ibid., 51; p. 246.

[18] Ibid., 39; p. 239.

[19] Malebranche, *Dialogues on Metaphysics and on Religion*, VII, 5; trans. M. Ginsberg (London: G. Allen and Unwin, 1923), p. 183.

action exerted by a body upon another body does not represent anything to our mind; we simply have no such idea; consequently, there is no such action. And what is more, there can be no such action, for its very supposition would involve a flat contradiction. What could we mean in saying that a body moves another body? The only possible meaning that such an expression could have would be that a certain body A causes another body B, which at first was existing in a certain place, to exist now in another place. But how could a material body cause another material body to be in the place where it is actually to be found? It is God's will which gave existence to bodies, as well as to all created things, and the same divine power that created them is still keeping them in existence, so much so that should this divine will cease to be, bodies themselves would necessarily cease to be. Now, it is impossible for us to conceive a body that is not somewhere, that is to say, that is not in a certain place; nor is it possible for us to conceive a body that is neither moving, nor at rest, neither changing its relations of distance to other bodies, nor keeping the same. So true is this, that "God himself, though all-powerful, cannot create a body which should be nowhere and which should not stand to any other body in some special relation." It is therefore one and the same thing to say that God's will is preserving the existence of a certain body, and to say that it preserves that same body as existing in the very place where it actually is. God, indeed, could not do differently; since "He cannot will that which cannot be conceived" namely, that which involves a manifest contradiction. But then, what is there left, that created bodies can do? A certain body is where it is because God's creative power is conserving it just where it is; in the next instant, God will conserve that same body in another place, if the body be moving, or in the same place, if the body be at rest. Consequently, bodies are in no wise the causes for other bodies being where they are, since they neither move these other bodies, nor are moved by them.[20]

It would be difficult to conceive a more lucid explanation of the logical consequences involved in Descartes' conception of matter. Pure extension is pure passivity, that is to say, it is by its nature exclusive of causality. When God first created the world, the world itself stood for nothing in its own creation, it simply was "being created". Every one understands that, in the very moment of their creation, things were not the causes of their own existence, of their own natures, or of their own location in space; God's will alone made them to be, to be what they were, and to be where they were. Most of us would admit that it was so at the moment of creation, but that, the moment of creation once passed, it is no longer so. "The moment of creation once passed!" says Malebranche, but "that moment never passes away. The conservation of created beings is . . . their continuous creation. . . . In truth, the act of creation never ceases, since in God, conservation and creation are but one and the same volition, and in consequence are necessarily followed by the same effects."[21] In short, just as bodies cannot be endowed with any kind of efficacy, "it is God alone who adapts the efficacy of His actions to the *ineffective actions* of His creations."[22]

A man who could find so perfect an expression of his thought will certainly not be charged with inconsistent and loose thinking; nor could his conclusions be rejected on the sole ground that they were unusual and disconcerting, which true conclusions often are; but it is still quite legitimate to ask him whether there was not something wrong in his very approach to the question. This is precisely what John Locke did, and he did it with his usual acuteness, both in his *Examination of Malebranche's*

[20] Ibid., VII, 6; pp. 184–85.
[21] Ibid., VII, 7; pp. 185–86.
[22] Ibid., VII, 10; p. 189.

Opinion of Seeing All Things in God, and in his *Remarks upon Some of Mr. Norris's Books wherein He Asserts P. Malebranche's Opinion of Our Seeing All Things in God*. Locke had clearly perceived the two main reasons why Malebranche had to uphold occasionalism: the desire to extol the absolute power of God, and the radical impossibility of finding in matter the cause of its own motion. Locke's answer to the first of those reasons is identically the same as that which had already been given by St. Thomas Aquinas, in the thirteenth century, to those who made man "altogether passive in the whole business of thinking". The parallel is so striking that I beg leave to quote Locke's text in full: "The infinite eternal God is certainly the cause of all things, the fountain of all being and power. But because all being was from Him, can there be nothing but God Himself? Or because all power was originally in Him, can there be nothing of it communicated to His creatures? This is to set very narrow bounds to the power of God, and, by pretending to extend it, takes it away." [23] So much for the theologian, but there is also something for the philosopher. Malebranche had been compelled to resort to occasional causes, because we have no clear and distinct idea of how one body can act upon another body, and still less upon a mind. But have we any clear and distinct idea of what an *occasional* cause could be? If it does not act upon God, it is not a cause; if it does, we shall arrive at the conclusion that God can give bodies a power to operate on His own infinite mind, but He cannot give them a power to operate on the finite mind of man, or on other things, which is an absurdity.[24] The trouble with Malebranche, as with all the Cartesians, was that he wanted to make everything clear and to know how everything is brought to pass; "but perhaps it would better become us, to acknowledge

[23] J. Locke, *Remarks upon Some of Mr. Norris's Books*, no. 15; ed. J. A. St. John, vol. 2, p. 667.
[24] Ibid.; p. 466.

our ignorance, than to talk such things boldly of the Holy One of Israel, and condemn others for not daring to be as unmannerly as ourselves." [25]

The lesson was not lost, and it was to bear unexpected fruit in the mind of David Hume. How could the deeply religious and almost mystical Father Malebranche, of the Oratory, have foreseen that his world would some day fall into the hands of a man to whom the existence of God could neither be successfully preached nor rationally proved? Yet this thing happened on the very day Hume became acquainted with Malebranche's philosophical conclusions. And what would become of the physical world of Malebranche if God, who is the keystone of its whole structure, were to be taken out of it? It would crumble to pieces; nothing would be left of it but disconnected fragments.

This is precisely what happened when David Hume took up the problem of physical causality where Malebranche had laid it down. Generally speaking, Hume was much more a continuator of Locke than of Malebranche; yet, on this precise point, there is little doubt that Malebranche's occasionalism played an important part in the formation of Hume's doctrine. Like his predecessor, Hume applied his analysis to the idea of cause and effect, with the result that he could find nothing essential in that idea but a relation of contiguity, or succession, between what we call cause and effect, plus the notion of a necessary connection between them. A certain body approaches another, touches it, and, without any sensible interval, the motion that was in the first body is now in the second. We see that it is so; we feel that it cannot be otherwise, and that, in similar circumstances, it will always be so. But why and how it is so, we have not the slightest idea, for the simple reason that we cannot even imagine what an impulse, or a production, could possibly be. [26] What is there in

[25] Ibid., no. 16; p. 469.
[26] D. Hume, *A Treatise of Human Nature*, bk. 1, part 4, sec. 3.

our mind, for instance, which answers to the word "efficacy"?
Nothing at all. Malebranche, to whom Hume himself expressly
refers us on that point, had conclusively proved that no philosopher had ever been able to explain the so-called "secret force
and energy of causes". Hence, Hume says, Malebranche's own
conclusion "that the ultimate force and efficacy of nature is
perfectly unknown to us, and that it is in vain we search for it in
all the known qualities of matter." And how indeed, Hume
concludes, could the Cartesians have given any other answer to
the question? They had established as a principle that we are
perfectly acquainted with the essence of matter; "as the essence
of matter consists in extension, and as extension implies not
actual motion, but only mobility; they conclude that the energy
which produces the motion cannot be in the extension." [27] One
could hardly wish for a more intelligent and acute observer; but
it is easy to see that the reason for which Hume had so closely
watched that philosophical game was that Malebranche's conclusion was to be his own starting point.

For, Hume tells us, this conclusion leads the Cartesians into
another, which they regard as absolutely inevitable. Since, according to them, matter is in itself entirely inactive and "deprived of any power by which it may produce, or continue, or
communicate motion", the power that produces the physical effects evident to our senses must be in the Deity. "It is the Deity
therefore, . . . who not only first created matter, and gave it its
original impulse, but likewise, by a continued exertion of omnipotence, supports its existence, and successively bestows on it
all those motions . . . with which it is endowed." But, says Hume,
if we have no adequate idea of "power" or "efficacy", no notion
of "causality" that we can apply to matter, where could we get
one that would apply to God? "Since these philosophers, therefore, have concluded that matter cannot be endowed with any

[27] Ibid., bk. 1, part 3, sec. 14.

efficacious principle, because it is impossible to discover in it such a principle, the same course of reasoning should determine them to exclude it from the Supreme Being."[28]

Thus, according to Hume, causality could no longer be considered as the transportation of a thing by another thing, or as the transportation of a thing by the power of God, but as a transportation of our own mind from an idea, which we call cause, to another idea, which we call effect. Custom makes us believe that an idea will soon be followed by another idea, and we mistake the force of our belief for a physical force to be found in things. Irrefutable conclusion indeed, which blasted, once and for all, the Cartesian school's last hope of maintaining even the slightest shadow of causality in the world. Owing to Hume's philosophical insight, the Cartesian cycle had thus been brought to a close; and it really was a cycle, because its end was in its very beginning—scepticism. Montaigne's scepticism at the beginning; Hume's scepticism at the end; in between, a tremendous effort, tirelessly renewed by a chain of philosophical and scientific geniuses, to no other effect than the wiping out of the external world by Berkeley and, for those like Hume who still believed in the existence of matter, the final dismissal of the principle of causality. What do I know apart from what I am being taught by custom? Montaigne had asked. The mind, God, and the world, as evidently as mathematics, if not more so, was Descartes' answer. But Descartes' geometry had turned the world into a mosaic of mutually exclusive substances, that could neither act nor be acted upon, neither know, nor be known. And now, after a steady scrutiny of that answer for a century, Hume had to write as its ultimate conclusion: "that all our reasonings concerning causes and effects are derived from nothing but custom."[29] On a deeper level, it was Montaigne's answer to his own question; but that answer was being repeated now in

[28] Ibid.   [29] Ibid., part 4, sec. 1.

another tone, not with the smiling carelessness of a man who does not know because he does not even want to know, but with the despondency of a great mind, who comes into the spiritual legacy of many other great minds, and, as soon as he looks at it, sees it shrivel into nothingness. "I am . . . affrighted and confounded with that forlorn solitude in which I am placed in my philosophy", says Hume at the end of the *Treatise*. What was Hume, after all, but a sad Montaigne?

Let us thank him, however, for having deeply felt and sincerely expressed what he himself called his "despair".[30] His voice was soon to be heard by a young professor of philosophy at the German university of Koenigsberg. The name of that man was Immanuel Kant. With him a new philosophical cycle was to begin, and it is to that cycle we now turn our attention.

[30] Ibid., part 7, sec. 8, conclusion.

PART THREE

THE MODERN EXPERIMENT

CHAPTER IX

THE PHYSICISM OF KANT

In 1756, Kant read Hume in a German translation, and as soon as he began to realize the meaning of Hume's scepticism, his own faith in the validity of metaphysical knowledge was badly shaken. "David Hume", Kant was to write many years later in his *Prolegomena*, "first broke my dogmatic slumber." Hume's critical observations on the principle of causality, generalized and extended by Kant to the whole body of metaphysics, brought him to the conclusion that, as positive knowledge, metaphysics was dead. The first page of the first preface to the *Critique of Pure Reason* takes it as an obvious and accomplished fact, which stands in no need of demonstration: "There was a time when metaphysic held a royal place among all the sciences. . . . At present, it is the fashion to despise metaphysic, and the poor matron, forlorn and forsaken, complains like Hecuba: 'But late on the pinnacle of fame, strong in my many sons, my daughters and my husband, I am now dragged away, penniless, exiled.' " [1]

Just as Montaigne had ushered a new sceptical age into the world, before Descartes, so Hume had done, immediately before Kant: "At present, after everything has been tried, so they say, and tried in vain, there reign in philosophy weariness and complete indifferentism, the mother of chaos and night in all

[1] Immanuel Kant, *Selections*, ed. Theodore Meyer Greene (New York: Scribner's, 1929), p. 2. The quotation is from Ovid, *Metamorphoses*, XIII, 506.

sciences." [2] What Kant had to face was a generalized despair of metaphysical knowledge; he had not to stage a revolution; he found one, and to limit the losses was to him the shortest way to bring it to an end.

It is to be noted that hope came to Kant from the same source whence it had come to Descartes—from science itself. Descartes had been cheered by the dim light he could perceive in the chaos of contemporary geometry; Kant was now descrying in the night of all sciences, "the spring or, at least, the prelude of their near reform and of a new light, after an ill applied study had rendered them dark, confused, and useless". [3] There was so striking a contrast between the obvious senility of metaphysics and the flourishing condition of positive science in the second half of the eighteenth century that nothing short of a fundamental blunder made by the metaphysicians themselves could account for their perplexities. Not only had mathematics maintained its old reputation of solidity, but physics, with Newton, had far surpassed its own fame. True enough, philosophers were beginning to question the validity of scientific knowledge itself, but they were extending to science the philosophical despair that was an attitude of philosophers towards science, not of scientists. To sum up the situation in a few words: all was well with science, but something was wrong with philosophy. What was it?

After groping his way through the problem for about fifteen years, Kant thought that he had at last found the answer to that question. What defines science as a specific ideal of human knowledge is self-criticism. Perceiving as true what can be demonstrated, science dismisses all the rest as idle speculation, with the twofold result that it is always progressing, and always respected. Not so with metaphysics, ethics, or religion. These

[2] Kant, *Selections*, pp. 2–3.
[3] Ibid., p. 3.

disciplines do not ground their right to our respect on the
evidence of their conclusions, but on the importance of the
subjects with which they deal. As Kant saw it, such an attitude
was a thing of the past. The time had come when men could no
longer feel interested in any discipline for the sublimity of its
ambitions, but only for the soundness of its demonstrations.
"Our age is, in every sense of the word, the age of criticism,"
Kant concludes, "and everything must submit to it. Religion,
on the strength of its sanctity, and law, on the strength of its
majesty, try to withdraw themselves from it; but by so doing
they arouse just suspicions, and cannot claim that sincere respect
which reason pays to those only who have been able to stand its
free and open examination." [4]

As early as 1763, in his *Inquiry concerning the Clearness of
Principles in Natural Theology and in Ethics*, Kant was able to point
to the fundamental mistake that had brought about the chaotic
condition then prevailing in philosophy. It is interesting to note
that he introduced his own view on the question by a quotation
from Bishop Warburton (1698–1779), who was still alive at the
time Kant was quoting him. Warburton had said that nothing
had done more harm to philosophy than mathematics; to which
Kant immediately added that though the *application* of mathematics be highly desirable wherever it is possible, the *imitation*
of mathematics as a method of reasoning is very dangerous
when tried in cases in which it is impossible to use it. [5] Philosophy and, especially, metaphysics happen to be such cases. The
object of mathematics is simple: it is quantitative; the object of
metaphysics is manifold and infinitely varied: it is qualitative.
The relation of a trillion to unity is very easy to understand,

[4] Ibid.
[5] Immanuel Kant, *Untersuchung über die Deutlichkeit der Grundsätze der
natürlichen Theologie und der Moral*; in Kant, *Werke*, ed. K. Vorländer (Leipzig: F.
Meiner, n.d.), vol. 5, 1; p. 126.

whereas analyzing the concept of freedom into its ideological units is a task which no teacher of wisdom has ever been able to achieve. You cannot apply a method to that which is not its specific object; this, Kant concludes, is the reason why mathematical philosophies pass away, while mathematics remains: "Metaphysics no doubt represents the hardest of all human intuitions; only it has not yet been written." [6]

When Kant reached that conclusion, he found himself a perfectly free mind; for he was free from the mathematicism of Descartes, and he had not yet made any mistake of his own. How long he remained in that highly desirable state we shall never know. Perhaps a year, or perhaps two; but it is more than probable that Kant himself never knew when he was free, for no sooner had he cast off the method of Descartes than he proceeded to chain himself to another one. The first rule of the new method was, not to begin by definitions as mathematicians do, but to seek in each object what can be perceived in it with immediate evidence. Each one of these immediately evident perceptions expresses itself in a judgment. The second rule was to enumerate separately all such judgments, and to make sure that none of them is contained within another, after which the remaining judgments can safely be laid down as the fundamental axioms on which all subsequent knowledge has to be grounded.

The *Inquiry* of 1763, wherein the rules of the new method were defined for the first time, is still well worth reading for any one who wants to understand Kant's philosophy. We are here witnessing the birth of the *Critique of Pure Reason*, at a time when Kant himself did not know that it was being born. But it was. By substituting empirical observation for abstract definitions as the first stage of philosophical knowledge, Kant was not shifting from mathematics to philosophy, but from mathematics to physics. As Kant himself immediately concluded: "The true

[6] Ibid.

THE PHYSICISM OF KANT

method of metaphysics is fundamentally the same as that which
Newton has introduced into natural science, and which has
there yielded such fruitful results."[7] On the very day and at the
very minute in which he wrote these simple words, Kant crossed
the deadline beyond which lies the waste land where no metaphysics can live. A new standard science had been appointed the
supreme judge of philosophy. But metaphysics is no more capable of physical than of mathematical demonstration; in honour
and conscience the verdict of its new judge was obliged to be a
condemnation.

There is nothing easier for us than to see this, but Kant
himself could not guess it; he had to learn it by experience. Far
from having misgivings about the future of metaphysical
knowledge, Kant set about proving, in the same *Inquiry* of 1763,
that metaphysics was capable of reaching conclusions whose
certitude amounts to a total and absolute conviction. At that
time he could see no difference whatever between the evidence
of the first principles of metaphysics and that of any rational
knowledge other than mathematics.[8] On the strength of that
conviction, Kant undertook to prove in two pages that the first
principles of natural theology are susceptible of the highest
philosophical evidence (*sind der gröszten philosophischen Evidenz
fähig*); he then proceeded to prove in slightly more than three
pages, that the first principles of ethics, though not yet susceptible of such evidence, should at least be considered as competent to reach it in time.[9] The future author of the *Critique*
could entertain such illusions because he still believed in some
sort of intellectual intuition by which he could perceive the
various objects of philosophical speculation. Assuming that we
have an intellectual intuition of space, of time, of the soul, and
of God, the physical method of Newton would remain applicable to such objects. It took Kant some time to realize that the

[7] Ibid., p. 129.   [8] Ibid., pp. 135–41.   [9] Ibid., pp. 141–46.

only form of intuition by which actual reality can be grasped was sensible intuition. He was not yet quite clear about it in 1770, when he wrote his dissertation *On the Form and Principles of the Sensible and Intelligible World*, but the discovery was near. All that which really exists, Kant there said, is *irgendwo und irgend-wann* (in a certain place and in a certain time),[10] but he still did not see that his position entailed the rejection of metaphysics. On the contrary, he presented a very deep and enlightening analysis of what a metaphysical method should be. But he had no right to use it, and the time had now come when, in the mind of Kant, Newton was bound to be victorious.

Kant must have become aware of that fact about the beginning of the period of complete silence extending from 1770 to the publication of the *Critique* in 1781. It became clear at this time that he not only considered Newton's method as the only valid method, but also that he took the fact for granted that the real world was exactly as Newton had described it. The *Critique of Pure Reason* is a masterly description of what the structure of the human mind should be, in order to account for the existence of a Newtonian conception of nature, and assuming that conception to be true to reality. Nothing can show more clearly the essential weakness of physicism as a philosophical method. The pure reason described by Kant could last no longer than the Newtonian physics, which it was its proper function to justify. Newton considered the existence of an absolute space and an absolute time as necessarily required by his physics;[11] consequently, Kant decreed that man should be credited with two forms of sensible intuition: space and time, in which all the objects of knowledge are given to the understanding. So long as

[10] Immanuel Kant, *De mundi sensibilis . . .*, in *Werke*, vol. 5, 2; p. 125.

[11] I. Newton, *Mathematical Principles of Natural Philosophy and His System of the World*, ed. F. Cajori (Cambridge University Press, 1934), def. 8, scholium, nos. 1 and 2.

our mind applies itself to objects so given, it can form a scientifically valid knowledge; when, on the contrary, it applies itself to mere mental presentations of possible objects, it does not form concepts of things, but mere ideas; and as these ideas have no objects, they do not constitute a scientific knowledge, but that illusory speculation which we call metaphysics.

The technical language of Kant is hard to master, but it is a great help to those who have once mastered it. Let us say, therefore, with him that man has both sensibility and understanding; and that sensibility itself immediately perceives given reality through two *a priori* forms—space and time. These forms are said to be *a priori* because we do not derive them from things, but impose them on things; the forms of our knowledge of reality make it an object of knowledge, and are therefore also the forms of experience itself. Now our understanding is similarly equipped with *a priori* principles, such as the notions of substance, or of causality, by which it connects the various objects given to us in space and time. These principles of understanding—the so-called categories—are no more derived from things than are space and time themselves; as Kant says, they are transcendent in respect to things; they are not drawn from experience, they make it. This very property of the principles of understanding, being the condition of all sensible experience, is likely to be the source of a dangerous illusion. As they can deal with really perceived objects, so can they deal also with our concepts of things, as if those concepts were themselves real things—which they are not. The transcendent nature of the principles of understanding thus becomes the source of what Kant calls a transcendental illusion. It is an illusion because, instead of connecting real objects together by means of concepts, we are then connecting concepts together by means of abstract ideas, and yet we believe that we are still dealing with things. It is a *transcendental* illusion because its very possibility is due to the fact that the principles of human understanding are not borrowed from any particular objects, but transcendent in respect of all possible objects. When applied to sensible intuitions, these principles give birth to scientific knowledge, which is the proper work of understanding; when applied to scientific concepts, they beget abstract ideas, and metaphysics, which is the proper work of reason. Thus devoid of concrete objects, metaphysics is both necessary and empty. It is necessary, because we cannot stop our understanding or prevent it from thinking in a vacuum; thus converted into reason, it will prove everything. But it is also empty, precisely because it will prove everything: that there is no God and that there is a God; that there is no soul and that there is a soul; that the world has a unity and that the world has no unity. As soon as the principles of understanding "transcend all the limits of experience and therefore withdraw themselves from all empirical tests", reason is bound to become "the battlefield of these endless controversies which is called *metaphysic*." [12]

Kant has, in his *Prolegomena*, retraced for us the train of thought that brought him to these conclusions. It began when Hume had first broken what Kant there calls his "dogmatic slumber". By generalizing on Hume's observation concerning the principle of causality, he came to the conclusion that scientific knowledge would be absolutely impossible unless such principles were considered not as derived from experience, which had been Hume's mistake, but as originating in pure understanding.[13] By thus shifting from experience to the intellectual conditions of experience, Kant hoped to achieve a threefold result: first, to rescue science from scepticism; secondly, to rid metaphysics of its pretensions to the title of objective knowledge; thirdly, to make it clear that though a mere illusion, metaphysics was an inevitable illusion.

[12] Greene, *Kant Selections*, p. 2.

[13] Immanuel Kant, *Prolegomena*, trans. E. B. Bax (London, 1883), pp. 6–7.

Thus brought face to face with questions that could be neither ignored nor rationally answered, Kant had no choice but to find a justification, and an answer, outside the order of rational knowledge. A man whom Kant had read, and whose lesson he had carefully kept in mind, could at least suggest a possible way out of that maze. There is a deep symbolism in the mad personal hatred of Jean Jacques Rousseau for Hume; Rousseau's aversion was undoubtedly pathological, but it had selected its object with unerring accuracy. Hume's scepticism was the embodiment of reason as destructive of the very principles of philosophical knowledge and morality. Rousseau's passionate appeal to feeling, and to moral conscience, against the natural blindness of reason, was to Kant the revelation of a wholly independent and self-contained order of morality. "O conscience, conscience, thou divine instinct . . . thou infallible judge of good and evil . . .",[14] Rousseau had exclaimed in one of his most famous books; "Duty! Thou sublime and mighty name . . . ," Kant was to exclaim in his *Critique of Practical Reason*.[15] Failing a rational justification of morality, and granting that morality is inseparable from human life, there is nothing else to do but to take morality as a self-justifying fact. But when morality does not flow from what we know, it becomes free to prescribe for us what we ought to believe. By adopting Rousseau's moral feeling, Kant was obligating himself to accept Rousseau's natural theology, as rationally unjustifiable but morally necessary. When, after cutting loose from metaphysics, ethics begins to dictate its own metaphysics, moralism appears upon the scene. The Kantian principle of the primacy of practical reason is a clear case of moralism, one of the classical escapes from scepticism for those who despair of philosophy.

[14] J. J. Rousseau, *Profession of Faith of a Savoyard Vicar*, trans. O. Schreiner (New York, 1889), p. 64.

[15] Greene, *Kant Selections*, p. 330.

The primacy of practical reason means that reason has to subscribe to a certain set of affirmations, though they be rationally undemonstrable, because their truth is postulated by the exigencies of moral life. The fundamental fact in morality is the feeling that certain things ought to be done, while certain other things ought to be avoided. Reason can and does teach us what we ought to do, but that we ought to do certain things is a fact which can be observed and described, but cannot be demonstrated. That fact's true name is duty. We call duty the necessity, recognized by any thoughtful mind, of acting, not only in conformity with the moral law, but from pure respect for moral law, independently of the pain or pleasure we may feel in so doing.

The first implication contained in the fact of duty is that we should be conceived as able to perform it. An act of pure duty, without any personal motives, is perhaps a psychological impossibility; but the desire to obey moral law because it is the law must at least enter into the composition of our moral decisions. Unless the word *ought* is to be wholly meaningless, what we ought, we also can. Now, to be able to determine oneself according to a certain law is to be free. Consequently, freedom must be presupposed as a property of the will of all rational beings.[16] Moreover, since man is not free as a member of the world of sense, which understanding is bound to conceive as strictly determined, it is to be supposed that man, as a moral agent, is a member of another world, purely intelligible, where no sensible motives can interfere with the exigencies of morality. We are thereby confronted with the necessity of accepting, as inseparably connected with practical reason, certain theoretical positions wholly "withdrawn from any possible insight of speculative reason."[17] The will to act from pure

[16] Ibid., p. 385.
[17] Ibid., p. 356.

respect for duty postulates the possibility of a perfect moral order; if that order is impossible in this life, it has to be possible in another; hence the soul is immortal. Again, such a perfect moral life, undisturbed by the ceaseless strife between reason and sensibility, must needs possess happiness—happiness, not as the end of morality, but as flowing from it. And what is moral law as cause of eternal happiness if not God? Thus God is postulated by practical reason, which means that reason has to posit His existence, although speculative, or theoretical reason can know nothing about it.[18] Obviously, the primacy of practical reason is more than an abstract formula; ethics is now charged with the obligation of solving metaphysical problems without consulting metaphysics. What had been held as true by the metaphysicians can neither be proved, nor disproved; but practical reason needs it; therefore, it is safe against the possible attacks of scepticism, its safety being fully protected by its rational irresponsibility.

A physicism supplemented by a moralism was neither an unknown nor an impossible position; but it had its difficulties. Kant had conceived his whole doctrine in such a way as to satisfy two postulates: the physics of Newton is possible, moral duty is possible. A philosophy thus conceived usually succeeds in carrying out its program, but as it is entirely governed by its postulates as by external requirements, its component elements necessarily remain more or less unrelated. In spite of his efforts to multiply the internal connections between the several parts of his doctrine, Kant never succeeded in giving it an organic unity. It was not a question of cleverness, or of genius; the thing simply could not be done. Having cut loose from metaphysics, Kantism could not grow from within like a tree; because it did not germinate internally, but copied models outside, Kantism could be only a set of mutually unrelated adaptations.

[18] Ibid., p. 360.

When other great minds surveyed it, Kantism appeared as a lofty structure, but devoid of internal necessity. There was a first chasm, within the *Critique of Pure Reason* itself, between sensibility and understanding. These two sources of knowledge are not only distinct, but heterogeneous, yet they belong to the same mind. Is it conceivable that no common root can be found within the very mind from which they spring? If there is none, how is it that, wholly distinct, they succeed in working together, as they do successfully in mathematics and physics? Kant, of course, had seen the question, but answer it he would not, and could not. He would not because that was not a question for criticism, which deals only with the *a priori* conditions of human knowledge, but for a metaphysic, which deals with the ultimate causes of reality. But he could not, because ascribing to sensibility and understanding a common origin would have wiped out their distinction; empirical knowledge would then become impossible, there would be no difference between physics and metaphysics, in short a metaphysical idealism would be the final result of the *Critique of Pure Reason*.

But there was another chasm, perhaps wider and deeper, between the two *Critiques*. It shows ignorance of the point in dispute to charge Kant with having unsaid in the second one what he had said in the first. Had he done so, we would not even open his books. What was postulated by the *Critique of Practical Reason* had never been turned by Kant into an object of understanding. To posit God as required by the fact of morality is not to *know* that God exists. The difficulty was more deeply hidden in the doctrine. According to the *Critique of Pure Reason*, nature is a system of substances strictly determined by the principle of causality; whatever it may be in itself, we cannot conceive it differently. The *Critique of Practical Reason*, on the other hand, contends that duty postulates an autonomous free will, capable of self-determination and free from natural necessity. This, indeed, is the meeting point of the two *Critiques*: because the world of sensible intuition is submitted to necessity, no sensible motives can enter a moral act without destroying at one and the same time both its liberty and its morality. The ethical strictness of Kant, which led him to consider pleasure and duty as incompatible, was not in him a mere consequence of Spener's pietism (we would say here, puritanism), it was imposed on him as a necessary consequence of his first *Critique*. Now nothing follows from the fact that a doctrine is inconsistent, but when a doctrine begins to heap up arbitrary difficulties by reason of its very consistency, one has a right to wonder what is wrong with it. Here, indeed, the difficulties were appalling, since they entailed a radical anti-nomy between man as living in the order of nature, and man as acting in the order of morality. After all, they are bound to be the same man. For what reason, in consequence of what un-told original sin, is man as a free citizen of the intelligible world condemned to live in the strictly determined world of matter? If he himself is the cause of that determination, why should his own understanding erect causal necessity as a perma-nent hindrance to his own free will? If we make nature to be what it is, why do we make it to be an obstacle to our own morality? As a matter of fact, this dramatic struggle in us between the law of nature and the law of morality looks a little too much like an Epistle to the Romans in philosophical garb. Having refused to hold metaphysical conclusions on metaphysi-cal grounds, Kant had been necessarily dragged from metaphys-ics to ethics, and from ethics to theology.

He lived long enough to discern at least from afar what would have been the normal outcome of his philosophical career. As we read the notes published in 1920 by Erich Adikes under the title of *Kant's Opus Posthumum*, we are led to suspect that, had he lived a little longer, even Kant might have finally given way to some sort of mystical urge. Having proved in his youth that we know nothing about God, old Kant was beginning to suspect that he himself might be God: "God is not a being outside me, but merely a thought in me. God is the morally practical self-legislative reason. Therefore, only a God in me, about me, and over me." A God who is both in us and above us, as moral law itself, is either nothing, or the legislative power of practical reason in us. "God can be sought only in us", says Kant, and further: "There is a Being in me which, though distinct from me, stands to me in relations of causal efficacy, and which, itself free, *i.e.*, not dependent upon the law of nature in space and time, inwardly directs me (justifies or condemns), and I, as man, am myself this Being. It is not a substance outside me; and what is strangest of all, the causality is a determination to action in freedom, and not as a necessity of nature." [19] What a metaphysico-theological maze! Newton would have been surprised to see such results flowing from his method. Philosophers who have been misled by the lure of positive science always end their lives in a queer world—that is a punishment for their mistake; but it never occurs to them that it is their philosophy that is queer—that is a reward for their honesty.

Yet, there is for them still another punishment—their disciples. At the beginning, master and disciple find nothing but pure joy in their mutual intercourse. Who can read without emotion those pages of his Diary where the young Fichte tells us how, penniless and unknown, he went to the great Kant and asked from him both advice and money. Kant had no money to give, but he gave advice. In order to attract his attention, Fichte had written a *Critique of All the Revelations*, and sent it to Kant as a letter of recommendation. What joy when Kant declared that it should be printed! Fichte wanted to revise it; but Kant said: "It is well written." "Can this be true?" Fichte asks himself in his

[19] Ibid., pp. 373–74.

Diary, "and yet Kant says so." [20] What usually brings such friendships to an end is that, whereas a master holds his conclusions as conclusions, his disciples receive them as premises, with the consequence that their own conclusions can never be the master's conclusions.

In the particular case of Kant, the gap left open by the *Critique of Pure Reason* between sensibility and understanding was obviously asking for a bridge. The move was so necessary that Reinhold had made it as early as 1789. When Fichte took up the same problem, he solved it in such a way that even Reinhold took off his hat and bowed to the new solution. But Kant kept his hat on and grumbled. Such as Fichte conceived it, the will of the *Critique of Practical Reason* was obviously enjoying its primacy and, instead of merely supplementing the *Critique of Pure Reason*, it was rebuilding it. In his *Fundamental Principles of the Science of Knowledge* (1794), Fichte had attempted to deduce both sense and understanding from the Ego, or "I", considered as their source. The Ego itself is essentially a will, which finds itself limited from without by the material world. In order to free itself from that limitation, the Ego brings forth the world of sense and understanding as a substitute for an otherwise unintelligible reality. Of course, the Ego is still limited, but since it has created the new obstacle, it is at least the master of its own limitation. On the strength of that first reduction, it becomes easy to reconcile even the two *Critiques*. There is no opposition between the necessity of nature and the freedom of the will, since the freedom of the will is the cause of that necessity. And just as the Ego has created nature, it can always remodel it and liberate itself more and more from that self-imposed limit by giving it more and more intelligibility. Our progressive knowledge of nature is our progressive liberation from it.

[20] H. Heine, *De l'Allemagne depuis Luther*, part 2; in *Revue des deux mondes* 4 (15 Dec. 1834): 654.

After reaching these conclusions, Fichte had still another problem to solve. How is it that the world of sense and of understanding, created by the Ego, happens to be the same for all of us? His answer was that the agreement among the products of individual wills was the result of the One Eternal Infinite Will, which creates the world *in* our minds, and *by* our minds. This unexpected offspring of the *Critique of Practical Reason* was a very interesting philosophical monster—a Spinozism of the will. After Rousseau's hymn to conscience and Kant's hymn to duty, there naturally follows Fichte's hymn to the will: "Sublime and Living Will! named by no name, compassed by no thought! I may well raise my soul to Thee, for Thou and I are not divided. Thy voice sounds within me, mine resounds in Thee." [21] Unless the philosophy of Kant means that, wrote Fichte to Schelling in 1799, it is meaningless; but another Kantian, Forberg, was writing on his side: "Fichte goes about affirming, repeating, that his system is no other than that of Kant. Yet I have it on the best authority and am in a position to give assurance, that the founder of the *Critique* is himself of another opinion." [22]

At the time when Fichte was thus disavowed by Kant, the young Schelling was Fichte's favourite disciple. When he published his *System of Transcendental Idealism* in 1800, Schelling was convinced that his book was but a confirmation of his master's doctrine. He merely wanted to know why the will is so ready to limit itself by a material obstacle. And his answer was that the will is an artist whose intelligible ideas need to embody themselves in a material reality. The world is a masterpiece and the philosophy of art, or esthetics, is the keystone of philosophy. The originality of the new doctrine became apparent in 1801,

[21] J. G. Fichte, *The Vocation of Man*, bk. 3, 3; in B. Rand, ed., *Modern Classical Philosophers* (Boston: Houghton Mifflin, [1924]), p. 530.

[22] X. Léon, *Fichte et son temps* (Paris: A. Colin, 1922), vol. 1, p. 415.

when Schelling published his *Philosophy of Nature*. In 1802, Fichte wrote to Schad that Schelling had *never* understood his philosophy. Schelling was very much surprised; but he was to feel quite indignant when, in 1806, he had to charge Fichte with having stolen a long series of propositions from his own *Philosophy of Nature*. What a triumph! Schelling had so correctly deduced these conclusions from Fichte's own principles that, four years later, Fichte was obliged to borrow them from the very book which he had publicly disavowed.[23]

The man who was to bring some sort of order into this chaos was Hegel. Author of a treatise *On the Difference between the System of Fichte and That of Schelling* (1801), he was intimately acquainted with both systems and could reasonably hope to find a way out of these contradictions. He discovered it, and revealed it to the world in his *Phenomenology of Mind* (1807). Many years later, lying on his death bed, Hegel was to say with some melancholy: "Only one man ever understood me; and he did not understand me either."

Confronted with the problem of reconciling so many varieties of metaphysics, Hegel was in very much the same situation as Nicolaus Cusanus in the fifteenth century. After describing what he calls the state of "unhappy", or "contrite", consciousness, which arises from such contradictions, he proceeded to show that there are typical attitudes in philosophy, objectively describable as mental phenomena, and whose exclusive self-assertion was the root of the evil. Each typical attitude is bound to assert itself as true; and to be sure it is true, but it is not *the* truth. "The truth is the whole", and the whole itself is nature, which reaches "its completeness through the process of its own development".[24] Having established this first conclusion, Hegel went straight to the source of all these metaphysical contradictions

[23] Ibid., vol. 2, pp. 501–2.
[24] J. Loewenberg, ed., *Hegel Selections* (New York: Scribner's, 1929), p. 16.

and, having found it in the Kantian antinomies of pure reason, with deep insight he tried to extract from them a remedy for the philosophical strife which they had caused. Nature is but the external manifestation of an absolute and eternal Idea, which expresses itself in space and time according to a dialectical law. As the One of Plotinus, the Idea which thus "alienates" itself in nature is finding its way back through the successive moments of its dialectical realization. Each term of a concrete antinomy thus becomes a necessary step to the final self-reassertion of the Idea. That was a master stroke, but it entailed the open recognition of the fact that contradiction was at the very root of reality. Contradiction had to be everywhere in things in order to turn the contradictions of philosophy into a true picture of reality.

At first sight, there was nothing alarming in such an attitude. It was but a "learned ignorance" and one more case of dogmatically established scepticism. But when Hegel justified his position in his *Encyclopedia of Exact Sciences* (1817), and later on in his *Philosophy of Law* (1821), the impact of the new doctrine on practical life was at once apparent. The truth is the whole, but the progressive realization of the whole supposes a progressive overcoming of all the partial contradictions from which its unity shall spring. So long as we are dealing with abstract reasoning, it is a harmless dialectical game, to posit a thesis, which raises an antithesis, both of which soon disappear in the unity of a synthesis. It is a pleasure to watch the synthesis, now turned into a thesis, rouse again its own antithesis, and so on indefinitely. I even grant that there is a metaphysical emotion in watching the progressive advance of the leading Idea towards its own actualization. But it should not be forgotten that contradiction is the very stuff of which such a world is made. Intelligible as part of the whole, each particular thing is unintelligible by itself; rather, by itself, it is but a self-affirmation grounded on the negation of the rest, and denied by the rest. If the realization of the Idea is the march of God through the world, the path of the Hegelian God is strewn with ruins.

In a metaphysical system wherein the whole of reality is included, such a doctrine does not limit itself to ideas, it applies to things. The conflict between philosophies then becomes a conflict between philosophers; the "battlefield of endless controversies" described by Kant under the name of metaphysics is, therefore, a battlefield of men, where each philosopher, as a particular moment of the universal law, has to be the antithesis of another, until both are resolved into the synthesis of a third. That which is contradiction between ideas is war between men, and in such a world, war is by no means an accident. It is law. The progressive actualization of the world-leading Idea entails the submission of individuals to the unity of the State. The ideal State itself is progressively working out its unity through the necessary oppositions between particular states. The State, then, in Hegel's own words: "is the march of God through the world",[25] and there again the path of God is strewn with ruins.

It could not possibly be otherwise. In a doctrine where philosophies are but abstract expressions of the civilizations from which they spring, these civilizations themselves express only the particular ideas of the corresponding states. Now, as term of an antinomy, each state is an individual, and "in individuality negation is essentially contained." Even a confederation of states, "as an individuality, must create an opposition, and so beget an enemy". In such a world, the concrete expression of the dialectical force which opposes its many terms is the armed soldier: "The military class", says Hegel, "is the class of universality."[26] There is something uncanny about a philosophy in which, as Hegel proves, even the gun is not a chance invention, but the necessary discovery of the impersonal weapon which allows states, taken as wholes, to carry on impersonal

[25] Ibid., p. 443.   [26] Ibid., p. 465.

wars against other states, also taken as wholes. The liberal-minded professors who teach Hegel's relativism in universities seem to believe that it is a school of toleration, where students can learn that there is a place for everything because everything is right in its own way. That is not Hegelian relativism; it is philosophical indifferentism. The dogmatic relativism of Hegel teaches something very different, and it is that, taken by itself, no particular thing can rightly assert itself except by destroying another, and until it is itself destroyed. "War", says Hegel, "is not an accident", but an element "whereby the ideal character of the particular receives its right and reality".[27] These are really and truly murderous ideas, and all the blood for which they are responsible has not yet been shed. Yet they are the last word of Hegelianism and the necessary conclusion of a school which, confining reason to the sphere of pure science, enslaved philosophy to the blind tyranny of the will.

[27] Ibid., p. 464.

CHAPTER X

THE SOCIOLOGISM OF A. COMTE

On the third day of the month of Dante in the sixty-sixth year of the Great Western Crisis, the French philosopher Auguste Comte was completing the list of the one hundred fifty volumes that make up his *Positivist Library*. In the *Positivist Calendar*, the third day of the month of Dante is the feast of Rabelais. Yet the *Positivist Library* was not a joke; it was a catalogue of the books which it is necessary and sufficient to read in order to acquire all the knowledge required by our social needs. Thirty volumes of poetry, thirty volumes of science, sixty volumes of history, and thirty volumes of what Comte called synthesis, make one hundred fifty volumes. The philosophical works in that library are listed among the thirty volumes of *Synthesis*, and do not comprise more than four or five volumes. Plato is not represented; nor are Leibniz, Spinoza, Locke, Kant; but one volume is reserved for the *Politics* and *Ethics* of Aristotle, a second volume for Descartes' *Discourse on Method*, preceded by Bacon's *Novum Organum* and followed by Diderot's *Interpretation of Nature*; Pascal's *Thoughts*, followed by those of Vauvenargues, and the *Counsels of a Mother* by Mme. de Lambert make up a third volume; the main works of Auguste Comte himself provide the matter for a fourth volume, and Hume's *Philosophical Essays* form an essential part of the last. At the origins of Comte, as at the origins of Kant, stands Hume.

Born in 1798, educated at the college of Montpellier, then a
pupil at the Polytechnic School, whence he was expelled because of subversive political opinions, Comte had been confronted, from early youth, with the social consequences of the
eighteenth-century philosophy. His starting point was not only
the breakdown of classical metaphysics, as it had been with
Kant, but also the breakdown of the very social structure which,
for several centuries, had both sheltered that form of Philosophy and been sheltered by it. Destroyed by the Revolution, the
France of the Kings had gone; but the Revolution itself had
failed to establish a new order of political life, and after the
glorious and tragic episode of Napoleon's Empire, the country
seemed to be headed for a return to the past. The Kings were
coming back, and were pretending to rule France as though
nothing had happened since 1789. Comte's whole career was to
be dominated by the settled conviction that after the Revolution a restoration was indeed necessary, but that at the same time
the past was irrevocably dead. Comte's thought is wholly contained in his adverbs; "irrevocably" means that the death sentence which was passed upon the old social régime could not
possibly be revoked by men, because it expressed a historic and
objective fatality.

This being the case, a restoration had to be a reorganization;
that is, the building of a new type of social order according to
new principles. Comte was not the only one to feel concerned
with the problem: De Bonald and de Maistre, Fourier, and
Saint-Simon had already suggested various remedies for the
political anarchy of the times; but Comte approached the situation as a born philosopher for whom the whole problem was
essentially a problem of ideas, solution of which must necessarily be a philosophical solution. To him, social and political
anarchy was but the outward manifestation of the state of
mental anarchy that had been prevailing ever since the old ways

of thinking had become obsolete. Although those old ways were gone, no new way had come to take their place, or to play, in a new social order, the part which metaphysics had played in the old. That was why no new social order could arise. When men do not know what to think, they cannot know how to live. Comte would show men how to live by teaching them what to think. This was, no doubt, a high ambition, but one from which Comte never shrank, and which he ultimately felt had been wholly fulfilled. From 1830 to 1842 the new reformer had published the six volumes of his *System of Positive Philosophy*; now he could inscribe the words of the French poet Alfred de Vigny as a motto for his *System of Positive Politics*: "What is a great life? A thought of youth fulfilled in maturity." Yet Comte's great life was but one more great dream, for an evil genius had attended the birth of his philosophy; and once again it was a dazzling scientific idea: not mathematics, or physics, but sociology. Comte's philosophy was to be a Sociologism.

The choice of a new standard science can not be considered as an entirely arbitrary decision in this case any more than it can in that of Abailard, Descartes or Kant. Taken at any one moment of its evolution, a society is always defined by three fundamental elements whose mutual relations are unchangeable, and which Comte described as follows. First of all, lying at the very root of each social group there is a definite state of intellectual knowledge. It is an obvious fact that a society in which fetishism reigns supreme is wholly different, in every element of its internal structure, from a society in which monotheism prevails; and that such a society, in its turn, must needs be different from another in which a monotheistic theology has been superseded by scientific knowledge. A social group is essentially constituted of families united by the same intellectual conception of the world. In connection with, and determined by, this factor of knowledge, there always appears a second

factor, which is a definite form of political government. It flows
from the first; for government is but the natural reaction of the
whole upon its parts, and since the whole is the common
intellectual outlook which ties together the members of the
community, any political régime is bound to express the belief
from which it springs. Finally there is the third element, which
also flows from the first two: a specific literary, artistic, commer-
cial and industrial civilization, born of both the ruling belief
and the political régime of that society. An easy way to remember this part of Comte's doctrine is to reverse it. In that case we
have Marxism, with a definite industrial situation at the root of
the system, whence springs a political régime, which is, in turn,
attended by its religious, artistic and philosophical justifications.
Reverse it again, and we are back to Comtism, with a definite
state of knowledge at the root of the system, an equally definite
industrial situation at the top, and, in between, a specific form
of art.[1] In short, just as Marxism is an historical materialism,
Comtism was an historical idealism, in which the whole structure of a given society, at a given time, is strictly determined by
the communion of beliefs on which it is founded. The ideological cohesion of these beliefs is one and the same with the
social cohesion.

   Such being the static structure of all social groups, let us now
consider the dynamic law of their development. Given the
position adopted by Comte, the development of human societies had to be conceived necessarily as that of a certain idea or,
rather, of a certain spirit. In point of fact, Comte conceived it
as the slow but almost regular process by which what he calls
"the positive spirit" has reached the complete awareness of its
own nature. What we call political or social history, together
with the history of art, literature, or philosophy, tells us of mere

[1] A. Comte, *Positive Philosophy*, trans. H. Martineau (New York, 1868),
bk. 6, chap. 11, pp. 685–86.

episodes incidental to the great central epic of the positive spirit. For this spirit existed from the very beginning when the human mind was still explaining all phenomena by the wills of deities. That was the so-called "theological state"; but the proof that the positive spirit was already there lies in the fact that, even during that primitive state, there was a progressive rationalization of theological beliefs, from fetishism to polytheism, and from polytheism to monotheism. This is so true that the transition from monotheism to the second state was almost imperceptible. This second is the "metaphysical state", in which abstract causes are substituted for gods, or for God, as an ultimate explanation of the world. In point of fact, says Comte, metaphysics is but the ghost of dead theologies. Yet it is a necessary interlude during which positive science reaches its complete maturity. Now the positive spirit is essentially the spirit of positive science, which feels no interest in gods, or in causes, because it is never concerned with the "why", but only with the "how". Laws, not causes, are the only valid explanations for all knowable facts. Such is the third and last of the three stages through which all human conceptions, and therefore all human societies, have to pass necessarily in the course of their development. The famous "law of the three states" was completely formulated by Comte as early as 1822, and was to remain the basis of his whole system: every branch of human knowledge successively passes through the theological or fictitious state, the metaphysical or abstract state, and the scientific or positive state.

   The discovery of that universal law was not only the foundation of Comte's sociology, but it also offered him the complete explanation of the social crisis in which he was living, and a safe means of bringing it to a close. Supposing a society in which theology reigns supreme, a corresponding social order is not only possible but necessary. The Middle Ages, for which Comte always entertained a romantic admiration, were a clear proof of the fact. A revealed truth taught by theology and received through faith was bound to bring about a theocracy in which the popes ruled the priests, and the priests the kings, and the kings the lords, and so on, in accordance with the laws of the feudal system. To this were added a Christian art and a Christian literature, so that the whole structure of mediæval society was permeated, quickened from within, and kept together by the same theological spirit. Not so in Europe at the beginning of the nineteenth century. Owing to the necessary growth of the positive spirit, mediæval theology had become a thing of the past. In due time it had given way to the metaphysical state, whose rise had been attended by the absolute monarchies of the seventeenth century, their art and their literatures. But the positive spirit marches on; its advance must bring about the disruption of the metaphysico-monarchical order, and this had, in fact, been the effect of the French Revolution. Metaphysics had now become obsolete, even as theology before it. Hume and the critical spirit of the eighteenth century had revealed its complete vanity to the world. The difficulty, however, was that the positive spirit had failed so far to produce a completely rounded interpretation of the world, whose general acceptance would become the common bond of a new social order. Who was to do for the positive state in the nineteenth century what St. Thomas Aquinas had done for the theological state in the Middle Ages, and what Descartes had done for the metaphysical state in the seventeenth century? The world was waiting for a prophet whose mission it would be to usher in the last and final age in which humanity was to live forever. Of course, you know the name of the prophet—Auguste Comte. But how was he to do it?

Gifted as he was with an immense power for abstract speculation, Comte began by showing why positive science had failed to provide mankind with a systematic view of the world. True, there were already many positive sciences, but there still remained one order of facts whose interpretation was purely metaphysical: the order of social and political facts. In a time when no one would have dreamt of dealing with matter without resorting to physics, chemistry, or biology, it was still the general belief that social facts obey no laws and that, consequently, any man can make any society to be what he wants it to be, provided only he has the power to do so. Hence the illusions of the belated conservatives, or of the reckless revolutionists, who draw plans for ideal and dreamlike cities without asking what the laws of social life actually are. Therefore the first task of our reformer was necessarily to extend the spirit of positive science to social facts; that is, to create the still missing science, sociology. By doing so, Comte hoped to achieve a twofold result. First, by taking politics out of its metaphysical and chaotic state and turning it into a positive science, he would initiate an era of social and political engineering. We can act upon matter because we know its laws; when we know social laws, it will be at least as easy to act upon societies. Next, having thus extended the positive spirit to the only class of facts still outside of its jurisdiction, Comte could proceed to build up a perfectly consistent system of human knowledge and to procure the scientific dogma required for the new social order. By driving metaphysics out of its last position, Comte had ensured the perfect uniformity of the whole of human knowledge; all ideas, all laws, being equally positive, could henceforth be reduced to a homogeneous system, whose ideological cohesion would be the social cohesion of humanity.

All well and good. Even realizing how delusive it is, I cannot withhold my sympathy for the pure enthusiasm of these young philosophers. There is nothing on earth more beautiful than the birth of an idea when, in its pristine novelty, it throws a new light on our old world. Whereas everything was out of joint, now everything has found its place, because logic revealed itself to Abailard, mathematics to Descartes, physics to Kant, or because the young Comte now discovers the science of social facts. But why should each one of them be so certain that he has at the same time discovered philosophy itself? We are now, I hope, much nearer to the answer of that important question than we were at the beginning of our inquiry, but before giving it we must pursue the sociological experiment of Comte and his successors to its bitter end.

There was nothing wrong in discovering sociology. A new science is always welcome, and though this science is not the most secure, it may in time become a very decent branch of knowledge, especially if it takes into account the fact that not animal groups, but human societies, are its object. The only trouble with Comte was that, after having conceived the possibility of such a science, he thought that he could achieve it all alone; and that, having more or less achieved it, he asked it to solve all philosophical problems. First of all, he asked it to make philosophy itself possible by reorganizing all human knowledge from within.

There is nothing arbitrary in the ventures of a philosopher, even when he is mistaken. Comte was in quest of a scientific dogma whose common acceptance would bring forth a new social order. At first glance, the whole body of scientific knowledge now completed by the discovery of sociology seemed to be in itself a sufficient answer to the question. Science was replacing metaphysics in human reason; the only thing to do was to wait patiently for the inevitable day when, the old ideas having completely vanished, all men would spontaneously adopt the same scientific outlook on the world. Then would the new social order naturally arise as a necessary offspring of the new mental unity.

This was a very tempting solution because it was so simple; but Comte never accepted it, and for a very profound reason.

Science, whereby he meant the body of all positive sciences from mathematics to biology and sociology, is an objective representation of what the world actually is; but if we look at it from the point of view of science, the world has no unity of its own. Every scientist naturally has the temper and the tastes of a specialist; he first specializes in his own science; then he begins to specialize in a special part of that same science, and he goes on restricting his outlook on the world until, at last, turning his back on all the other sciences and their results, he finds himself engaged in the exhaustive investigation of some microscopic detail which has now become the whole of reality so far as he is concerned. This is the reason why, already in Comte's time, the teaching of the sciences in universities was absolutely chaotic, no one science being related to any other, and each professor holding his own bit of the world, as a dog his bone, with an unfriendly look at those who would touch it. In short, the natural tendency of science is not towards unity, but towards an ever more complete disintegration. Such facts point to an intrinsic heterogeneity of the world. True enough, everything is strictly determined, but the sum total of all those determinations does not make up a whole. Now, even though the physical world, as expressed by positive science, is not a coherent system of things, yet a society, to be a real society, must be a coherent system of men; this is impossible, however, unless its fundamental outlook on the world has some sort of unity. A primitive tribe is a whole because of its fetish; a theological civilization is one because of its god; a metaphysical society is swayed by the Author of Nature; but if it has nothing to live by except science and its disconnected laws, society will inevitably find itself condemned to a state of a complete disintegration; in fact, it will not be a society at all.

This train of thought led Comte to the conclusion that, although all the material of the future dogma had to be borrowed

from science, science alone could never produce the dogma itself. What was needed now, above and beyond positive science,
was a positive philosophy—a strictly unified system of thoughts,
each of which would be a scientifically demonstrated truth, and
all of which, taken together, would constitute a completely
rounded explanation of reality. All the data of the problem with
which we have been dealing from the beginning of this book are
here before our eyes, numbered and defined by Comte with an
amazing lucidity. Men no longer believe in theology; they also
know that metaphysics is a thing of the past; yet they need a
philosophy; but the only thing that remains for them is not philosophy, but science; hence the problem: how will science give us
a philosophy? That which makes Comte's case highly significant
is the fact that, having thus asked the question, he was clear-
sighted enough to give it the right answer: science alone will not
and cannot give us a philosophy. Unless we look at science from
a non-scientific point of view, our positive knowledge will never
be reduced to unity. Now if we do not look at things from the
point of view of things, as science does, the only alternative is to
look at them from the point of view of man. To express the
same idea in Comte's own terminology, let us say that since no
"objective synthesis" is attainable, the only possible synthesis is a
"subjective synthesis". Consequently, philosophy has to be the
subjective synthesis of positive knowledge from the point of
view of man and his social needs.

Being compelled to take that fatal leap, Comte did it as
scientifically as possible. First he pointed out the fact that the
youngest of all positive sciences, sociology, was the science of
man. Nor was it by chance that the science of man had been the
last to be discovered; for the positive knowledge of societies, which
are the most complex of all facts, presupposes the positive knowledge of all other facts, and hence all the other sciences had to be
discovered before sociology. But then, and for the same reason,

human social life is the only fact from which we can view all the others with the certainty of not overlooking any that is fundamental. Thus science itself invites us to unify positive knowledge from the point of view of humanity. The consequences of this subjective interpretation of science in Comte's doctrine are simply amazing. In order to draw a subjective synthesis from positive knowledge, Comte had first to reduce it to what he calls the theoretical and abstract sciences: mathematics, astronomy, physics, chemistry, biology, and sociology. Such sciences deal with laws, not with things; should we take into account such concrete sciences as mineralogy, botany or zoology, we would again lose ourselves in the heterogeneous character of reality. Let us therefore stick to the abstract sciences and eliminate all the rest as unfit for a philosophical synthesis. From the point of view of science itself this was, of course, an arbitrary move. In his book, *The Classification of the Sciences* (1864), H. Spencer raised a strong protest against the "anthropocentric" character of Comte's classification.[2] Spencer was right; how could one, in the name of science, eliminate half the sciences for the benefit of the other half? But Comte was not wrong: if you do nothing to science, how are you to turn it into a philosophy?

Having proceeded to this drastic reduction in the number of the sciences, Comte found himself confronted with the still more difficult task of reducing those that remain to a synthetic unity. To ask sciences themselves to restrict their activities to what furthers the social needs of man would have been a waste of time. Science cares not for man, but for things, and to the pure scientist it is just as important to know one thing as it is to know another, provided only that it falls within the scope of his own science. The consequence was that every one of the fundamental sciences themselves had to be reorganized from within to suit the

[2] L. Lévy-Bruhl, *The Philosophy of Auguste Comte*, trans. F. Harrison (New York: Putnam, 1903), p. 54.

needs of the philosopher. Comte called this operation the "regeneration" of a science, by which he meant: to cause the spiritual rebirth of science by infusing into it a proper dose of subjective spirit. Unfortunately the subjectively regenerated sciences looked so queer that the scientists failed to recognize them in their new positive garb. Astronomy, for example, was reduced to the study of the solar system, because this is the system in which man happens to live; as to so-called sidereal astronomy, Comte branded it as a "grave scientific aberration". Later on he submitted astronomy to a still more drastic reduction by restricting it to the study of the earth and of the other celestial bodies in their relation to the earth. For the earth is *our* planet, the *human* planet, and therefore our astronomical studies should be concentrated around it. In the same way chemistry should be simplified: first, by supposing that all composite bodies are made up of two simple bodies, or of any number of other complex bodies, which may in turn be resolved into two simpler ones; next, by cutting off the study of practically all those innumerable chemical bodies which are unworthy of our attention.

When a science had gone through this process of regeneration, what little of it was left had still to face the last, and by far the most dangerous, of its trials: its actual incorporation into the subjective synthesis. As Comte had said at the end of his *System of Positive Philosophy*: "The essentially philosophical point of view finally assigns no other end to the study of natural laws than that of providing us with such a representation of the external world as will meet the essential requirements of our intelligence, insofar as is consistent with the degree of accuracy required by the whole of our practical needs." [3] As soon as he set about to build up his subjective

[3] A. Comte, *Cours de philosophie positive*, vol. 6, p. 642. Comte, himself, suggested later that "Système de philosophie positive" would have been a better title.

synthesis, it became apparent that practical needs would not
tolerate much intellectual accuracy. After all, Comte had now
reached a point at which reason had nothing more to say. Were
a scientist to say to him: "Since you are so fond of the spirit of
science, which you call the positive spirit, why does not positivism let science alone? As a scientist, I strongly object to any
one tampering with science on any ground whatsoever, even in
the highest interests of man. You do not want science to be the
handmaid of theology; I do not want it to be the handmaid of
humanity, for the result will be the same in either case, science
will be destroyed." What rational arguments could Comte have
opposed to such an attitude? Absolutely none. The ultimate
reason why science should be regenerated to suit the social
needs of humanity cannot possibly be found within science
itself; the less you interfere with science, the better it feels; and
the more you love science, the less you feel like sacrificing it to
anything else. The only justification for such a venture could be
not a reason, but a feeling; in point of fact, it could be no other
feeling than love for humanity. By thus making love the ultimate foundation of positivism, Comte was repeating, in his
own way, and for reasons that were entirely his own, Kant's
famous move decreeing the primacy of practical reason. Obviously Comte owed nothing to Kant, but, left as he was with the
task of contriving a philosophy without metaphysics, he had no
choice other than some sort of moralism. Comte's moralism
was to be the sentimentalism which asserts itself at the beginning of his *Discours sur l'ensemble du Positivisme*: "The necessity
of assigning with exact truth the place occupied by the intellect
and by the heart in the organization of human nature and of
society leads to the decision that affection must be the central
point of the synthesis." And again: "The foundation of social
science bears out the statement made at the beginning of this
work, that the intellect under Positivism accepts its proper

position of subordination to the heart. The recognition of this, which is the subjective principle of Positivism, renders the construction of a complete system of human life possible." [4] The initial condemnation of metaphysics in the name of science, posited by such philosophies as the only type of rational knowledge, invariably culminates in the capitulation of science itself to some irrational element. This is a necessary law, inferable from philosophical experience, and wholly confirmed by what is often called Comte's second career.

The popular explanation of his sentimental subjectivism is, of course, quite different. When, after going through the six volumes of the *System of Positive Philosophy*, the reader stumbles upon the motto of *A General View of Positivism*: "We tire of thinking and even of acting; we never tire of loving", he cannot help wondering what lies behind it. The obvious answer is: a woman; and, in fact, there was one. In Comte's case, *cherchez la femme* is a perfectly superfluous piece of advice, for the problem is not to find her, but to get rid of her and of what he calls "her angelic influence". As Comte says in his inimitable manner: "My career had been that of Aristotle—I should have wanted energy for that of St. Paul, but for her." [5] One should never quarrel with prophets about the source of their inspiration. Comte tells us that Clotilde de Vaux was to him a "new Beatrice". It is a rather good comparison, for it reminds us that though Beatrices are plentiful, very few find their Dante; and so long as there is no Dante, there is no *Divine Comedy*: Clotilde never inspired Comte except with his own ideas. Let us therefore pay due homage to the new Beatrice, without forgetting that the second part of Comte's career flows, not from Clotilde

---

[4] A. Comte, *A General View of Positivism*, trans. J. H. Bridges (London: G. Routledge, 1908), pp. 15 and 40.

[5] A. Comte, *The Catechism of Positivism*, trans. R. Congreve (London: J. Chapman, 1858), preface, p. 19.

de Vaux, but from the first part of his career, and that with an organic necessity.

As early as 1826, that is eighteen years before he met Clotilde, Comte had laid down the principles of his social and religious reformation in his *Considerations on Spiritual Power*. Anticipating the time when the new positive dogma would have been formulated, he could already foresee the necessity of organizing a new clergy, whose proper function it would be to teach the new truth and to facilitate the rise of a positive social order. As soon as his *System of Positive Philosophy* and his *Positive Politics* were completed, the next move obviously was for Comte to establish a positive spiritual power and, of course, to assume its direction. From that time on, instead of being simply the central principle of his subjective synthesis, humanity became for Comte an object of worship, the positive god, or Great Being, of the new religion whose self-appointed pope he was. The science of sociology thus gave rise to sociolatry, with love as the principle, order as the basis, and progress as the end. As he grew older, Comte felt more and more convinced of the holiness of his religious mission. On Sunday, October 19, 1851, he concluded his third course of philosophical lectures on the General History of Humanity with what he modestly calls "a summary of five hours". The memorable conclusion of that summary was this uncompromising announcement: "In the name of the Past and of the Future, the servants of Humanity—both its philosophical and practical servants—come forward to claim as their due the general direction of this world. Their object is to constitute at length a real Providence in all departments—moral, intellectual, and material. Consequently they exclude, once and for all, from political supremacy all the different servants of God—Catholic, Protestant, or Deist—as being at once outdated and a cause of disturbance." [6]

[6] Ibid., p. 1.

Having thus excommunicated all the other religions, the High Priest of Humanity set about organizing the new cult. His first thought was for his immortal predecessors, the great men of the eighteenth century, whose destructive work had been carried on so consistently, both in religion and in politics, that, after them, a total and direct reorganization of society had become an absolute necessity. It was not for Voltaire, or Rousseau, whose vague metaphysical deism had given rise to "superficial and immoral sects" wholly alien to the positive spirit, but rather for the great and immortal school of Diderot and Hume. "Hume", says Comte, "is my principal precursor in philosophy",[7] and now we know why his *Essays* are among the few philosophical books listed in the catalogue of the *Positivist Library*. But the most important point lies not there, but in the necessary connection which Comte perceived between Hume's complete destruction of metaphysics and religion, and his own reconstruction of religion and politics on the basis of a new philosophy. As compared with Hume, Kant, whose "fundamental conception had never really been systematized and developed except by Positivism", was merely an accessory to Comte. Comte, not Kant, had brought the great Western crisis to a close, since, starting from the universal and absolute negation of Hume, he had at last reached what he calls "the noble object of his wishes, a religion resting on demonstration".[8]

In contrast to Kant, Comte had been both his own Fichte and his own Hegel. This notable fact accounts not only for his lack of enthusiasm for Kant's work, but also for the fact that the two schools broke down in two opposite ways. Kant had to cut loose from Fichte, because he refused to be dragged from positive knowledge to metaphysics and from metaphysics to religion. John Stuart Mill and Littré had to cut loose from Comte, because they refused to be dragged by him from positive phi-

[7] Ibid., p. 7.   [8] Ibid., p. 6.

losophy to a new theology and a new religion. The disciples of
Kant had travelled too fast and too far for him, Comte was
travelling too fast and too far for his early followers. Hence the
endless controversy in which Mill and Littré were obliged to
oppose Comte on the same point, though not for the same
reasons.

Mill had been an independent, but very close, follower of
Comte during the first part of the latter's career. He was very
much in favour of a positive philosophy, whereby he meant a
complete reliance on scientific knowledge coupled with a decided agnosticism in metaphysics as well as in religion; but as
soon as he heard of the subjective synthesis, Mill accused Comte
of yielding to an inordinate passion for abstract unity. He then
withdrew from the school on the ground that Comte's positive
politics and positive religion had really nothing to do with his
positive philosophy. Comte, Mill concluded, was at least as great
as Descartes and Leibniz, who, of all great scientific thinkers,
"were the most consistent, and for that reason the most absurd,
because they shrank from no consequences, however contrary
to common sense, to which their premises appeared to lead".
Yes, Comte was as great as they, and hardly more extravagant;
only, writing in an age "less tolerant of palpable absurdities",
those which he committed, though not in themselves greater, at
least appeared more ridiculous.[9]

Littré also wanted a philosophy based upon science and nothing else, but he took exception to the comparison drawn by Mill
between Comte and the old metaphysicians. According to Littré,
Descartes and Leibniz were wrong because, having laid down
wrong principles, they had consistently pursued them to their
last consequences; whereas, said Littré, Comte had laid down
true philosophical principles, but had failed to follow them in a

[9] J. S. Mill, *A. Comte and Positivism* (London: Trübner, 1865), last lines of
the book.

consistent way: "In the case of both Descartes and Leibniz, the principle was responsible for the consequences; in the case of Mr. Comte, the consequences were arbitrary, but the principle itself remained safe." [10] Littré concluded accordingly that true positivism must be exclusively restricted to Comte's scientific philosophy without any admixture of subjective religion.

Mill and Littré were good men, but they were no match for Comte. Naturally, he was deeply hurt, but that at which he marvelled above all was their shortsightedness. They wanted a positive philosophy free from all subjectivism; in other words, they wanted an "objective synthesis." But *that* was a "palpable absurdity"! Were we to remove from his positivism all its subjective elements, the positive politics and the positive religion would, of course, go, but the positive philosophy itself would also have to go. Comte knew his own doctrine from the inside, and he could not forget how he had made it. Remove the subjective purpose of reorganizing the sciences to suit the social needs of humanity, and nothing will remain but disconnected scientific knowledge, a chaos of unrelated sciences, most of them useless, and the few useful ones themselves encumbered with irrelevant speculation. In short, science would be left, not philosophy. If you reject positive politics and positive religion because of their subjectivity, you must also reject positive philosophy, and for the same reason; if, on the contrary, you accept positive philosophy in spite of its subjectivity, what right have you to condemn positive politics and positive religion? Philosophy is a synthesis; all synthesis is subjective; positive philosophy is a subjective synthesis of objective facts, and this is why it is a philosophy; therefore, you must either take the whole as it is, or leave it

Comte's sociologism is one of the most striking philosophical experiments recorded by history. Reduced to its simplest

[10] E. Littré, *Auguste Comte et J. S. Mill* (Paris, 1867), pp. 5–6.

expression, it means that if you give up metaphysics as incompletely rational, there remains no other choice but to "regenerate" science on a non-scientific basis, which entails the loss of science; or strictly to maintain the complete objectivity of scientific knowledge, which entails the loss of philosophy. Mill and Littré were right in refusing to tamper with the absolute objectivity of science, for the very existence of science was at stake; but Comte also was right in replying that, having identified rational knowledge with objective scientific knowledge, Mill and Littré could not reject all subjectivity and still have a philosophy. Such being the case, men naturally chose to lose philosophy, thus opening the age of intellectual disorder and social anarchy in which we ourselves are now groping our way.

CHAPTER XI

THE BREAKDOWN
OF MODERN PHILOSOPHY

When Oswald Spengler first published *The Decline of the West*, many readers of his now famous book felt at variance with more than one of its conclusions; yet few among them would have thought of questioning the fact that the West was actually declining. Most of them had already known it for a long time. Not in the least because of the World War; on the contrary, the War had been a time of enthusiasm and complete self-dedication to a sacred cause, when old fears and solicitous misgivings as to the future of Western culture had been forgotten. I know that it is now fashionable to laugh at that sacred cause; yet there are still a few people who remember how they were then trying to redeem war by giving it a meaning, and who remember what that meaning was. A certain idea of man, and a corresponding ideal of social life, were not to be allowed to perish. Yet it now seems clear that even at that time Western culture was steadily following its process of dissolution, and we know it from within, by a sort of immediate and personal experience. For we are the bearers of that culture; it cannot be dying, and dying in us, without our being aware of it.

In its broadest sense, what we call Western culture is essentially the culture of Greece, inherited from the Greeks by the Romans; transfused by the Fathers of the Church with the religious teachings of Christianity, and progressively enlarged by countless numbers of artists, writers, scientists and philosophers from the beginning of the Middle Ages up to the first third of the nineteenth century. It would be a waste of time to look for a turning point in its history—in the continuous stream of historical events every point is a turning point—but it can safely be assumed that the French Revolution marks the time when the more clearsighted among the representatives of Western culture began to feel that there was something wrong with it. They offered various diagnoses, and they began to suggest remedies. For the reasons we have noted, Comte failed to provide Europe with a living dogma; his new scientific religion was still-born, and he died, a self-appointed pope, with a very small number of disciples. On the whole, his Reformation was a failure, but Comte had at least seen clearly that the European crisis was essentially a crisis of Western culture: Can a social order, begotten by a common faith in the value of certain principles, keep on living when all faith in these principles is lost?

The meaning of that question will be illustrated best by a summary description of what may be called, for brevity's sake, the Western creed. Its most fundamental feature is a firm belief in the eminent dignity of man. The Greeks of classical times never wavered in their conviction, that of all the things that can be found in nature, man is by far the highest, and that of all the things important for man to know, by far the most important is man. When Socrates, after unsuccessful attempts to deal with physical problems, made up his mind to dedicate himself to the exclusive study of man, he was making a momentous decision. "Know thyself" is not only the key to Greek culture, but to the classical culture of the Western world as well. What the Greeks left to their successors was, a vast body of knowledge mainly related to man's nature and his various needs: logic, which is the science of how to think; several different philosophies, all of them culminating in ethics and politics, which are the sciences of how to live; remarkable specimens of history and political eloquence, related to the life of the city. As to what we today call positive science, the greatest achievements of the Greek genius were along the lines of mathematics, a knowledge which man draws from his own mind without submitting to the degrading tyranny of material facts; and medicine, whose proper object is to ensure the well-being of the human body. And they stopped there, checked by an obscure feeling that the rest was not worth having, at least not at the price which the human mind would have to pay for it: its freedom from matter, its internal liberty.

Of the heirs to Greek culture it can truly be said, that while they enlarged and deepened their heritage, they always respected its nature and never thought of displacing its centre of gravity. When the Romans added the lofty structure of Roman Law to it, man and the betterment of human life still remained their essential interest. As to Christianity, though it be true that God was its ultimate goal and its centre of reference, the fact remains that it conceived man, created by God in his own image and likeness, as the most perfect of all earthly beings, with no higher duty than to achieve his own salvation. And why is man an image of God? Because, says St. Augustine, he has a mind. All the Greek philosophers would have gladly subscribed to that statement.

Hence the second fundamental feature of Western culture, which is a definite conviction that reason is the specific difference of man. Man is best described as a rational animal; deprive man of reason, and what is left is not man, but animal. This looks like a very commonplace statement, yet Western culture is dying wherever it has been forgotten; for the rational nature of man is the only conceivable foundation for a rational system of ethics. Morality is essentially normality; for a rational being to act and to behave either without reason or contrary to its dictates is to act and behave, not exactly as a beast, but as a beastly man, which is worse. For it is proper that a beast should act as a beast, that is, according to its own nature; but it is totally unfitting for a man to act as a beast, because that means the complete oblivion of his own nature, and hence his final destruction.

It is hardly possible to realize the continuity that prevails throughout the whole history of Western culture, unless one keeps in mind the important part played by the Church in the work of its transmission. The Greek and the Latin Fathers of the Church had so carefully preserved the classical notion of man that when St. Thomas Aquinas, in the thirteenth century, undertook to build up a complete exposition of the Christian truth, he did not scruple to borrow for his technical equipment from the pagan Aristotle, whose logic, physics, biology, ethics and metaphysics were then transformed by his mediæval disciple into as many elements of a Christian synthesis.

The Reformation of the sixteenth century was to wreck that stately edifice, whose two component elements then fell apart, Christianity on the one side and Greek culture on the other. Yet, not only Catholic humanists, such as Erasmus, but even Protestants, such as Melanchthon, immediately set about re-building it. Luther himself, despite his fierce attacks upon pagan culture, was fond of Ovid, and he always remained partial to Cicero. The humanists who, more or less consciously, swerved from Christianity to paganism, were either going back to what seemed to them the pure doctrine of Aristotle, or testing the truth value of the doctrines left by the Stoics and Epicureans. Throughout the Renaissance and until the middle of the nine-teenth century, the classical tradition remained the common ground on which both pagans and Christians could still meet and carry on fruitful intellectual intercourse. Even the most brilliant scientific discoveries were made by men who, like Descartes, Pascal, Fermat, Leibniz and Newton, had learned little more at school than classical Latin, a philosophy which more or less resembled that of St. Thomas or Aristotle, and the elements of mathematics. So long as, and in so far as, science itself kept faith with its own nature, it remained the healthy exercise of reason, reason seeking to know because knowing is its natural function. Even the most stupendous progress made by the physical and biological sciences entailed no disruption in the continuity of Western culture. While man remained in control of nature, culture could still survive. It was lost from the very moment nature began to control man.

Such a development was by no means inevitable, but the progressive growth of natural science had made it more and more probable. The growing interest taken by men in the practical results of science was in itself both natural and legitimate, but it helped them to forget that science is knowledge, and practical results but its by-products. Moreover, the constant accumulation of hitherto unknown facts, and of their recently formulated laws, was destroying the old balance between the human and the physical sciences, to the advantage of the latter. This, however, was not the main point. It lay rather in the fact that before their unexpected success in finding conclusive explanations of the material world, men had begun either to despise all disciplines in which such demonstrations could not be found, or to rebuild those disciplines after the pattern of the physical sciences. As a consequence, metaphysics and ethics had to be either ignored or, at least, replaced by new positive sciences; in either case, they would be eliminated.

A very dangerous move indeed, which accounts for the perilous position in which Western culture has now found itself. The European burnt his old ships before making sure that the new ones would float. Moreover, the first article of the scientific creed is the acceptance of nature such as it is. Far from making up for the loss of philosophy, the discovery of the scientific substitutes for it leaves man alone with nature such as it is, and obliges him to surrender to natural necessity. Philosophy is the only rational knowledge by which both science and nature can be judged. By reducing philosophy to pure science, man has not only abdicated his right to judge nature and to rule it; but he has also turned himself into a particular aspect of nature, subjected, like all the rest, to the necessary law which regulates its development. A world where accomplished facts are unto themselves their own justification is ripe for the most reckless social adventures. Its dictators can wantonly play havoc with human institutions and human lives, for dictatorships are facts and they also are unto themselves their own justification.

Europe had been heading for such trouble ever since Comte and Hegel stretched physical determinism to embrace social facts. The situation created by Comte and Hegel was indeed paradoxical. Their philosophies were philosophies of history, whose essential purpose was to describe the progressive unfolding of a certain spirit, or an idea, from the beginning of the world to our own day. But there, somehow or other, history came abruptly to a close. The positive spirit having completely emancipated itself from theology and metaphysics, humanity with Comte had reached the last of its three states; therefore, after Comte, nothing new could possibly happen, except that men would live forever and ever in a positivist paradise. Hegel was leading his readers to the same conclusion in a different way. The absolute Hegelian Idea first transforms itself into nature, where it loses self-awareness, then further expresses itself in man, where, owing to man's thinking power, it comes to itself again through science, history and philosophy.[1] But this return of the Idea to itself through man had become with Hegel an accomplished fact. Since his philosophy had proven "that this Idea reveals itself in the World, and that in that World nothing

[1] J. Loewenberg, *Hegel Selections*, p. 370.

else is revealed but this, and its honour and glory",[2] not only had Hegel's question about the ultimate design of the world received its answer, but also the world itself had achieved its ultimate design. Thus both in Comte and in Hegel there was an amazing discrepancy between the method, nay the very spirit, of the doctrine, and the conclusion to which it led. Two philosophies of change culminated in eternal stability; two complete relativisms terminated in self-satisfied dogmatisms. "Nothing is absolute, all is relative" had been one of Comte's favourite formulas; but he never added: including Positivism. Yet, after the death of Comte and of Hegel, history went on as before, and their disciples naturally began to wonder why.

In the case of Comte, the answer could easily be discovered. Having borrowed from positive science, and especially from sociology, the fundamental notions of his doctrine, French Positivism was bound to disintegrate into positive natural science on the one hand, and positive social science on the other. The first of these products of the decomposition of Comtism is represented in France by the so-called "absolute positivism"; the second, by the sociology of Durkheim and his school. French sociology is, or, at least, would fain be, a positive science of sociological facts, including even philosophy and ethics. Morals are facts; their so-called philosophical justifications are also facts; in short, men act as they must act and they think as they must think, given the social group in which they live—"What do we do?" is a sensible question which sociology can answer; but "What ought we to do?" is not a scientific question, and hence there is no answer to it. In Professor L. Lévy-Bruhl's own words: "There is no answer to the demand: give us an ethical system! because the demand has no object."[3] As to absolute positivism,

[2] Ibid., p. 349.

[3] L. Lévy-Bruhl, *Ethics and Moral Science* (London: A. Constable, 1925), p. 216.

it is, basically, a mere scientism which is made up of commentaries on the conclusions of science;[4] but, strangely enough, scientists fail to see the necessity of such commentaries on science when they are made by men who are not themselves scientists, and who consequently possess a superficial acquaintance with science. The upshot of French Positivism is a complete elimination of philosophy and its problems; it is, in short, one of the possible forms of philosophical suicide.

It is a harmless one; in this sense at least, that ignoring as it does all philosophical questions, the French Positivism allows the world to follow its own laws without interfering with them. The disciples of Hegel were of an altogether different type, and they had to be, on account of the peculiar nature of his dialectical method. Instead of reaching the harbour of a golden age after centuries of straightforward progress, the Idea of Hegel could find itself only by fighting its way through the course of the antinomies. In short, Hegel's method had been that of a revolutionist aiming at conservative results. Now, it so happened that among his disciples there were revolutionists aiming at revolutionary results. The method of Hegel, but not his conclusions, appeared to them as highly suitable to their own ends, for they failed to see why the course of the world's history should come to an end with the Prussian monarchy of Frederick William the Third. In other words, since the world was still changing, Hegelianism was obviously not the concluding word by which all antinomies were brought to a close; rather, it was one of the terms of a new antinomy, the antinomy between the obvious fact of social change and the necessary conclusion that, according to Hegelianism, social change should have come to an end. Hegelianism was caught in the wheels of its own method; as Engels was later to write, "it had to be 'sublated' in its own

---

[4] É. Gilson, "Sur le positivisme absolu", in *Revue philosophique* 68 (1909): 63–65; and Professor A. Ray's answer, ibid., pp. 65–66.

sense, that is, in the sense that while its form had to be annihilated through criticism, the new content which had been won
through it had to be saved." [5]

No one could see how to do it until light began to shine from
an unexpected direction. In 1841, ten years after the death of
Hegel, Ludwig Feuerbach published his *Essence of Christianity*,
soon followed, in 1845, by his *Essence of Religion*. He had first
been a student in theology and, in a way, he always remained an
inverted theologian. After beginning as a free Hegelian in philosophy, Feuerbach resolutely turned his back on the Absolute
Idea and devoted himself to the exclusive study of man. As he
himself says, instead of a *theo*logian, he became an *anthropo*logian.
In spite of opinions to the contrary, Feuerbach was not an
irreligious man; on the contrary, he considered man as an essentially religious animal. The brutes have no religion, man alone
has one; consequently religion must have its base in the essential
difference between man and the brute. Now there is no other
difference except the consciousness which man has of his own
nature. Man's self-consciousness has no other object than himself; when, therefore, man says God, he actually means man. In
short, God has not created man in his own image, but man has
created God in his own image and likeness: the worship of man
under the name of God is the very essence of religion. [6]

The doctrine of Feuerbach aimed at the destruction of all
supernaturalism, and was expressly contrived to achieve it. Let
us convince man that he is the supreme reality, he will no longer
look for happiness above himself, but within himself; being to
himself the Absolute, he will lose all supernatural wishes and,

[5] F. Engels, *Ludwig Feuerbach and the Outcome of Classical German Philosophy*,
vol. 15 of Marxist Library (New York: International Publishers [Union of
Soviet Socialist Republics], 1935), p. 29. See the pertinent remarks of J.
Loewenberg, *Hegel Selections*, pp. xiv–xv.

[6] L. Feuerbach, *The Essence of Christianity*, trans. M. Evans (New York,
1855), chap. 1, pp. 21–22.

as Feuerbach himself says, "he who no longer has any supernatural wishes has no longer any supernatural beings either." [7]
The new religion was, therefore, not a worship of society, like
the Sociolatry of Comte; it was a worship of human nature, an
"Anthropolatry". To those disciples of Hegel who were striving
to reconcile the ever-changing nature with the absolute immo-
bility of the Idea, the message of Feuerbach came as a revelation. What was the Hegelian Idea, after all, but the ghost of
God? If, as was now obvious, the entire supernatural order had
to go, the Hegelian Idea had to go also; but then nothing
remained but nature, and its endless dialectical development.
The Hegelian antinomy itself was thus overcome, or "sublated"
(*aufgehoben*) and the way was open for a new philosophical
conception of reality.

Among those who greeted Feuerbach as their deliverer was a
young man by the name of Karl Marx. Many years later, in
1886, his friend, and with him the co-founder of Communism,
Frederick Engels, could still vividly describe the joy of their
discovery. "Then came Feuerbach's *Essence of Christianity*. . . .
The spell was broken, . . . and the contradiction, shown to exist
only in our imagination, was dissolved. One must himself have
experienced the liberating effect of this book, to get an idea of
it. Enthusiasm was general; we all became at once Feuerbachians." [8]
What Engels says here is undoubtedly true, but he passed through
an important stage without stopping, and unless we pause and
consider it a little while, the rest of the story will lose its
intelligibility.

When the *Essence of Christianity* came upon the scene, says
Engels, "With one blow it pulverized the contradiction, in that,
without circumlocutions it placed materialism on the throne

---

[7] L. Feuerbach, *The Essence of Religion*, trans. A. Loos (New York, 1873),
p. 71 (conclusion of the book).

[8] Engels, *Ludwig Feuerbach*, p. 28.

again." [9] In point of fact, construing Feuerbach as a materialist is one of Marx's most personal contributions to the development of modern philosophy. Feuerbach himself would have resented it. Against the crude mechanical materialism of the eighteenth century, he always maintained that materialism was "the foundation of the edifice of human essence and knowledge . . . but not the building itself. Backwards, I fully agree with the materialists; but not forwards." [10] Marx and Engels were not slow in perceiving that Feuerbach had verged on the materialism of the future, even though he himself was not able to see it. In fact, both Marx and Engels also rejected the "shallow and vulgarized form" of materialism "which was preached on their tours in the 'fifties by Büchner, Vogt and Moleschott." [11] Their own materialism was a development of the limited materialism of Feuerbach: all that which is, is either material by itself, or rooted in and strictly determined by, something which is itself material. Stretched forward by Marx, the materialism of Feuerbach could now be extended from the mechanical interactions of matter to biological problems and even to social life, including even philosophy.

A second modification of Feuerbach's limited materialism submitted it to a still more radical change. The material order of nature, as Marx understood it, was conceived as having a history, that is to say, as following a Darwinian evolution, whose law was essentially the same as that of Hegel's dialectics. This was a wholly logical decision. In the doctrine of Hegel, world history is not the history of nature, but of the absolute Idea as expressing itself in nature and in man; now that the Idea itself had vanished, Hegel's dialectic must be understood as the law of the evolution of matter in time, and of all the biological and social phenomena rooted in matter and determined by it.

[9] Ibid., p. 28.   [10] Ibid., p. 35.   [11] Ibid., pp. 35–36.

It is not easy to start a new idea, but it is still more difficult to
stop it. Here at last is the complete philosophical justification of
dialectical materialism. How many thinkers of all times and of
all nationalities have made it possible, no one can say. When
Engels reviewed his historical ancestors, he began by stating that
"materialism is the natural-born son of Great Britain. The
British schoolman, Duns Scotus, had already asked, 'whether it
was impossible for matter to think'. In order to effect this
miracle, he took refuge in God's omnipotence; *i.e.*, he made
theology preach materialism. Moreover, he was a nominalist.
Nominalism, the first form of materialism, is chiefly found
among the English schoolmen." [12] I am afraid Engels was mis-
taking Duns Scotus here for Ockham, but since Duns Scotus
was a Scotsman, and Ockham an Englishman, Engels' mistake
confirms rather than destroys his thesis. In any case, whatever its
remoter origins may be, the immediate philosophical anteced-
ents of Communism were exactly those described by Engels.
Lenin himself endorsed the view of Engels, when he quoted
German philosophy, English political economy and French socialism as the three sources and the three constituent parts of
Marxism. The philosophical source itself, the only one with
which we are now dealing, Lenin describes as "the system of
Hegel, which had led in its turn to the materialism of Feuerbach".
Hence Lenin's conclusion that "the historic materialism of Marx
is one of the greatest achievements of scientific thought." [18]
"Historic" refers to the evolutionist interpretation of Hegel's
dialectics; "materialism" refers to the Marxist interpretation of
Feuerbach. The agreement is complete between the testimony

[12] Ibid., p. 84.

[13] The essay of Lenin's is translated in K. Marx, *Capital, the Communist
Manifesto, and Other Writings*, ed. Max Eastman (New York: Modern Library,
1932), p. xxii. See also the criticism of the materialism of the German worker
Dietzgen by Lenin, in his *Materialism and Empirio-Criticism: Critical Notes concerning a Reactionary Philosophy* (London, 1927), pp. 205–10.

of the founders and leaders of Communism and the evidence of historical facts.

But Communism does not only presuppose Hegel's philosophy; it entails a definite philosophy of its own, and to define it in Marx's own terms is also to witness the failure of modern philosophers: "The phantasmagorias in the brains of men are necessary supplements of their material life-process as empirically establishable and bound up with material premises. Morals, religion, metaphysics and other ideologies, here no longer retain a look of independence. They have no history, they have no development. . . . It is not consciousness that determines life, but life that determines consciousness." In short: "The mode of production of the material subsistence conditions the social, political and spiritual life process in general." [14] Since, as is stated at the very beginning of the *Communist Manifesto*, "the history of all hitherto existing society is the history of class struggles", [15] the Hegelian phenomenology of mind henceforward must be a mere phenomenology of the abstract expressions of social classes, and Hegel's dialectic the ideological reflection of a Darwinian class struggle. Philosophy is a commentary upon civil wars, and their necessary justification.

Unfortunately, there is nothing which a universal relativism, such as that of Hegel, could not justify. If all that is real is also rational, Communism is rational, but no more than its contrary. Strangely enough, after criticizing Hegel for attempting to stop the course of history, Karl Marx did the very same thing. He never considered class struggle as an end, but as a means to usher in the Golden Age, when classes and their antagonism will be excluded, and even political power will no longer be needed. [16]

[14] K. Marx, *Capital* . . ., pp. 9–11. See also Engels' *Preface to Manifesto of the Communist Party*, pp. 318–19, where the influence of Darwin is clearly seen.

[15] K. Marx, *Capital* . . ., p. 321.

[16] Ibid., p. 2. Compare pp. 313–14 and 343.

The fact remains, however, that where there is class struggle, there are two classes; in order to bring their antagonism to an end, one of them has to be "sublated" (*aufgehoben*); the only question is, which is to "sublate" which? In point of fact, the correct Hegelian answer to the question would be: both must be "sublated" by their common absorption in a new totality. When a certain state feels that class struggle has lasted long enough and does not wish to achieve social peace by the dictatorship of one of these classes, it naturally decrees its own dictatorship as the only means to bring the strife to an end.

Such is the reason why neo-Hegelianism has become the philosophy of Fascism in the writings of G. Gentile, just as it was the official doctrine of Communism in the writings of Marx, of Engels and of Lenin. The Communists strongly resent what they call the philosophical pretensions of the "Social-fascists". Yet the latter can put up a very good case, for even though we dismiss Hegel's absolute Idea, there is nothing to prove that nature is purely material. Hegel minus Feuerbach remains an open possibility. Again, supposing that we take Hegel minus the Idea and plus Feuerbach, then what is left is a social Darwinism, whose only law is natural selection and where the survival of the fittest will ultimately settle all theoretical discussions. Now, who is the fittest? This is not a question for philosophy to answer; life and history alone will show it. Benedetto Croce was fully justified in writing, a good many years ago, that "when historic materialism is stripped of all survivals of purposiveness and of providential plans, it can support neither socialism nor any other practical orientation of human life."[17] On the ground of this evidence, as early as 1899, Gentile had parted company with Croce himself in a very acute criticism of the philosophy of Marx,[18] and when later Fascism got the upper

[17] B. Croce, *Sulle concezioni materialistiche della storia*, p. 15.
[18] G. Gentile, *La filosofia di Marx* (Pisa: E. Spoerri, 1899).

hand in Italy, Gentile's Hegelianism was fully justified in welcoming it in the name of Hegel's theory of the state. For if the state is anything at all, it is something permanent; it is law, and it is force: law to achieve order within, and force to protect itself against its adversaries from without. By saying that the state asserts its own autonomy in war,[19] Gentile was merely repeating what we have seen to be the authentic Hegelian conception of the state. If the state "is the march of God through the world", it is the only legitimate heir to the late transcendent Idea; and nothing else but the state can "sublate" social antinomies into its own unity. Thus understood, Hegelian Fascism is much more than a political party; in Gentile's own words, it is "before anything else a total conception of life", *una coucezione totale della vita*. Schools ought not to teach it as politics, but as a religion, for "the state is the great will of the nation, and therefore its great intelligence." Such a "Statolatry," though it sees itself as an antidote to the blindness of materialism,[20] is but the advent of another blindness. The state has monopolized intelligence as well as all the rest; from the Great Intelligence, we shall receive even philosophy.

What has been the reaction of independent philosophy to such state dogmatisms? Judging from its practical results, the answer is: almost nothing. True enough, since the second half of the nineteenth century there have never been as many philosophers and professors of philosophy writing books and articles about all possible questions. Yet, in spite of that tremendous philosophical inflation and notwithstanding its crushing technical superiority, independent philosophy has failed to produce a single constructive doctrine, which could act as a rule of public order and private morality. If our long inquiry proves anything at all, the reason for that failure is at hand; but

[19] G. Gentile, *Che cosa è il Fascismo?* (Florence: Vallecchi, 1925), p. 34.
[20] Ibid., pp. 34–38 and 95–116.

instead of stating it myself, I prefer, for the last time, to consult facts.

Whatever else it may be, Communism is emphatically *not* a scepticism. I wish I could make clear that I am not here alluding to the spirit of heroism and self-sacrifice by which the noblest among its representatives were and still are animated. We are here dealing with philosophy, and nothing else. Now it is a fact that, as a philosopher, Lenin has always been fighting against two main adversaries: Berkeley, the immaterialist, and Hume, the agnostic. More than forty times, in his *Materialism and Empirio-Criticism*, Lenin came back to this central position in his philosophy, that Hume had begotten Kant, who in turn had begotten Mill, Mach, Huxley, Cohen, Renouvier, Poincaré, Duhem, James, and all the exponents of what he calls the "Humean agnosticism". In a clumsy way, but with penetrating philosophical insight, Lenin insists that despite the petty changes "made in the terminology or argument of preceding systems" all these doctrines are, basically, so many variations of the fundamental philosophy of Hume.[21] Had he to write it today, Lenin would not be obliged to modify his judgment. At any rate, an American editor of Engels did not hesitate very recently to declare that "to this day, all those philosophical tendencies which in England and the United States parade under the name of 'philosophy,' such as pragmatism, neo-realism, behaviourism, etc., are admittedly nothing but various shades of agnosticism. But all of them in the final analysis are rooted in the philosophy of Hume."[22] This at least is a point on which Communism and Fascism wholly agree, as can be seen from Gentile's untiring

[21] Lenin, *Materialism and Empirio-Criticism*, chap. 2, "The Theory of Knowledge", p. 82. Compare, among many other passages, pp. 14–17, 84–85, 100, 133–35; 160–62. A more detailed exposition should take into account the line of distinction drawn by Lenin between the distinct influences of Berkeley and of Hume; see ibid., p. 161. On James, see p. 296, note 15.

[22] P. Ludas, in his preface to Engels' *Ludwig Feuerbach*, p. 10.

attacks against what he calls "the agnosticism of the schools", and from his burning pleas in favour of an openly dogmatic and constructive teaching, given by uncompromising, intransient masters in universities whence broadmindedness will be severely excluded.[23]

Nothing is more logical than such an attitude. In a society where the freedom of individuals is reduced to their coincidence with the state, intellectual freedom has to reduce itself to the coincidence of each particular intellect with that of the state. It is Averroïsm or Spinozism gone mad. The only thing that can be said to the credit of the so-called liberal philosophers is that ever since 1850 most of them have realized that the recent extension of positive science to social facts was bound to bring about this new fatalism. The classical notion of man and the whole ideal of Western culture were at stake. Was Adam the divinely appointed manager of nature, or only one of its parts? Was Job a tragic figure, or was he merely ridiculous? Prometheus was obviously to be bound again to his rock; or rather, he was binding himself with the chains which he himself had forged. The forging of them was the only use he had ever made of his liberty.

The liberal philosophers were sound in their previsions. Unfortunately, themselves the sons of Kant and Hume, they had lost faith in the rational validity of all metaphysical knowledge. Thus left without any set of philosophical convictions concerning man, his nature and his destiny, they had nothing wherewith to oppose the progressive encroachments of science on the field of human facts. This is the reason why, for want of a rational metaphysics by which the use of science could be regulated, the liberal philosophers had no other choice than to attack science itself and to weaken its absolute rationality. The source of modern agnosticism is the fear of scientific determinism in the

[23] Gentile, *Che cosa è il Fascismo?*, pp. 163–66.

hearts of men who, by breaking metaphysical rationalism, had broken the very backbone of human liberty. Not only Mach, and the Machians, so heartily hated by Lenin, but also all who were not merely rehearsing stale philosophies, therefore devoted themselves to the task of proving the limited character of both scientific rationality and natural determinism. At the same time when Vaihinger was turning Kant's categories into convenient means of handling empirical facts, Emile Boutroux was writing his famous thesis *On the Contingency of the Laws of Nature* (1876), a title which is in itself a complete manifesto. His most illustrious pupil, Henri Bergson, repeated the same experiment, but on a larger scale, when he published in 1889 his still more famous thesis *On the Immediate Data of Consciousness*. The determinism criticized by Boutroux was that of Comte; the particular form of determinism discussed by Bergson is rather that of Spencer and his mechanical Darwinism. Boutroux's position, with its ultimate appeal to moral duty, had been a clear case of moralism, but that of Bergson, with its criticism of intellectual knowledge in the name of intuition, was a revival of old philosophical mysticisms. At the same time and quite independently of Bergson, but influenced by the neocriticism of Renouvier, William James was elaborating a pragmatic conception of knowledge, where ideas were not true, but became true in proportion to their practical verification.[24] Even scientists were joining the chorus. P. Duhem, a Catholic, and a physicist of good repute, deemed it necessary to revive the nominalistic interpretation of science and to pit Ockham once more against St. Thomas Aquinas. Last and not least, the great mathematician, H. Poincaré, laid strong emphasis on the conventional character of scientific laws, and even of scientific facts, at the same time when Bertrand Russell was reaching the conclusion

[24] On the various aspects of the pragmatist movement, see R. B. Perry, *The Thought and Character of William James*, 2 vols. (Boston: Little, Brown, 1935).

that "mathematics may be defined as the subject in which we never know what we are talking about, or whether what we say is true." [25] I said last, because all enumerations should come to an end, but the unsound welcome recently given by some philosophers to the merely "statistical" interpretation of physical laws is a safe indication that too many among us are still looking at irrationality as the last bulwark of liberty.

This, I am afraid, is a mistake. Losing science will not give us philosophy. But if we lose philosophy itself, we must be prepared to lose science, reason, and liberty; in short, we are bound to lose Western culture itself together with its feeling for the eminent dignity of man. "It is possible", says Professor Perry, "that philosophy is now nearing the close of a great phase that began with Descartes, and that what it has been customary to term *modern*, as distinguished from *mediæval* and *ancient* philosophy, will soon cease to be modern." [26] Personally, I even hope that it will soon cease to be at all. For what is now called philosophy is either collective mental slavery or scepticism. There still are men who hate both, and who will not lament the passing of that alternative. But it will not pass away so long as the title of Vaihinger's book remains the program of our philosophical teaching: *The Philosophy of the* AS IF, *being a system of the theoretical, practical and religious fictions of mankind, on the basis of an idealistic philosophy.* [27] Against the crude, yet fundamentally sound craving of Marxism for positive and dogmatic truth, the scepticism of our decadent philosophy has not a chance. It deserves to be destroyed as it actually is in the minds of many among our

[25] B. Russell, "Recent Work on the Principles of Mathematics", *The International Monthly* 4 (1901): 84.

[26] R. B. Perry, *Philosophy of the Recent Past* (New York: Scribner's, 1926), p. 221. It will prove useful to read, in the same volume, the remarkable analysis of the "post-Kantian cycle", pp. 145–46.

[27] Vaihinger wrote his book around 1875, but it was not published until after his death in 1911.

contemporaries who embrace Marxism because it is the only dogmatism they know. Not something less rational, or less constructive, but something more rational and more comprehensively constructive is required to meet its challenge. The time of the "As ifs" is over; what we now need is a "This is so", and we shall not find it, unless we first recover both our lost confidence in the rational validity of metaphysics and our long-forgotten knowledge of its object. Therefore, let the dead bury their dead, and let us turn ourselves towards the future, for it will be what we shall make it: either an aimlessly drifting wreck, or a ship holding a steady course with a rational animal at the wheel.

PART FOUR

THE NATURE AND UNITY
OF PHILOSOPHICAL EXPERIENCE

CHAPTER XII

THE NATURE AND UNITY
OF PHILOSOPHICAL EXPERIENCE

At the beginning of his "Life of Sertorius", Plutarch observes
that some people are fond of collecting the strikingly similar
events that happened in the lives of famous men. The author of
the *Parallel Lives* was obviously one of them, and he could see
two different explanations for such coincidences: "If the multi-
tude of elements is unlimited, fortune has, in the abundance of
her material, an ample provider of coincidences; and if, on the
other hand, there is a limited number of elements from which
events are interwoven, the same things must happen many
times, being brought to pass by the same agencies." [1] After
reviewing several different phases of the history of Western
philosophy, we find ourselves confronted with the same problem that was worrying the mind of old Plutarch. Strikingly
similar movements can be observed in the course of that history,
and they bring forth strikingly similar results. What is behind
these historical coincidences? Is it mere chance, or do they
testify to the presence of intelligible laws?

In discussing this problem, the question that first arises touches
the very nature of the facts with which we have been dealing
from the beginning of this book. All of them were borrowed
from what we call history of philosophy, but it is not yet clear
what history of philosophy itself is. More than once, in order to

[1] *Plutarch's Lives*, trans. B. Perrin (New York, 1919), vol. 8, p. 3.

throw more light on the meaning of certain philosophical movements, we have resorted to significant episodes in the lives of their authors. I wish I could have done it more often, for the biography of a philosopher is of great help in understanding his philosophy; but that is the history of a philosopher, not of his philosophy. Furthermore, it was impossible to outline these successive philosophical positions without referring to the books in which they are formulated. This should also be done with the utmost care and accuracy, for it is the basis on which all history of philosophy ultimately rests; yet it is the literary history of philosophical writings, not the history of philosophy. Again, in order to stress certain sequences of ideas, and to make clear their ideological articulations, we had to detach them from the philosophical organisms whose parts they were. This, of course, is always detrimental to such organisms, and highly objectionable from the point of view of the philosophers themselves. A philosophical doctrine is not defined merely by its general spirit, its fundamental principles and the consequences to which they actually lead its author. It is made up of many other elements which enter its structure and share in determining its concrete individual nature. What a philosopher has not seen in his own principles, even though it may flow from them with absolute necessity, does not belong to *his* philosophy. The possible consequences which the philosopher has seen, but which he has tried to evade, and has finally disavowed, should not be ascribed to him, even though he should have held them on the strength of his own principles; they are no part of *his* philosophy. On the other side, all those subtle shades of thoughts which qualify the principles of a philosopher, soften their rigidity and allow them to do justice to the complexity of concrete facts, are not only part and parcel of his own doctrine, but are often the only part of it that will survive the death of the system. We may wholly disagree with Hegel, or with Comte, but nobody can read their encyclopedias without finding there an inexhaustible source of partial truths and of acute observations. Each particular philosophy is, therefore, a co-ordination of self and mutually limiting principles which defines an individual outlook on the fullness of reality. Its historian has to describe it as such, but this is the history of *a* philosophy, it is not yet the history of philosophy itself.

The philosophical events which have been described in the previous chapters cannot be wholly understood in the sole light of biography, of literary history, or even of the history of the systems in which they can be observed. They point rather to the fact that, in each instance of philosophical thinking, both the philosopher and his particular doctrine are ruled from above by an impersonal necessity. In the first place, philosophers are free to lay down their own sets of principles, but once this is done, they no longer think as they wish—they think as they can. In the second place, it seems to result from the facts under discussion, that any attempt on the part of a philosopher to shun the consequences of his own position is doomed to failure. What he himself declines to say will be said by his disciples, if he has any; if he has none, it may remain eternally unsaid, but it is there, and anybody going back to the same principles, be it several centuries later, will have to face the same conclusions. It seems, therefore, that though philosophical ideas can never be found separate from philosophers and their philosophies, they are, to some extent, independent of philosophers as well as of their philosophies. Philosophy consists in the concepts of philosophers, taken in the naked, impersonal necessity of both their contents and their relations. The history of these concepts and of their relationships is the history of philosophy itself.

If this be true, the recurrence of similar philosophical attitudes is an intelligible fact, and a comparative history of philosophy becomes a concrete possibility. If such a possibility is to materialize, however, philosophy alone will have to be taken into account, and it should be compared with nothing else but philosophy itself. Two doctrines may resemble one another because one of them is the historical source of the other; this is an important fact to know for him who writes a history of these philosophies, but it has little to do with the history of philosophy itself. Coming after Kant, it is easier for us to realize the full implications of philosophical criticism, and we are very much indebted to him for having explicitly stated the whole case; but once stated in its abstract purity, the essence of criticism stands by itself, and even though we learn in Kant what it is, we do not learn it from Kant, but from itself. In short, just as did Kant himself, we bow to its internal necessity.

Proceeding, as they do, from the same illusion, the untiring efforts of historians, sociologists and economists to account for the rise of philosophical ideas by historical, sociological and economic factors seem ultimately headed for a complete failure. True enough, philosophical doctrines that have been conceived in the same society, or in social groups whose structure is comparable, will be themselves comparable, insofar at least as they bear the mark of their origin. There is such a thing as a "spirit of the time", and all the elements of a given culture, taken at a certain moment of its history, have a share in its composition. But the "spirit of the time" accounts for the contingent and transitory elements of philosophical doctrines, not for what they have of permanent necessity. The trouble with explanations of that sort is not that they do not work, but that they always work with the same infallible success. Any philosophy can be explained away by its time, its birthplace and its historical setting. Any philosophy can be accounted for by the collective representations that prevailed in the social group in which it was conceived. And any philosophy can as successfully be traced back to the economic structure of the nation in

which the philosopher himself was born. Whatever method
you choose, it works beautifully. But it ascribes the birth of
Aristotelianism to the fact that Aristotle was a Greek and a
pagan, living in a society based on slavery, four centuries before
Christ; it also explains the revival of Aristotelianism in the
thirteenth century by the fact that St. Thomas Aquinas was an
Italian, a Christian, and even a monk, living in a feudal society
whose political and economic structure was widely different
from that of fourth-century Greece; and it accounts equally well
for the Aristotelianism of J. Maritain, who is French, a layman,
and living in the "bourgeois" society of a nineteenth-century
republic. Conversely, since they were living in the same times
and in the same places, just as Aristotle should have held
the same philosophy as Plato, so Abailard and St. Bernard, St.
Bonaventura and St. Thomas Aquinas, Descartes and Gassendi,
all these men, who flatly contradicted one another, should have
said more or less the same things. Whether it prefers to stress the
political, or the social, or the industrial, or the racial prerequi-
sites for the rise of philosophical doctrines, historicism, in all its
forms, is inconsistent with these obvious facts. In short, the
ultimate explanation of the history of philosophy has to be
philosophy itself.

If this be true, the constant recurrence of definite philosophical attitudes should suggest to the mind of its observers the
presence of an abstract philosophical necessity. As an American
philosopher recently wrote: "Granted that there is no such thing
as an historical determinism, it still remains true that history
contains a metaphysical determinism. The history of philosophy
contains more than the interplay of isolated opinions; it contains the inner history of ideas." [2] Now the most striking of
the recurrences which we have been observing together is the

[2] A. C. Pegis, *Proceedings* of the Eleventh Annual Meeting of the American
Catholic Philosophical Association (Washington, D.C., 1937), p. 27.

revival of philosophical speculation by which every sceptical crisis was regularly attended. As it has an immediate bearing on the very existence of philosophy itself, such a fact is not only striking, it is for us the most fundamental fact of all. If there is a metaphysical necessity behind this, what is it?

The reality of the fact itself seems to be beyond question. Plato's idealism comes first; Aristotle warns everybody that Platonism is heading for scepticism; then Greek scepticism arises, more or less redeemed by the moralism of the Stoics and Epicureans, or by the mysticism of Plotinus. St. Thomas Aquinas restores philosophical knowledge, but Ockham cuts its very root, and ushers in the late mediæval and Renaissance scepticism, itself redeemed by the moralism of the Humanists or by the pseudo-mysticism of Nicolaus Cusanus and of his successors. Then come Descartes and Locke, but their philosophies disintegrate into Berkeley and Hume, with the moralism of Rousseau and the visions of Swedenborg as natural reactions. Kant had read Swedenborg, Rousseau and Hume, but his own philosophical restoration ultimately degenerated into the various forms of contemporary agnosticism, with all sorts of moralisms and of would-be mysticisms as ready shelters against spiritual despair. The so-called death of philosophy being regularly attended by its revival, some new dogmatism should now be at hand. In short, the first law to be inferred from philosophical experience is: *Philosophy always buries its undertakers.*

Against this law, the ready objection is that, this time at least, the pitcher went once too often to the well. It is in the very nature of objections against philosophy to be unphilosophical; but philosophy itself is bound to answer in a careful and thoughtful way even arbitrary objectors.

That is the reason why, at the very time when he was denouncing the illusory character of metaphysical knowledge, Kant sought the root of that illusion in the very nature of reason itself. Hume had destroyed both metaphysics and science; in order to save science, Kant decided to sacrifice metaphysics. Now, it is the upshot of the Kantian experiment that, if metaphysics is arbitrary knowledge, science also is arbitrary knowledge; hence it follows that our belief in the objective validity of science itself stands or falls with our belief in the objective validity of metaphysics. The new question, then, is no longer, Why is metaphysics a necessary illusion, but rather, Why is metaphysics necessary, and how is it that it has given rise to so many illusions?

It is an observable character of all metaphysical doctrines that, widely divergent as they may be, they agree on the necessity of finding out the first cause of all that is. Call it Matter with Democritus, the Good with Plato, the self-thinking Thought with Aristotle, the One with Plotinus, Being with all Christian philosophers, Moral Law with Kant, the Will with Schopenhauer, or let it be the absolute Idea of Hegel, the Creative Duration of Bergson, and whatever else you may cite, in all cases the metaphysician is a man who looks behind and beyond experience for an ultimate ground of all real and possible experience. Even restricting our field of observation to the history of Western civilization, it is an objective fact that men have been aiming at such knowledge for more than twenty-five centuries and that, after proving that it should not be sought, and swearing that they would not seek it any more, men have always found themselves seeking it again. A law of the human mind that rests on an experience of twenty-five centuries is at least as safely guaranteed as any empirically established law. Of course, nature itself may change, but we are dealing with nature as it now is; and observation teaches us that though the pattern and even the content of ideas may change, the nature of the human intellect has remained substantially the same, even after crises from which it should have emerged completely transformed. Let this, therefore, be our second law: *by his very nature, man is a metaphysical animal.*

The law does more than state a fact, it points to its cause. Since man is essentially rational, the constant recurrence of metaphysics in the history of human knowledge must have its explanation in the very structure of reason itself. In other words, the reason why man is a metaphysical animal must lie somewhere in the nature of rationality. Many centuries before Kant, philosophers had stressed the fact that there is more in rational knowledge than we find in sensible experience. The typical attributes of scientific knowledge, that is, universality and necessity, are not to be found in sensible reality, and one of the most generally received explanations is that they come to us from our very power of knowing. As Leibniz says, there is nothing in the intellect that has not first been in sense, except the intellect itself. As Kant was the first both to distrust metaphysics and to hold it to be unavoidable, so was he also the first to give a name to human reason's remarkable power to overstep all sensible experience. He called it the *transcendent* use of reason and denounced it as the permanent source of our metaphysical illusions. Let us retain the term suggested by Kant; it will then follow that whether such knowledge be illusory or not, there is, in human reason, a natural aptness, and consequently a natural urge, to transcend the limits of experience and to form transcendental notions by which the unity of knowledge may be completed. These are metaphysical notions, and the highest of them all is that of the cause of all causes, or first cause, whose discovery has been for centuries the ambition of the metaphysicians. Let us, therefore, state as our third law, that *metaphysics is the knowledge gathered by a naturally transcendent reason in its search for the first principles, or first causes, of what is given in sensible experience.*

This is, in fact, what metaphysics is, but what about its validity? The Kantian conclusion that metaphysical knowledge is illusory by its own nature was not a spontaneous offspring of human reason. If metaphysical speculation is a shooting at the moon, philosophers have always begun by shooting at it; only after missing it have they said that there was no moon, and that it was a waste of time to shoot at it. Scepticism is defeatism in philosophy, and all defeatisms are born of previous defeats. When one has repeatedly failed in a certain undertaking, one naturally concludes that it was an impossible undertaking. I say naturally, but not logically, for a repeated failure in dealing with a given problem may point to a repeated error in discussing the problem rather than to its intrinsic insolubility.

The question then arises: Should the repeated failures of metaphysics be ascribed to metaphysics itself, or to metaphysicians? It is a legitimate question, and one that can be answered in the light of philosophical experience. For indeed that experience itself exhibits a remarkable unity. If our previous analyses are correct, they all point to the same conclusion, that metaphysical adventures are doomed to fail when their authors substitute the fundamental concepts of any particular science for those of metaphysics. Theology, logic, physics, biology, psychology, sociology, economics, are fully competent to solve their own problems by their own methods; on the other hand, however, and this must be our fourth conclusion: *as metaphysics aims at transcending all particular knowledge, no particular science is competent either to solve metaphysical problems, or to judge their metaphysical solutions.*

Of course Kant would object that, so far, his own condemnation of metaphysics still holds good, for he never said that metaphysical problems could be solved in that way; he merely said that they could not be solved at all. True, but it is also true that his condemnation of metaphysics was not the consequence of any personal attempt to reach the foundations of metaphysical knowledge. Kant busied himself with questions about metaphysics, but he had no metaphysical interests of his own. Even during the first part of his career there was always some book between this professor and reality. To him, nature was in the books of Newton, and metaphysics in the books of Wolff. Anybody could read it there; Kant himself had read it, and it boiled down to this, that there are three metaphysical principles, or transcendental ideas of pure reason: an immortal soul to unify psychology; freedom to unify the laws of cosmology; and God to unify natural theology.[3] Such, to Kant, was metaphysics; a second-hand knowledge, for which he was no more personally responsible than for the physics of Newton. Before allowing Kant to frighten us away from metaphysics, we should remember that what he knew about it was mere hearsay.

In fact, what Kant considered as the three principles of metaphysics were not principles, but conclusions. The real principles of metaphysics are the first notions through which all the subsequent metaphysical knowledge has to be gathered. What these first notions are cannot be known unless we begin by bringing forth some metaphysical knowledge; then we can see how it is made and, lastly, we can form an estimate of its value. Now our analysis of the concrete working of various metaphysical minds clearly suggests that the principles of metaphysics are very different from the three transcendental ideas of Kant. The average metaphysician usually overlooks them because, though he aims at the discovery of the ultimate ground of reality as a whole, he attempts to explain the whole by one of its parts, or to reduce his knowledge of the whole to his knowledge of one of its parts. Then he fails and he ascribes his failure to metaphysics, little aware of the fact that now is the proper time for him to metaphysicize, for the most superficial reflection on his failure would take him to the very root of metaphysics.

[3] Greene, *Kant Selections*, pp. 164–65.

When Thales said, six centuries before Christ, that everything is water, though he certainly did not prove his thesis, he at
least made it clear that reason is naturally able to conceive all
that is as being basically one and the same thing, and that such a
unification of reality cannot be achieved by reducing the whole
to one of its parts. Instead of drawing that conclusion, the
successors of Thales inferred from his failure that he had singled
out the wrong part. Thus Anaximenes said that it was not water,
but air. It still did not work. Then Heraclitus said it was fire, and
as there were always objections, the Hegel of the time appeared,
who said that the common stuff of all things was the *inde-
terminate*, that is, the initial fusion of all the contraries from
which all the rest had been evolved. Anaximander thus completed the first philosophical cycle recorded by the history of
Western culture. The description of the later cycles could not
take us further, for it is already clear, from a mere inspection of
the first, that the human mind must be possessed of a natural
aptitude to conceive all things as the same, but always fails in its
endeavour to conceive all things as being the same as one of
them. In short, *the failures of the metaphysicians flow from their
unguarded use of a principle of unity present in the human mind.*

This new conclusion brings us face to face with the last and
truly crucial problem: What is it which the mind is bound to
conceive both as belonging to all things and as not belonging to
any two things in the same way? Such is the riddle which every
man is asked to read on the threshold of metaphysics. It is an
easy one, as, after all, was that of the Sphinx; yet many a good
man has failed to say the word, and the path to the metaphysical
Sphinx is strewn with the corpses of philosophers. The word
is—Being. Our mind is so made that it cannot formulate a
single proposition without relating it to some being. Absolute
nothingness is strictly unthinkable, for we cannot even deny an
existence unless we first posit it in the mind as something to be

denied. "If any man", says J. Edwards, "thinks that he can conceive well enough how there should be nothing, I will engage, that what he means by nothing, is as much something, as anything that he ever thought of in his life."[4] This, I think, is true. But if it is true that human thought is always about being; that each and every aspect of reality, or even of unreality, is necessarily conceived as being, or defined in reference to being, it follows that the understanding of being is the first to be attained, the last into which all knowledge is ultimately resolved and the only one to be included in all our apprehensions. What is first, last and always in human knowledge is its first principle, and its constant point of reference. Now if metaphysics is knowledge dealing with the first principles and the first causes themselves, we can safely conclude that *since being is the first principle of all human knowledge, it is a fortiori the first principle of metaphysics.*

The classical objection to this statement is that, from such a vague idea as that of being, no distinct knowledge can be deduced. This is true, but it is not an objection. To describe being as the "principle of knowledge", does not mean that all subsequent knowledge can be analytically deduced from it, but rather that being is the first knowledge, through which all subsequent knowledge can be progressively acquired. As soon as it comes into touch with sensible experience, the human intellect elicits the immediate intuition of being: *X* is, or exists; but from the intuition *that* something is, the knowledge of *what* it is, beyond the fact that it is something, cannot possibly be deduced, nor is it the task of the intellect to deduce it. The intellect does not deduce, it intuits, it sees, and, in the light of intellectual intuition, the discursive power of reason slowly builds up from experience a determinate knowledge of con-

[4] C. Van Doren, ed., *Benjamin Franklin and Jonathan Edwards: Selections from Their Writings* (New York: Scribner's, 1920) p. 222.

crete reality. Thus, in the light of immediate evidence, the intellect sees that something is, or exists; that what exists is that which it is; that that which is, or exists, cannot be and not be at one and the same time; that a thing either is, or it is not, and no third supposition is conceivable; last, but not least, that being only comes from being, which is the very root of the notion of causality. Reason has not to prove any one of these principles, otherwise they would not be principles, but conclusions; but it is by them that reason proves all the rest. Patiently weaving the threads of concrete knowledge, reason adds to the intellectual evidence of being and of its properties the science of *what* it is. The first principle brings with it, therefore, both the certitude that metaphysics is the science of being as being, and the abstract laws according to which that science has to be constructed. Yet the principle of a certain knowledge is not that knowledge; and the first principle of human knowledge does not bring us a ready-made science of metaphysics, but its principle and its object.

The twofold character of the intellectual intuition of being, to be given in any sensible experience, and yet to transcend all particular experience, is both the origin of metaphysics and the permanent occasion of its failures. If being is included in all my representations, no analysis of reality will ever be complete unless it culminates in a science of being, that is, in metaphysics. On the other hand, the same transcendency which makes the first principle applicable to all experience entails at least the possibility of overstepping the limits by which concrete and particular existences are distinguished. This indeed is more than an abstract possibility, it is a temptation, precisely because it is true that the notion of Being applies to all real or possible experience. Yet, if it is also true that everything is what it is, and nothing else, existence belongs to each and every thing in a truly unique manner, as its own existence, which can be shared in by nothing else. Such is the first principle, both universally applicable, and never applicable twice in the same way. When philosophers fail to perceive either its presence or its true nature, their initial error will pervade the whole science of being, and bring about the ruin of philosophy.

When, owing to some fundamental scientific discovery, a metaphysically minded man first grasps the true nature of a whole order of reality, what he is thus grasping for the first time is but a particular determination of being at large. Yet the intuition of being is always there, and if our philosopher fails to discern its meaning, he will fall a victim to its contagious influence. That which is but a particular determination of being, or *a* being, will be invested with the universality of being itself. In other words, a particular essence will be credited with the universality of being, and allowed to exclude all the other aspects of reality. This is precisely what happened to Abailard, to Ockham, to Descartes, to Kant and to Comte. They were truly labouring under a transcendental delusion; Kant himself knew it, but he was wrong in thinking that such an illusion was unavoidable, for it can be avoided; and he was still more wrong in viewing that illusion as the source of metaphysics, for it is not its source but the cause of its destruction; and not only of the destruction of metaphysics, but, for the same reason and at the same time, of the ruin of the very science which has thus been unduly generalized. If every order of reality is defined by its own essence, and every individual is possessed of its own existence, to encompass the universality of being within the essence of this or that being is to destroy the very object of metaphysics; but to ascribe to the essence of this or that being the universality of being itself, is to stretch a particular science beyond its natural limits and to make it a caricature of metaphysics. In short, and this will be our last conclusion: *all the failures of metaphysics should be traced to the fact, that the first prin-*

ciple of human knowledge has been either overlooked or misused by the metaphysicians.

Their failure is bound to be our failure, if we repeat their mistake by resorting to a false first principle in philosophy. The most tempting of all the false first principles is: that *thought*, not *being*, is involved in all my representations. Here lies the initial option between idealism and realism, which will settle once and for all the future course of our philosophy, and make it a failure or a success. Are we to encompass being with thought, or thought with being? In other words, are we to include the whole in one of its parts, or one of the parts in its whole? If intellectual evidence is not enough to dictate our choice, history is there to remind us that no one ever regains the whole of reality after locking himself up in one of its parts. Man is not a mind that thinks, but a being who knows other beings as true, who loves them as good, and who enjoys them as beautiful. For all that which is, down to the humblest form of existence, exhibits the inseparable privileges of being, which are truth, goodness and beauty.

Thus understood as the science of being and its properties, metaphysics will not be found in a new system of tomorrow, or in the resurrection of some system of the past. The three greatest metaphysicians who ever existed—Plato, Aristotle and St. Thomas Aquinas—had no system in the idealistic sense of the word. Their ambition was not to achieve philosophy once and for all, but to maintain it and to serve it in their own times, as we have to maintain it and to serve it in ours. For us, as for them, the great thing is not to achieve a system of the world as if being could be deduced from thought, but to relate reality, as we know it, to the permanent principles in whose light all the changing problems of science, of ethics and of art have to be solved. A metaphysics of existence cannot be a system wherewith to get rid of philosophy, it is an always open inquiry, whose conclusions are both always the same and always new, because it is conducted under the guidance of immutable principles, which will never exhaust experience, or be themselves exhausted by it. For even though, as is impossible, all that which exists were known to us, existence itself would still remain a mystery. Why, asked Leibniz, is there something rather than nothing?

If such is the ultimate teaching of philosophical experience, the spectacle of so many blunders, ending invariably in the same scepticism, is more suggestive of hope than of discouragement. Far from being a science long since exhausted, metaphysics is a science which has, as yet, been tried by but few. What passed by its name was almost always something else, and it is better that we know it; that is, if we are to realize that the misadventures which regularly befall that something else are wholly unrelated to the true nature of metaphysics. If properly understood, the history of philosophy can help us to realize it, for it is the privilege of a truly philosophical history of philosophy that, in its light, not only philosophical truth, but even philosophical error becomes intelligible, and to understand error as such is also to be free from it. There is, and there always will be a history of philosophy, because philosophy exists only in human minds, which them-selves have a history, and because the world of knowledge and action to which the first principles apply is a changing world, but there should be no history of the first principles themselves, be-cause the metaphysical structure of reality itself does not change. *Perennis philosophia* is not an honorary title for any particular form of philosophical thinking, but a necessary designation for phi-losophy itself, almost a tautology. That which is philosophical is also perennial in its own right.

It is so because all philosophical knowledge ultimately depends on metaphysics. Whether you say with St. Thomas Aquinas, that metaphysics has for its own object "being and its properties"; or with Jonathan Edwards, that it entails "the consent of being to

Being", in both cases metaphysics remains the knowledge of the first principle, and of all the rest in the light of that principle. Thus grounded on existence as on the most universal object of intellect, it is its permanent duty to order and to regulate an ever wider area of scientific knowledge, and to judge ever more complex problems of human conduct; it is its never-ended task to keep the old sciences in their natural limits, to assign their places, and their limits, to new sciences; last, not least, to keep all human activities, however changing their circumstances, under the sway of the same reason by which alone man remains the judge of his own works and, after God, the master of his own destiny.

To learn this from history is also to solve the problem which vexed the minds of E. Troeltsch and of a whole generation of historians: How to overcome historicism? It enables us, therefore, to free ourselves from historical relativism and opens a new era of constructive philosophical thinking. Where it deals with contingent and irreversible facts, history is, and has to be, historicism, for, although everything happens according to intelligible causes, not everything happens according to universal laws; but where, as is here the case, it reaches those necessary connections of ideas which are philosophy itself, history automatically overcomes both itself and historicism. May that liberation in truth be the common reward of our long journey through what has often been a barren metaphysical landscape. For helping me, as you have so lavishly done, by your attentive and sympathetic fidelity, even the warmest thanks would remain an inadequate recompense. Were it in my power to do so, I would rather leave you with a gift. Not wisdom, which I have not and no man can give, but the next best thing: the love of wisdom, for which philosophy is but another word. For to love wisdom is also to love science, and prudence; it is to seek peace in the inner accord of each mind with itself and in the mutual accord of all minds.

BIBLIOGRAPHY

The following bibliographical indications will include (1) easily obtainable editions of philosophical writings, either in the original English text, or in some reliable English translation; (2) for each one of the doctrines under discussion, one or two among the best books devoted by modern historians of philosophy to their detailed and objective interpretation. Books or articles already quoted in the footnotes of the present volume will not be quoted again in the Bibliography, unless they be of a more than episodic importance. All of them can be found by using the subsequent Index of Proper Names. Bibliographical indications have been listed according to the Parts and Chapters of the present book.

PART I

CHAPTER I

DEUTSCH, S. M. *Peter Abälard, ein kritischer Theologe des zwölften Jahrhunderts*. Leipzig: S. Hirzel, 1883.

McKEON, R. *Selections from Medieval Philosophers*, vol. 1, pp. 202–58. New York: Scribner's, 1929.

DE RÉMUSAT, C. *Abélard, sa vie, sa philosophie et sa théologie*, 2 vols. Paris: Didier, 1855.

SYKES, T. G. *Peter Abailard* (esp. pp. 88–112). Cambridge University Press, 1932.

CHAPTER II

DE BOER, T. J. *The History of Philosophy in Islam* (esp. pp. 55–62). Translated by E. R. Jones. London: Luzac and Co., 1933.

ENDRES, J. A. *Forschungen zur Geschichte der frühmittelalterlichen Philosophie*. Münster in Westfalen: Aschendorff, 1915.

―――. *Petrus Damiani und die weltliche Wissenschaft*. Münster in Westfalen: Aschendorff, 1910.

GILSON, ÉTIENNE. *La Philosophie de Saint Bonaventure*. Paris: J. Vrin, 1926. English translation: New York: Sheed and Ward, 1938.

HUSIC, I. *A History of Medieval Jewish Philosophy*. New York: Macmillan, 1930.

MAÏMONIDES, MOSES. *The Guide for the Perplexed*. Translated from the original Arabic text by M. Friedländer. 2d ed. New York: Dutton, 1928.

CHAPTER III

HOCHSTETTER, E. *Studien zur Metaphysik und Erkenntnislehre Wilhelms von Ockham*. Berlin: W. de Gruyter, 1907.

KRAUS, J. *Die Universalienlehre des Oxforder Kanzlers Heinrich von Harclay*. In *Divus Thomas* 10 (1932): 36–58, 475–508; and 11 (1933): 228–314.

MCKEON, R. *Selections from Medieval Philosophers*, vol. 2, pp. 351–421. New York: Scribner's, 1929.

MOODY, E. A. *The Logic of William of Ockham*. New York: Sheed and Ward, 1935.

PELSTER, F. *Heinrich von Harclay, Kanzler von Oxford, und seine Quästionen*, in *Miscellanea Francesco Ehrle*, Rome, 1924, vol. 1, pp. 307–56.

VIGNAUX, P. "Nominalisme". In Vacant-Mangenot, *Dictionnaire de théologie catholique*, vol. 11, cols. 717–84. Paris: Letouzey et Ané, 1951– .

CHAPTER IV

BUSSON, H. *Les Sources et le développement du rationalisme dans la littérature française de la Renaissance (1588–1601)*. Paris: Letouzey, 1923.

―――. *La Pensée religieuse française de Charron à Pascal*. Paris: J. Vrin, 1933.

CHARBONNEL, J. R. *La Pensée italienne au XVIe siècle et le courant libertin*. Paris: Champion, 1919.

KARRER, OTTO. *Meister Eckhart: Das System seiner religiösen Lehre und Lebensweisheit*. Munich: J. Müller, 1926.

LAPPE, J. *Nicolaus von Autrecourt, sein Leben, seine Philosophie, seine Schriften*. Münster in Westfalen: Aschendorff, 1908.

PFEIFFER, F. *Meister Eckhart's Sermons*. Translated by C. de B. Evans. London: J. M. Watkins, 1924–1931.

TOFFANIN, G. *Storia dell' Umanesimo dal XIII al XVI secolo*. Naples: F. Perella, 1933.

VANSTEENBERGHE, E. *Le Cardinal Nicolas de Cues*. Paris: Champion, 1919.

VIGNAUX, P. *Nicolas d'Autrecourt*. In *Dictionnaire de théologie catholique*, vol. 11, cols. 561–87.

PART II

CHAPTER V

EATON, R. M. *Descartes Selections*. New York: Scribner's, 1927.

GOUHIER, H. *La Pensée religieuse de Descartes*. Paris: J. Vrin, 1926.

HAMELIN, O. *Le Système de Descartes*, 2d ed. Paris: F. Alcan, 1926.

MARITAIN, J. *Le Songe de Descartes*. Paris: Corréa, 1932.

CHAPTER VI

GIBSON, A. B. *The Philosophy of Descartes*. London: Methuen, 1932.

GILSON, ÉTIENNE. *R. Descartes: Discours de la méthode, texte et commentaire*. Paris: J. Vrin, 1930.

MOUY, P. *Le Développement de la physique Cartésienne*. Paris: J. Vrin, 1934.

OLGIATI, F. *Cartesio*. Milan: Vita e Pensiero, 1936.

CHAPTER VII

GILSON, ÉTIENNE. *Études sur le rôle de la pensée médiévale dans la formation du système cartésien*. Paris: J. Vrin, 1930.

GOUHIER, H. *La Philosophie de Malebranche et son expérience religieuse*. Paris: J. Vrin, 1926.

GOUHIER, H. *La Vocation de Malebranche*. Paris: J. Vrin, 1926.

MALEBRANCHE, N. *Dialogues on Metaphysics and on Religion*. Translated by M. Ginsberg. London: Allen and Unwin, 1923.

RAND, B. *Modern Classical Philosophers*. Boston: Houghton, Mifflin, 1924.

CHAPTER VIII

GIBSON, J. *Locke's Theory of Knowledge and Its Historical Relations*. Cambridge University Press, 1917.

HENDEL, C. W. *Hume Selections*. New York: Scribner's, 1927.

LAIRD, J. *Hume's Philosophy of Human Nature*. London: Methuen, 1932.

LAMPRECHT, S. P. *Locke Selections*. New York: Scribner's, 1928.

LOCKE, J. *The Works of J. Locke*. Edited by J. A. St. John, *The Philosophical Works*, 2 vols. London: G. Bell, 1877.

WILD, J. G. *Berkeley: A Study of His Life and Philosophy*. Harvard University Press, 1936.

PART III

CHAPTER IX

DELBOS, V. *La Philosophie pratique de Kant*. Paris: F. Alcan, 1905.

GREENE, T. M., ed. *Kant Selections*. New York: Scribner's, 1929.

LOEWENBERG, J. *Hegel Selections*. New York: Scribner's, 1929.

RAND, B. *Modern Classical Philosophers*. Boston: Houghton, Mifflin, 1924.

STACE, W. T. *The Philosophy of Hegel: A Systematic Exposition*. London: Macmillan, 1924.

CHAPTER X

LÉVY-BRUHL, L. *The Philosophy of Auguste Comte*. Translated by F. Harrison. New York: Putnam, 1903.

COMTE, A. *Positive Philosophy*, 2 vols. Translated by H. Martineau. New York, 1868.

———. *The Catechism of Positivism*. Translated by R. Congreve. London: J. Chapman, 1858.

LITTRÉ, E. *A. Comte et J. Stuart Mill*. Paris, 1867.

MILL, J. STUART. *A. Comte and Positivism*. London: Trübner, 1865.

CHAPTER XI

ENGELS, F. *Ludwig Feuerbach and the Outcome of Classical German Philosophy*. Vol. 15 of *Marxist Library*. New York: International Publishers (Union of Soviet Socialist Republics), 1935.

FEUERBACH, L. *The Essence of Christianity*. Translated by M. Evans. New York, 1855.

———. *The Essence of Religion*. Translated by A. Loos. New York, 1873.

LENIN, W. L. *Materialism and Empirio-Criticism: Critical Notes concerning a Reactionary Philosophy*. London, 1927.

PERRY, R. B. *Philosophy of the Recent Past*. New York: Scribner's, 1926.

PART IV

CHAPTER XII

BAUDIN, E. *Introduction générale à la philosophie*, vol. 1, *Qu'est-ce que la philosophie?* Paris: de Gigord, 1927.

BRENTANO, F. *Die vier Phasen der Philosophie und ihr augenblicklicher Stand*. Edited by Oskar Kraus. Leipzig: F. Meiner, 1926.

———. *Ueber die Gründe der Entmutigung auf philosophischem Gebiete*. In *Ueber die Zukunft der Philosophie*. Leipzig: F. Meiner, 1929.

MARITAIN, J. *An Introduction to Philosophy*. Translated by E. I. Watkin. London: Sheed and Ward, 1932.

———. *St. Thomas Aquinas: Angel of the Schools*. Translated by J. F. Scanlan. London: Sheed and Ward, 1931.

———. *Distinguer pour unir, ou les degrés du savoir*. Paris: Desclée De Brouwer, 1932. English translation: *The Degrees of Knowledge*. New York: Scribner's, 1938.

INDEX OF PROPER NAMES